Praise for *Career and Corporate Cool*™

"Rachel Weingarten has a keen eye for the unwritten rules of today's workplace—and a wicked sense of humor."

—Elaine Pofeldt, Senior Editor,
Fortune Small Business

"With one part fashionista, one part career guru, and one part hip older sister you always wish you had, Weingarten has a well-manicured finger on the workplace zeitgeist. *Career and Corporate Cool*™ is a must-have for every professional struggling to reconcile their inner geek with their inner cool kid while negotiating today's ever-evolving business arena."

—Emma Johnson, MSN.com
Personal Finance

"*Career and Corporate Cool*™ helped me realize that I don't need a Y chromosome to be on the same playing field as my male colleagues, or to connect with our male demographic, but rather the confidence as a woman with her own perspective, to voice my ideas. Now my new mantra is 'May the best idea (not man) win.'"

—Carrie Brzezinksi,
Maxim Magazine Marketing

"Great tips, funny insights, and sneaky ways to infuse more cool into all aspects of your life—from the way you look to the way you work. You want cool? Weingarten's got cool."

—Ted Spiker, Contributing Editor,
Men's Health

"Rachel Weingarten has taken the intimidation out of creating your own style—a daunting task for so many women! By taking it one step further and showing you how to use your own style to boost your career, she has proved that good clothes really *do* open all doors!"

—Casey Gillespie, Editorial
Director, *Zink* Magazine

career *and* corporate cool™

How to Look,
Dress,
and Act
the Part—
at every stage
of your career. . .

rachel c. weingarten

John Wiley & Sons, Inc.

Published by John Wiley & Sons, Inc., Hoboken, New Jersey.
Published simultaneously in Canada.

Wiley Bicentennial Logo: Richard J. Pacifico

For general information on our other products and services or for technical support, please contact our Customer Care Department within the United States at (800) 762-2974, outside the United States at (317) 572-3993 or fax (317) 572-4002.

Wiley also publishes its books in a variety of electronic formats. Some content that appears in print may not be available in electronic books. For more information about Wiley products, visit our web site at www.wiley.com.

Library of Congress Cataloging-in-Publication Data:
Weingarten, Rachel C.
    Career and corporate cool™ : how to look, dress, and act the part at every stage of your career / Rachel C. Weingarten.
      p. cm.
  ISBN 978-0-470-12034-7 (cloth)
    1. Business etiquette. 2. Self-presentation. 3. Clothing and dress. I. Title.
  HF5389.W45 2007
  650.1—dc22

                             2007004999

Printed in the United States of America.
10 9 8 7 6 5 4 3 2 1

This book is dedicated to my parents,
Judith Weingarten and David Weingarten.

My mother has always been a *career* trailblazer
and brings impeccable style, wit, and savvy
to everything that she says or does.

My father taught by example what it means
to honor *corporate* commitments
and never ceases to amaze me
with his ever-evolving take on popular culture.

Both of them, on a daily basis, redefine the meaning of *cool*.

Contents

Acknowledgments

Thank you:

- Much like snowflakes with their unmatchable character traits, this book was greatly enhanced by the unique input of each and every person who offered their personal perspectives, ideas, and insights. To find out more about them and for links to their businesses or projects, please visit the Career and Corporate Cool web site at www.careerandcorporatecool.com.
- A gushing thank-you to editor extraordinaire Emily Conway, Jocelyn Cordova, Christine Kim, Paul McCarthy, Miriam Palmer-Sherman, and everyone at John Wiley & Sons, Inc., who collectively embody everything that is Career and Corporate Cool.
- A refreshing *sisterhood is powerful* thank-you to Rebecca "Kiki" Weingarten—best friend, critic, round-the-clock life and career coach, and coolest sister ever.
- A frozen treat to the always coolheaded Bev Bennett, who lived through the first and subsequent incarnations of this book and concept and offered encouragement, counsel, and inspiration throughout.
- My life would be lukewarm without the support, wisdom, and friendship of Russell Barnett, Carrie Brzezinski, Gerry Byrne, Elizabeth Card, Jim Edwards, Anthony Elia, Jill Evans, Heidi Fischer, Carrie Foster, Debbie Geiger and the Geiger-ettes, Stacy Gulisano, Phil Katz, Ita and Avram Lawrence, Jeff McAdams, Michael Main, Jenna Muller, Ken Paulin, Sandra Payne, Erik Sherman, and Blossom Steinberg. Okay, and WJW for old times sake.
- Icy spicy loving to everyone at GTK Marketing Group who picked up a whole lot of slack while I took time off to write this book.

- A somewhat belated thank-you to the extremely cool Teril Turner and everyone at Henri Bendel, who not only have great and classic style but also seem to effortlessly create magic in everyday life.

- I thank most of the people that I went to high school with and/or met in the early days of my career, whose antiquated and frozen-in-time beliefs and conventions forced me to strive to be more than just another pretty girl answering phones for a living; and in the end, I thank Gil Shriki for knowing this and more all along.

- Big hugs to my coolio "coworkers" at UPS, FedEx, Airborne, DHL, and the USPS. It's a lonely endeavor to write a book, and I don't know how I could have gotten through it without the friendly faces and timely delivery of much-needed research materials.

Introduction

I know what you're thinking. *Career and Corporate Cool*—that can't possibly be right. Sure, people have cool careers, but for the most part *corporate* and *cool* have been mutually exclusive and more of a contradiction in terms—until now, that is.

While the corporate world used to be more of an exclusionary boy's club, the rise of feminism saw women working toward equality both at home and in the workplace. (However, according to the American Association of University Women's website, college-educated women still only earn about 75 percent as much as college-educated men, which equates to a shocking wage gap of 25 cents on the dollar.) As women first entered the corporate environment en masse they tried to emulate their male colleagues in both business practice and fashion choices. While imitation may indeed be the sincerest form of flattery, the business wardrobe they adopted was more depressive than expressive.

Way back in the 1980s, business clothes for women were usually composed of "power suits" consisting of ill-fitting jackets with linebacker shoulder pads, worn with fussy polyester blouses with loopy bows meant to be more feminized versions of ties. SUV-sized running shoes paired with both athletic socks and stockings completed this shudder-inducing ensemble. Fast-forward to the Internet era when laid-back work attire meant an influx of male coworkers clad in aloha shirts worn with more baggy shorts and hairy knees than you'd see on

1

a bus full of tourists. Women, meanwhile, wrestled with the concept of jeans versus skirts, the appropriateness of spaghetti straps, and hotly debated issues like the benefits of flip-flops versus high-heeled pumps with toe cleavage.

From movies like *Working Girl* to TV shows like *Melrose Place*, *Sex and the City*, and *Friends*, celluloid working heroines were usually portrayed as über fashion-forward or quirky caricatures. Aggressive stereotypes abounded of the professional working woman as frighteningly chic fashionistas with unlimited budgets for overpriced accessories. As for the rest of us? Not so much.

Historically as well as in our own time, strong, successful women have usually followed the less fashionable, more practical route. Hillary Clinton is known for her practical pantsuits, while Condoleeza Rice was teased mercilessly in the press for wearing a pair of black over-the-knee boots. Martha Stewart was publicly chastised for carrying a $4,000 handbag to her trial, and praised widely for leaving prison clad in a poncho crocheted by a fellow inmate. In other words, dressing well and dressing appropriately for your career and public/private persona can be two different things entirely.

For most people, *career* and *corporate* relate to a daytime dynamic, while *cool* is what happens after hours. A career draws respect or derision depending on perspective, while the combined concept of corporate and cool as a unit challenges more accepted pairings like Laverne and Shirley, Bert and Ernie, or peanut butter and jelly for maximum recognition factor. People, concepts, ideas, or accepted practices may be fine on their own, but unexpectedly can work so much better together.

For the purposes of this book, *career* refers to much more than just the occupation for which you are trained, and *corporate* means a lot more than hundreds of people crammed into a work environment. It means *your* work environment—be it your laptop at the local Starbucks, a three-person office, or a Fortune 500 company. Take the old adage of "Clothes make the man," add a much-needed shot of attitude adjustment, and you're on the right track.

You've likely tried on several careers on your way to becoming the professional that you are today. Maybe you took a few years off and spent some time on the mommy track and are just finding your way back to the nine-to-five. Maybe your job requirement or environment has changed and your two-person office now contains 300 coworkers and you're trying to figure out just where you fit in. Perhaps this is the first time in your working life that you can actually take a breather and look back at your success rate to date and wonder what to say or do, or how to dress to signify that you're ready for the next step—whatever it is. Or maybe you just want to sharpen the tools in your professional and always evolving arsenal.

I went through a lot of different careers until I found the one (okay, two) that fit me perfectly. But even now, I'm constantly put in new situations, meeting new people in different countries or with entirely new corporate cultures, and trying to figure out how to mesh my own work style with their requirements.

While an off-color joke won't play well in a cubicle environment, if you're a professional comedian, piling four-letter words and describing bodily fluids in depth is likely part of your job requirement. If you work for a Fortune 500 company, you've probably received memos detailing companywide sexual harassment policies that warn against touching or even speaking to anyone in a manner deemed inappropriate. By contrast, if you're a massage therapist you're likely touching naked strangers on a daily basis. If you're a CEO you probably shouldn't powder your nose in public, while if you're a makeup artist people will become mesmerized every time you touch up your lipstick.

We all strive to look our best, but generally only models and actresses actually have to be thin and beautiful as a job requirement—for the most part, their career depends on their surface. Yet a majority of women's magazines seem to cater to and encourage the cult of insecurity that many women fall prey to—that niggling internal voice or external ad that seems to tell them they're too fat or too tall, too awkward or loud, or perhaps just not as worthy or wonderful as their coworkers or friends.

Photographer Ronnie Andren refers to himself as a "street photographer" because of his fondness for shooting images of the average person on the street, though he's perhaps better known as the man behind *Glamour* magazine's "Do's & Don'ts" monthly images of

Nice To Meet Me...

women looking their best or worst. Though Andren regularly captures images of some of the most fashionable women in the world at glossy events like New York's Fashion Week, his ideal of feminine beauty is far from what might be considered perfect. Andren says, " The first thing that I notice about a woman is the way that she carries herself, the way that she moves through a crowd, her smile, her confidence, whether or not she's comfortable with herself and what she's wearing." Only after that does Andren notice or pay attention to "what she's wearing, her face, or even her size or body shape."

Most careers have a dress code, be it written or unwritten. At a recent press event it was fairly easy to spot the women who worked at *Vogue* magazine, with their long legs, sleek hair, oversized handbags, and undersized waists. At an advertising conference, the ad guys were almost identically clad with their just-interesting-enough hair (with a slight razor cut), indistinguishable European shirts (small checks or larger checks), eyeglass frames in bold colors with titanium accents, and expensive Italian loafers.

Some work uniforms are subtle, observes Ken Paulin, who as president of L.A. Promo spends a lot of time on the sets of major networks and studios where, he observes, "Some women walk around the lot dressed up as actresses, while others dress up as executives. They all play their parts, and dress up in the way that they're expected to." Some uniforms are more obvious, like those worn by Lisa Henderson, a lawyer in Edinburgh, Scotland. When in court, Henderson is required to wear a calf-length black robe over her clothing and a powdered horsehair wig with two pigtails down the back. She complains of chronic bad-hair days, and a wig line that takes hours to fade, though she always adds her own touches to the look. "When I don my wig and gown I feel as though I'm an actor playing a role. I don't feel that the wig and gown compromise my femininity as I always wear a nice shapely suit, high heels, and red lipstick in court. In fact, I feel as if I'm dressing up!"

Sonia Brown, a letter carrier for the U.S. Postal Service, doesn't mind wearing a uniform to work because she never has to "worry if what I'm wearing goes with my shoes." On the weekends, Brown wears a different kind of uniform, which she feels better reflects her true self, as a member of a women-only motorcycle club, which gives her "a chance to be free from everything."

Even unemployed people, it would seem, have their own uniform, as imagined by illustrator Todd Rosenberg. He says of his much beloved "Odd Todd," the slightly scruffy, blue-bathrobe-clad cartoon character, born of Rosenberg's own lengthy stint of unemployment: "In some ways he's living the American dream. Doing what you want all day long. Unconcerned what other people think. And not having to answer to anyone. I think there's just a little of him in all of us."

There is no one right way to speak, communicate, dress, or interact, but there *is* a right way for *you* to speak, communicate, dress, or interact to show others that you are at the top of your game in your chosen profession, and a force to be reckoned with.

There is no one definitive cool career. There is no one definitive corporate culture. For that reason, there is no one definitive Career and Corporate Cool ideology, but many practical tips and steps from people in all different walks of life who have figured out how to make their jobs more than just a way to pay the bills, but rather a passion, a facet of themselves, a fun and fulfilling vocation.

Career and Corporate Cool isn't for everyone. It isn't for the unimaginative, the chronically dull, or the corporate drones. It is, however, for women and men who want to stand out while fitting in.

Chapter 1

What Is Career and Corporate Cool™?

And Where Can I Get Some?

> *Nothing gives one person so much advantage over*
> *another as to remain always cool and*
> *unruffled under all circumstances.*
>
> —Thomas Jefferson

Cool Is As Cool Does

Ask 100 different people to define the word *cool* and you'll get 100 different answers. I did. One person might define *cool* as a concept, another as a state of mind, while still another will wax rhapsodic about cool books, cool clothing, or their icy cool taste in music. But the one thing that they all agree on? While you might never be able to quite put your finger on what makes someone cool, you'll always know cool when you see it.

While outward appearances may present the impression of cool, it's an unwavering self-confidence that makes you truly and enduringly cool. For the most part, being cool means being completely comfortable in your skin, with your attitudes and beliefs, but most of all in a way that will enrich not only your life but that of others around you.

So What Is It All About?

I interviewed scores of unbelievably cool people for this book, not only those with names you'd recognize but men and women who in some way exemplify the ideals of Career and Corporate Cool. Maybe you use their products on a daily basis; perhaps you've read their books, surfed on their web sites, voted for a candidate whose campaign they've managed, watched a concert that they've produced—or maybe you've never heard of them before. Whether or not the people who have shared their thoughts and hard-earned wisdom here are household names, they each possess a unique way of presenting themselves to the world and in their professional lives that makes them stand out in their chosen professions and beyond. You may or may not agree with them, but you will likely learn from them, their experiences, their generous advice, their mistakes, and their great successes—I know that I have.

A Short History of Cool

To put cool into perspective, one must understand how cool came to be. The concept of cool was born sometime in the mid-twentieth century. During the 1950s cool was a movement, a revolution, an evolution of sorts. Cool was part beatnik, part hipster, part poignant, part optimistic, part fatalistic, part groundbreaking, part old world. Cool in its infancy was about redefining boundaries or ignoring the fact that any limits might have existed in the first place. Cool was born of jazz, and in the beginning cool was poetry with a different cadence or rhythm; cool was art that didn't necessarily make sense but made you feel things you didn't know existed; cool was rebellion; cool was a form of self-acceptance and lack of self-consciousness.

Jack Kerouac epitomized cool, yet lesser known Beat muse Neal Cassady was probably a whole lot cooler. Marlon Brando may have been the first popular actor to rock a leather jacket and jeans, but it was James Dean who made them cool. Cool was dichotomy—cool was Elvis doing his duty not only as a performer, but also as a patriot. Cool became hippies, speaking out and sitting in. Cool was the rise of not only hemlines, but also of feminism. Cool was trying to redefine the societal roles of past generations.

Cool across the pond had a completely different connotation. Cool was Carnaby Street with lithe lovelies like Twiggy, and mods and rockers vying and posturing. Cool was Beatlemania, the Rolling Stones, and the British invasion that followed. Cool wasn't comfortable. Cool wasn't about fitting in. Cool was staying true to your own identity, even if it meant reinventing yourself to find yourself.

If the 1960s were about rediscovery and rebirth, the 1970s were about celebrating self with Studio 54 epitomizing the excess of the era. Living the louche lifestyle of the beautiful set, regulars including Bianca Jagger, Halston, Elton John, Truman Capote, and Cher, danced the New York nights away under a sculpture of the man in the moon with a giant cocaine spoon. The huddled masses were firmly kept away from the beautiful people while movies like *Saturday Night Fever* detailed the disco dreams of the ordinary and heavily accented bridge and tunnel set. This polyester-encased, disco-crazed, drug-induced haze that was the 1970s nearly stopped the evolution of cool in its tracks.

If television staple Arthur Fonzarelli, aka "The Fonz," personified cool to millions of middle-class households, it was nearly inevitable that a seminal sitcom like "*Happy Days*" would decades later inspire the expression "jump the shark" to describe the millisecond in pop culture collateral when it all goes wrong, when cool irreversibly becomes lukewarm and, even worse, irrelevant.

The 1980s saw a resurgence of cool, albeit in the form of irony. The raucous punk rock movement of the previous decade begat a second British invasion, and clothes from the neon to the studded followed suit. The collective gas and energy crises of the 1970s were followed by a generation of excess, ambitious ventures, bloated egos, larger-than-life personalities, and linebacker-size shoulder pads. Club kids ruled, we discovered Madonna, and modern-day F. Scott Fitzgeralds like Jay McInerney and Tom Wolfe chronicled this brash and slick generation of movers and shakers—until October 19, 1987, also known as Black Monday or the worst stock market crash in modern history.

Suddenly, sobered Americans struggled to find cool new icons. Anti-apartheid activist Nelson Mandela, perhaps one of the single coolest symbols of peaceful rebellion and 24-karat rhetoric, was released from prison after 27 years, but even this great victory did nothing to quell the unrest of the decade. The first Gulf War was fought, south-central Los Angeles erupted in riots, and Olympic hopeful Nancy Kerrigan was clubbed in the knee under the orders of archrival Tonya Harding. Our innocence was tested when American terrorists bombed the federal building in Oklahoma City and high school students went on a shooting spree at Columbine High School. Popular culture veered dizzly between defanged, de-ganged hip-hop icons, boy bands, and grunge gods. Kurt Cobain, lead singer of Nirvana, perhaps best symbolized the confused and somewhat muddled 1990s when he committed suicide. The Internet arrived, quietly at first, to early adopters and geeks, and when the initial rush of euphoria and unfounded investments subsided, we were all left wondering what came next.

We went from partying like it was 1999, to worrying about Y2K, and then facing the greatest tragedy to occur on native soil on September 11, 2001. The first decade of the new millennium brought about dizzying changes in everything from lifestyle to trends, communication, and technology.

So where does that collectively leave us in terms of the evolution of cool? They say that every generation has the heroes it deserves, and we still seem to be looking for someone and something to believe in. Our own generation is blessed in ways that previous ones could only have dreamed of. From the comfort of our homes we can access the most superior entertainment, sustenance, and companionship. We can travel weekly to our long distance jobs, or telecommute, freelance, or volunteer. A cool career or way of life is no longer dictated or limited by upbringing, affluence, education, race, or proximity.

Go to Cool

If you believe our family lore, I was always obsessed with the concepts of cool and entrepreneurism. As the youngest of three children, I was always scrambling to keep up with my older brother and sister. By the time I was two years old, my older siblings were already spending a full day in school. My mother often tells the story of how I would plaintively plead with her, as my sister and brother were getting on the school bus, "Rachel go cool," my way of saying that I, too, really wanted to get out of the house and go where the big kids were going. I also learned the importance of cool accessories at that tender age, when my mother bought me my own bright floral print lunchbox and packed a daily lunch for me.

My mother, a serial entrepreneur in a time way before Martha Stewart made it chic to be a capable woman in commerce, opened her first business, a yarn shop, when I was two and a half years old. I loved spending time with my mom at the store, where I like to think that I absorbed her unerring style and meticulous eye for color, and detail. When I was finally old enough to go to school, I would get off the school bus at her store, where I would play at being a shop-keeper; somehow, by osmosis, I picked up the principles of the retail trade. In other words, in the first few years of my life, I went directly from my early pursuit of cool to my first experience in entrepreneurism—and I haven't looked back since.

Nurturing the Cool Person Within

Since I'd like for us to stay friends, I won't regale you with too many stories of the many shopping trips that I made to Paris with my mother when I was in my late teens. By that time my mom had opened a high-end boutique where each and every garment was hand-picked for her clients. She had progressed from crafts to accessories to high fashion, and along the way she had started designing for some of New York's top design houses. It was almost a natural progression for me to follow suit, and while still in my teens I designed a line of denim fashions for a cult brand.

My point? For me, being in the fashion world was second nature. While growing up, my sister, brother, and I were usually dressed in color-coordinated clothing when we were with my mother, and if by some chance our clothing did clash, we weren't permitted to stand next to each other, but rather had to have the nonoffensively clad sibling act as a buffer zone.

I live and breathe color, cut, style, and texture the way the child of an accountant might instinctively hold her breath through tax season, or the way that the offspring of a poet laureate might recite prose. By the same token, aside from a brief stint as a jewelry designer, my father devoted his life to educating others, and until he retired a few years ago. My father never took time off during the 45 years that he spent as a teacher and school administrator, with summers spent running a camp so that he could pay for our private school tuition. Both of my earliest work influences have helped to shape the businessperson that I am today. I was never seduced by the flightiness of the fashion or beauty industries, but rather tempered by my parent's work ethic. In high school, I worked Sundays teaching art at the Y and at my mother's store after school to earn pocket money.

We all have early influences and experiences that set us apart from others, the qualities and conditions that serve to shape us, toughen us, and make us unique or better than the predictable pack. When creating your Career and Corporate Cool persona, it's important to tap into not only the career and lifestyle that you desire, but also your roots—the conditions, family members, friends, ideologies, idols, and earliest influences that have shaped your core being—and make you intrinsically cool whether you realize it or not.

Gerry Byrne, communications legend and founder of the Quills Literacy Foundation and Quill Awards, is a very formidable person indeed. I remember meeting him for the first time over lunch at Michael's, a celebrated New York eatery known as a mecca for power schmoozing and the place to see and be seen for anyone in the publishing industry. Byrne was seated at the center table, where others had to flutter in his peripheral vision to get noticed. One of the first things I noticed about him was his presence—quietly powerful. The second was his handshake and demeanor—both strong, commanding, and very much in control.

Byrne told me that he credits his early years as a marine with giving him the cornerstone of "honor, courage and commitment that has carried over into my personal and business life." He believes that he entered the business world with a different head on his shoulders than a graduate degree or PhD in leadership would have afforded him. "When you're twenty-three or twenty-four years old with a group of marines out at Paris Island, and you're responsible for the group, it's an experience that you can't even describe. It makes you into something that sticks with you." For better or worse, each and every life experience that you've had has somehow transformed you into the person that you are now. Those early lessons and tools, the heartaches, the ridiculous successes—add them up and they compose the essence of your being. If you're fortunate, you've learned to whittle down any bitterness and disappointment to become and keep evolving into the truest, purest, coolest essence of yourself.

Musician Ben Folds doesn't quite fit into the mold of rock star, though he does seem to have tantrums at times, and has cursed at audience members (while chastising them for shouting out song requests when he was clearly playing another tune). While he's best known for his sweet and sarcastic lyrics and virtuoso piano playing, Folds actually briefly attended the University of Miami on a percussion scholarship. Folds eschews a traditional piano bench and instead sits on a drum stool, and usually ends his sets by tossing said stool onto his piano keyboard. He has said in concert that he's broken his own rules by writing songs about the three topics he'd rather have avoided: political songs, advice songs, and love songs. His lyrics reflect his love/hate relationship with his past. In "The Best Imitation of Myself" he ponders taking a class to lose his southern accent, while in "Jesusland" he seems to reflect on the seeming hypocrisy of the so-called heartland.

One of the best concerts I've ever attended was a Ben Folds concert in Prospect Park in Brooklyn. It was a sweltering summer night, and Folds was suffering from laryngitis—in theory, far from perfect circumstances. Folds habitually leads his audience in singing the chorus of his songs in two- to three-part harmonies. For him, he explained, it's the almost rapturous feeling and pure pleasure of hearing voices joined in song. On that brutally hot night, as I sang along with hundreds of strangers under the stars, the feeling was practically elemental.

Does Folds, clad in some variation of his usual reddish-maroon pants, nerdy glasses, and awful haircut, qualify as what might traditionally have been considered a "cool" rock star? He was and is all that and more. His style is uniquely his own and seemingly thumbs its nose at the traditional leather and tattoos that have become the mainstream uniform of wannabe hipsters and rock gods alike. Folds led the audience in song because it pleased him to do so, and made hundreds of sweaty, cranky strangers feel as though they were part of something larger, part of a group, part of the whole. And for that one moment in time, old or young, hip or woefully unchic, sophisticated or clueless, every member of that audience was a rock star, too.

How very cool indeed.

Some Cool Thoughts

Hot means explosive; cool means calm.

Hot means lacking in control; cool means controlling the action.

Hot means ready for a meltdown; cool means the ability to sit back and assess a situation before making a potentially rash decision.

Hot means sweaty and uncomfortable when in the spotlight; cool means having all eyes on you and knowing that you won't disappoint.

Hot means sticking to a clichéd script or traditional role of women and men in the workplace; cool means rewriting that same script to make sure that it works best for you in your personal or professional life.

Hot means an inability to evolve; cool means knowing how to assess a situation and act accordingly.

Hot means using only your looks or attributes to move ahead in your career; cool means understanding that you are more than just a pretty face, but also a sexy brain and a gorgeous personality.

Hot is ephemeral; cool is eternal.

Hot is trendy; cool is classic.

Being hot isn't always an attainable or sustainable goal, but being cool is forever.

CAREER

At different points in your life you probably wanted to be a ballerina or a doctor, an artist or a professional athlete, depending on your particular set of life experiences, economic factors, and familial pressures or influences. Karen Ahaesy, the founder of Los Angeles–based agency Axis Media Public Relations, works with a lot of celebrities on a regular basis but is most inspired by her Scottish-born mother's work ethic. "My mother was the first and youngest in her family to leave her country and come to America. She had to struggle to get on her feet, get acclimated to American life and American culture, and she built a very successful career in the States. By watching her, I knew that hard work was a must and nothing would be handed to me."

The professional that you are right now has inimitable skills and intrinsic elements of cool. Take some time to figure out the different factors that contribute to what makes you cool and what in your life keeps you from feeling cool.

CORPORATE

It can be excruciating to try to distinguish yourself professionally in an environment that encourages conformity. Jillian Kogan, who as a Director of Production Events and Concert Services at MTV Networks has what is considered to be one of the coolest jobs in existence, feels that she needs to break out of the rigid corporate structure of her job through her outlet as an artist. When asked about the potential difficulties in balancing both of her careers, she admits that "We all need motivators and coaches and even just people to inspire us." Let your friends, mentors, and coworkers inspire you in your professional life.

COOL

You can't fake cool, but you can tap into the unique elements of your personal experiences that distinguish you from the rest.

Chapter 2

Who Are You?

Quizzes and Questions to Help You Define Your Personal Style

> *The world belongs to the enthusiast who keeps cool.*
> —William McFee

Cool Moments

The late monologist Spalding Gray (who was a really cool guy) used to talk about "perfect moments" in life, times when either the stars were all aligned or the elements were all in place—tiny moments carved out of life when everything seemed blissfully, perfectly cool. Can you recall a perfect moment in your own personal or professional life in the recent past? Don't strain to try to encompass a perfect year, month, week, or even day, but rather an isolated perfect moment when all was right in your world.

How did it feel, and what made it so great?

What were the elements that came into play that made it so absolutely perfect?

If you go by Gray's theory, you don't have to try to make things perfect, but when they are, take a moment to notice and appreciate them. Cool can't be forced, but it can be incorporated into your work day.

Cool Influences

Okay, I promise not to make you work too hard while reading this book, but take a few minutes to get to know your Career and Corporate Cool self, and try to fill in the following section. (Indulge me—it's really fun!)

Make a list of the five coolest things that have happened to you, or your five coolest experiences—anything from traveling to your dream destination, to being hired without an interview. Don't worry, I won't grade you on it.

The Five Coolest Things That Ever Happened to Me

1. _____

2. _____

3. _____

4. _____

5. _____

Okay, let's take this a step further. Now make a list of the five coolest people you know or wish you knew. This can be anyone from your next-door neighbor, who volunteers for a soup kitchen while holding down a full-time job and has perfectly behaved children, to the stars of your favorite nighttime soap opera.

The Five Coolest People I Know or Wish I Knew

1. Rachel Weingarten.

Oh come on, I feel like we practically know each other by now. (Heavy sigh.) Fine, be like that. List the five *other* coolest people.

1. _____

2. _____

3. _____

4. _____

5. _____

Uh-huh. I can tell that you're warming up to this. Now let's go for the five coolest things about your current job. Include anything—your fabulous coworkers, proximity to great shopping, summer Fridays, whatever springs to mind.

The Five Coolest Things about My Job

1. _____

2. _____

3. _____

4. _____

5. _____

Now list the five least cool things about your job. (Come on—you knew this was coming, and yes, you do have to limit it to only five things.)

The Five Least Cool Things about My Job

1. _____

2. _____

3. _____

4. _____

5. _____

We're nearly done. Off the top of your head, make a really quick list of the five worst, most painfully uncool elements about your life.

The Five Least Cool Things about My Life

1. _____

2. _____

3. _____

4. _____

5. _____

Okay, this is the last one, and it's a good one. List the five coolest things about yourself—and no false modesty please, just shameless self-flattery.

The Five Coolest Things about Me (and by "me" I mean "you"!)

1. _____

2. _____

3. _____

4. _____

5. _____

An Analysis of Cool

If you spend some time reading and rereading your lists, a pattern will start to emerge. Or you can spend some time trying to figure out how to understand what your greatest likes and dislikes say about you now, and about the obscenely cool person that is lurking within.

If you look at the coolest things that have happened in your life, you'll likely notice that they share a certain high point. Perhaps they all occurred at a certain time in your life—during college or while on vacation. Maybe they are work or family successes.

What about the five coolest people that you know or wish you knew—what common traits do they share? Are they all brilliant strategists? Do they find time to give back to their communities no matter how busy their schedule? Do they all share your DNA? Are they great dressers?

On to the five coolest things about your job. Notice any patterns here? Did you talk about your ability to express yourself? Your cool new computer? Your coworkers?

What about the five worst things about your job? Are you dissatisfied with your salary? Your work conditions, cubicle life, the fact that John Cusack doesn't occupy the cubicle next to yours? Your home office? Your lack of a social life?

Here's a really tough one, to spend time really delving into the five least cool things about your life. Do you hate where you live, or who you live with (even if you live alone)? Do you wish that you had more time to work out, to travel, or to pursue a creative outlet?

Okay, now bask in the glow for a minute. What about the five coolest things about yourself? Did you talk about what a generous person you are? A devoted friend? Your almost photographic memory for celebrity gossip? Your ability to stay calm in a crisis?

For extra credit, how do you think you might answer these questions five years from now?

This is the key to moving forward: retaining and enhancing the existing cool elements of your personal and professional life, slowly getting rid of the really bad ones, incorporating the best habits of your friends and idols, and moving toward an overall sense of contentment.

Born Cool

Halle Berry. Catherine Zeta Jones. Vera Wang. Cher.

What do these four iconic and very cool women have in common?

Dark, glossy tresses? Not even close. An ability to weather torrents of media attention while retaining their seemingly effortless sense of chic? Hmmm, you're getting warmer.

What these four women, and a majority of the exquisitely coiffed and clad women in the world, have in common is in fact a not-so-well-kept and somewhat dirty little secret. You see, these women are desperately hoping that years of looking perfect has caused you to forget their early years filled with fashion fiascos and clothing catastrophes.

Decades before Halle Berry made history as the first black woman ever to win a Best Actress Academy Award (clad in that spectacular Elie Saab dress), she was an apple-cheeked teen beauty queen—poofy hair, poofy skirts, and all.

Flash back to the early 1990s when young Welsh beauty Catherine Zeta-Jones starred as Mariette Larkin in *The Darling Buds of May*, one of the United Kingdom's most beloved television series. There was laughter, there were tears, there was Catherine with a frizzy do and an unfortunate wardrobe, and sadly her sartorial suicide was not limited to her time in front of the camera.

There's no denying the fact that the divine Ms. Vera Wang, who at the tender age of 23 became the youngest fashion editor of *Vogue* magazine, breathed new life into the traditional wedding dress with her modern silhouettes and updated takes on the classic sheath. As for her own wedding day? Well, gentle reader, seek out Vera's own wedding pictures and understand once and for all why Ms. Wang dedicated her life to bridal couture. She must have taken one look at her own wedding album and sworn that no other blushing bride should ever again be subjected to the miles of meringue-like flounces and endless frills worn by Vera on her own wedding day.

There is a lesson to be learned from these tales of frightful frocks and fashionable redemption, and the lesson is this: No one is born cool. (Well, that's not entirely true. By virtue of his name, architect Rem Koolhaas was very likely born cool.) If you take only one lesson from this book, here's hoping this is the one. I'll repeat myself in case you still don't believe me: *No one* is born cool!

People may be genetically gifted with looks, talent, or intellectual prowess. They may have a last name like Rockefeller, Kennedy, or Winfrey. But contrary to popular belief, not one of them was born cool, because cool of that magnitude isn't achieved without a coterie of "-ists." From hair and fashion stylists to makeup artists to personal trainers and personal assistants, it takes more than a village to make these women stand out from the Botox-enhanced pout and Pilates crowd. Like most super chic women and men, they learned through trial and error (and in some cases the 1980s) how to look, dress, and act the part. They spent years defining and refining their personal style. They tried on different careers, set and redefined their goals, and changed what wasn't working until they became the icons that we know and love. They make it look effortless now, but they actually make a career of being what we take for granted as impeccably dressed, always-in-control symbols of cool.

Oh, and as for Cher? She, too, went through decades of beaded and rhinestoned excess, dangerous-looking shoes, and spangly hair accessories. She then seemed to radically grow up and star in movies like *Silkwood*, *Mask*, and, in an Academy Award winning performance, *Moonstruck*. Then she completely transformed her style to wearing tailored Chanel suits by day and Armani sheaths at night—oh yes, and following a whirlwind courtship I married George Clooney and we lived happily ever after.

As you've correctly surmised, that last sentence is complete fiction. Cher never changed her dubious dress sense and, sadly, Mr. Clooney and I are not now, nor have we ever been, an item. But back to Cher. The fashion world may perpetually vilify her sartorial sense, but that never affects her choices in clothing. For better or worse (or, in the case of that dangerous-looking Bob Mackie Mohawk headdress at the 1986 Academy Awards, just plain scary), Cher trusts her gut on what works or doesn't work for her and doesn't seem to give a damn about what the rest of us or the fashion and entertainment media think. That's a sense of cool and confidence that no amount of money can buy.

Some Like It Hot

While the ubiquitous Paris Hilton may have appropriated the use of the word *hot* to describe everything from minute pocket pooches to overpriced blinging baubles, for a majority of people in the business world it's being cool that matters most. It's one thing to be considered a hot commodity but quite another and less desirable quality to be known as a hothead. Being considered a hottie may be the desired

There's No Such Thing As Basic Black...

reputation while on spring break, but in the workplace it's being cool, calm, and collected that counts.

A few years back a really tacky web site gained popularity. The purpose of said web site was for attractive young women and men to upload images of themselves and then invite ratings, compliments, or criticism from total strangers. One wonders at the wisdom of offering oneself up to critique and commentary on a medium that popularized the expression *flaming* or *flame wars* to describe the volleys of hostile and critical message board posts and e-mail exchanges between total strangers that sometimes run rampant on the Web. Why let others judge you on your looks or pixelated appearance alone? You're worth more than just the way you appear to others, and you're certainly more substantive than the way that you might allow yourself to be pigeonholed by a society obsessed with outward appearance.

In the mid 1980s New York based fashion designer Donna Karan appeared in commercials for Dry Idea deodorant. She offered her three basic tenets to the fashion industry, which can be applied to good business or great style:

1. Never confuse fad with fashion.
2. Never forget it's your name on every label.
3. When you're showing your line to the press, never let them see you sweat.

Whether you face your strongest critics on a daily basis or you are in fact your own toughest critic, the key isn't necessarily only appearing to be perfectly cool and in control, but rather always giving the impression of utter cool, calm, and control.

Smart versus Pretty—Can You Be Both?

Like one of my business idols, Estée Lauder, I've never felt that I was less of a smart, strong woman just because I also wanted to be a pretty and well-groomed one. I unabashedly obsess over lip gloss the way that Carrie Bradshaw once worshipped stiletto shoes, and Arianna Huffington still professes to do. For that reason, I suppose, I've spent a good portion of my personal and professional life buying, applying, or marketing makeup and other accoutrements of beauty and style.

Like most women, I have a love/hate relationship with my looks. Like most smart women, I also have a love/hate relationship with some of the fashion and beauty advertising and copy aimed at women. Much of it, instead of celebrating or, at the very least, accepting our unique features or figure flaws, coyly provides us with a whole new set of insecurities.

While researching my book *Hello Gorgeous! Beauty Products in America '40s–'60s*, I came to realize that in many ways, the more that advertising geared toward women changes, the more it stays the same. In the mid-twentieth century, a woman was assured that a spritz of perfume, a swipe of lipstick, and a dusting of powder would render her irresistible. Flip through a fashion magazine these days and you'll notice that most of the advertisements are eerily similar (and all seem to feature Kate Moss)—or are they? Though the premise of promise remains the same, aside from a handful of ads touting a "campaign for real beauty" or a short lived celebration of "thunder thighs," advertisements today feature models and ideals that bear precious little resemblance to the average woman.

Fashion magazines from both the mid-twentieth century and our own are bursting with advertisements promising a younger, fresher, more lovable version of yourself. Back in those days, luscious lovelies like Sophia Loren and Marilyn Monroe represented the desired beauty ideal despite their fleshy thighs, jiggly arms, and rounded tummies. In our own times, however, it can be hard to recognize formerly familiar famous faces and figures as they become molded with silicon and whittled by the plastic surgeon's scalpel.

In the dawn of my career, I did a stint as a celebrity makeup artist. Back then supermodels were mostly mortal, and catwalks contained healthy size 8s instead of scary size 0s. Cindy Crawford recently told me that a great part of her beauty ideal has always been to look not just pretty but "healthy and real." While she has publicly admitted to indulging in the occasional Botox injection, she is as luminous in person as in print. Crawford in her 40s is much more than just a pretty face. She's a savvy businesswoman, wife, and mother, who has capitalized on her popularity and initial recognition for looks alone to forge relationships with companies like Remington.

In the days prior to mainstream nip-and-tuck treatments, while beauty wasn't necessarily in the eye of the beholder, it was frequently more attainable. And as far as we knew, models weren't literally dying to be fashionable. In late 2006, two models died as a result of eating disorders; 21-year-old Brazilian model Ana Carolina Reston weighed only 88 pounds at the time of her death, while Uruguayan Luisel Ramos died of heart failure brought on by anorexia, leaving the fashion world in an uproar. The organizers of Madrid Fashion Week responded by banishing underweight models from appearing on the catwalk. British supermodel Erin O'Connor was said to have challenged designers who insisted on skeletal supermodels and urged them to accept some of the responsibility for the pressure on models to be unrealistically and unhealthily thin.

Fashion designers from Giorgio Armani to Karl Lagerfeld got into the fray, the former defending his preference for "slender" models, the latter musing that the lightweight lasses "have skinny bones." Armani was said to prefer thinner models because he wants the dresses he designs to seem to "float and flow with the body," much like the shapeless black burkas worn by Muslim women who are themselves subject to the whims of controlling men.

Back in the 1970s a woman's body was also a battleground. *Roe v. Wade* determined that a woman had the right to choose, while Title IX ensured that girls and women could compete in school sports. But for all of our rights, do we always choose wisely? If the 1970s were about choice, the 1980s were about fitting in at the workplace and the1990s were about figuring out how to have it all. Through it all, though, there have always been the warring factions of smart versus pretty.

Echoing Barbie's sentiment that math is hard, recent articles have declared that many female Ivy League graduates intended to opt out of the workforce, while an inflammatory editorial appeared on Forbes.com cautioning men against marrying career women. Both seemed to suggest that many women return full circle to the ideals of 1950s suburbia and the stay-at-home mommy track.

So what's a post-modern woman to do? While most of America seems to be steadily losing its battle with obesity in its obsession to supersize everything, Hollywood and the fashion world run rampant with taut faces, six-pack abs, and implanted everything else. I remember getting ready for an appearance on CNBC as an expert on the cosmetic industry, discussing male grooming products. I panicked about having a double chin on camera. It never once occurred to me to doubt my ability as an expert to answer questions on the fly, to quote detailed facts, studies, and statistics, and to make accurate analyses and predictions on a multibillion-dollar industry. I never doubted my knowledge, presence, wit, or attire. It was only my appearance that left me insecure.

An accident some years ago forced me out of my career as a makeup artist and I segued into the marketing game. On rare occasions, though, I can still be sweet-talked into making up famous faces. I remember styling a magazine cover that featured a triple threat of feminist literature, including Helen Gurley Brown and Erica Jong. While the *Fear of Flying* author seemed almost timid by comparison, the octogenarian Gurley Brown was as bold as her fire-engine red lipstick and suit (worn with fishnet stockings).

When I gently reminded her that we'd known each other in my makeup days and that she had always complimented me on my beautiful skin, she replied, "You can't take any credit for your looks. You had nothing to do with it." She continued, "What have you done to distinguish yourself since then?"

What indeed. It gave me pause to realize that for a woman who had created a glossy magazine dedicated to the obsessive and almost quaintly antiquated self-improvement of women's external appearance and sex life, looking good was far from enough. Evolving, learning, and growing as a human being and business professional, along with looking good, was what mattered most.

And the third subject of the magazine cover? Well, she seemed to forget the much-loved chestnut of feminism: "Sisterhood is powerful." Instead of getting to know any of the others involved with the shoot, she all but ignored us in favor of cozying up to the more famous names that she recognized. Lesson learned: In networking, business, and life, it's always a good idea to be equally polite and respectful to everyone that you meet—you never know who they are, who they know, or where they're going.

CAREER

A great career is like any great relationship—it isn't always perfect, and sometimes it takes a bit of hardship to make you appreciate just what you've got. It's okay to look back and laugh at past naiveté and style sense. It's okay to make some mistakes. It isn't okay to coast or be complacent about poor grammar, sloppy work habits, or professional relationships that have deteriorated.

CORPORATE

Unlike Tom Cruise's star-making turn as the cocky pilot in the flick *Top Gun*, not every office needs a Maverick or a rock star. If your company is built on teamwork, then learn how to become a valued member of the team, instead of hogging the limelight for yourself. There is strength in numbers, and it can be a pretty lonely climb to the top on your own. Share the job, share the credit.

COOL

What words would your best friends use to describe you? How about your boss? Significant other? Online friends? If the same words come up again and again, then for better or worse you've branded yourself as reliable, flighty, witty, or charming. Act the way that you want to be described. Redefine your brand—look what it did for Herbal Essence shampoo!

Chapter 3

Culture Club

Understand and Adapt to Your Firm's Unique Corporate Culture without Becoming Just Another Cog

> *Man was born to be rich, or grow rich by use of his faculties, by the union of thought with nature. Property is an intellectual production. The game requires coolness, right reasoning, promptness, and patience in the players. Cultivated labor drives out brute labor.*
>
> —Ralph Waldo Emerson

Turn and Face the Changes

Depending on what you read or who you talk to, you'll find numerous studies and statistics stating that the average person goes through anywhere from seven to a dozen or more different jobs or career changes in her lifetime. It can be hard to pinpoint specifics, though, since even the Bureau of Labor Statistics doesn't have a definitive description of what exactly a career change is. Does a career change mean making a radical change from lawyer to creative artist, or simply moving from a corporate gig to a freelance position?

What causes us to become restless and ready to make these changes, or to want to stay rooted where we are? Is it the company we work for? Are we unfulfilled with our current vocation? For most people, different internal and external elements factor into their major life decisions, ranging from personal factors like health scares, marriage or divorce, children or lack thereof, to job environment changes, market fluctuations, emerging careers (look at how the advent of the Internet affected career choice), lack of fulfillment—the list goes on. Different occurrences allow people to make different and often life-altering decisions. Success or great disappointments, triumphs or tragedies, great world events, or even just low-grade ennui can affect people and their daily dynamics, allowing some to spend an entire lifetime at a dead-end albeit well-paying job, while others flit from career to career without finding the right fit.

Follow Your Bliss

With no intention of sounding overly twee, I propose that every generation has its modern miracles—outstanding inventions or events that radically change the professional playing field. From the cotton gin to legalized birth control, from the Industrial Revolution to the Internet, humanity has been witness to major and minor daily changes that build up and then revolutionize and continue to alter the way that we live, interact, and create commerce.

The late educator and writer Joseph Campbell is best known for his study of myth and his exhortation to "Follow your bliss," to find what you might not have even realized was lost or lacking in yourself. "If you follow your bliss, you put yourself on a kind of track that has been there all the while, waiting for you, and the life that you ought to be living is the one you are living. Wherever you are—if you are following your bliss, you are enjoying that refreshment, that life within you, all the time." The Joseph Campbell foundation website http://www.jcf.org/bliss.php cites this most famous quote by Campbell, said in an interview with Bill Moyers. Campbell originally stated "follow your bliss" in his book *The Power of Myth* (Doubleday, 1988).

I've always had mentors in my life and unofficial heroes, and it occurs to me that the one thing they've all shared, besides an ability to make the impossible seem effortless, was a love and great passion for their chosen vocation. After listening to scores of tales of self-discovery and self-actualization, I realized that the common thread was finding a way to make work fun, and to keep trying until you find the job, career, vocation, or calling that engages you in every way possible. Most people never reach this point, though I know that you can and will, because *you* keep trying to find the life, the career, the love, the passion, the creativity, the fulfillment in each and every minute of each and every day.

Your Personal Brand Hallmarks

Hopefully, following your bliss is what led you to this point in your life, and what also led you to pick up this book in a bookstore crammed with titles all vying for your attention (and my publisher and I thank you for making that choice). Whatever point you are at in your career, you've likely developed specific ways of doing things and a particular way of interacting with others in your personal and professional life. Perhaps you're used to taking your cues from coworkers. If you work in the health care field you might understand the great financial rewards potential, or perhaps you fight your inner demons trying to figure out how to make health care more accessible. If you're a junior executive, you might be trying to figure out how best to work your way up the corporate ladder without stepping on too many feet on your way up. If you teach, perhaps you're navigating the dichotomy of a dress code for teachers but not students. Karen Ahaesy, founder of Los Angeles–based agency Axis Media Public Relations, advises: "Be yourself. Don't try to act or say things that you think others want to hear. Listen to yourself and project that accurately and confidently. People will notice."

A corporate culture is often a constantly evolving and growing component of a corporation. John Sencion, cofounder of Flight 001, admits that "Our culture is being cultivated as we speak. We certainly are getting better as time goes by. Early on we made the decision to open many stores and in order to do that you have to be more polished and formulaic in order to make it work."

Urban Outfitters is an example of a company that tries to remain "indie" but even they are "organized indie." Tim Westergren, the founder and CEO of Pandora Media Inc., has created something called "The Music Genome Project" a highly individualized service available on Pandora.com in which people can customize their musical choices and create personalized radio stations. Westergren doesn't simply pay lip service to this credo, though: "Our mantra as a company is to treat people with the utmost respect—to treat them as individuals and honor their individuality, and to speak to them with a human voice. I think though, that actually doing this effectively requires that everyone in the company really believe in and internalize this credo. It isn't so just because you decree it. We hire people who share these values, and we continually reinforce them. I think maintaining a sense of humility is vital."

But what about companies that seem to have a very specific culture or way of doing things? Michael Main, a managing partner at Chapterhouse, a Chicago-based health care strategy consultancy, disavows the notion of a great or all-encompassing corporate culture but rather believes that "Employees own culture—not leaders. Leaders, however, own the hiring and retention of their employees. Investing in people with the right values, treating them with honesty and support, and giving them what they need to deliver on the organization's strategy will serve to germinate and grow a healthy culture from the ground up."

Doing the Right Thing

Perhaps you work in the jewelry industry and wrestle with the thought of so-called blood diamonds, or you might be a fashion designer who drapes her creations on painfully thin models while your own daughter struggles with keeping her weight down. People at collection agencies sometimes abide by a corporate culture that advocates using threats or language meant to threaten—it's just part of their job.

Every day you make calculated decisions, whether you realize it or not. You decide on a daily basis whether you will continue to play by other people's rules or set your own. For the most part, you seek a happy medium—a career and employer that fulfills you monetarily while putting your unique skill set to work.

Hopefully your company stresses an overall message that you find reflects your own philosophy, one that in some way enhances or contributes to the greater good. Companies like Enron once stood for the greater good, providing employment for over 21,000 people, yet somehow their highest corporate team players twisted the overall company mission to suit their own personal gain. Films like *All the President's Men*, *Erin Brockovich*, and *The Insider*, among others, chronicle the struggle of real-life people to fight for justice, to do battle with their own personal issues, and to expose corruption for the ultimate greater good. Not all companies have a guidebook to follow—some play it by ear; some evolve on a daily, weekly, or monthly basis. One of the toughest decisions that you'll ever have to make at any point in your career is determining whether your employer's corporate culture works with your beliefs and ideals, and whether you are willing to compromise to fit in or bring any potential inequality or inconsistencies into the public eye.

Do the Write Thing: E-Mail Etiquette

Hopefully, you've found your niche, your cozy little career that fits you like a second skin, with plenty of room to grow and breathe. At that point you can start to play around a bit—not enough to jeopardize your job, but enough to create the right kind of impression with everyone with whom you choose to interact.

Most of us spend hours each day on immediate correspondence. From e-mail to instant messaging, your work correspondence has both your company and personal name on each and every message. As with much else in the workplace, with correspondence that is meant to expand your brand presence, check to see if there is one correct way of addressing people.

Much has been written about the correct way to start an e-mail. Accepted salutations include variations of "Hello," "Hi," "Dear," "Hey," "Hey There," and "Greetings." But to some, "Dear" can seem old fashioned, "Hello" a little too perky, and "Hey" a bit disrespectful. Follow the lead of your employer or supervisor, or at the very least the person who initiated the conversation. Follow their lead throughout, as e-mail intimacy can build up almost immediately, with plenty of room for awkwardness and misunderstandings. Because we're such a multicultural society, avoid any clear gender greetings like "Sir" or "Madame," since not only might these be construed as old-fashioned, but you might also be insulting the recipient with a generic and dated "Dear Sirs."

Also find out if there is one accepted signature at your place of business. If not, compose your own. Your e-mail signature is a free billboard to get your message out there; it's also a good way to give people your contact information.

Mine looks like this:

Rachel Weingarten, President
[GTK] Marketing Group—Good To Know!
www.gtkgroup.com (URL)
[e] rachel@careerandcorporatecool.com
[p] xxx.xxx.xxxx [f] xxx.xxx.xxxx [c] xxx.xxx.xxxx
[Read my book]: *Career and Corporate Cool* (www.careercorporate
cool.com)
This e-mail is confidential (and more legal stuff).

The top line identifies me, and the next one gives my company name and our tagline. These are followed by the company's URL, then by my e-mail address, phone number, fax, and cell phone number; the brackets contain our company logo. Last comes a shameless self-promotion for my book or current project. I then separate the signature from the content and also from the legal disclaimer (have your legal department draw one up for you).

One of my favorite e-mail signatures belongs to Robert Klara, the features editor at *Brandweek* magazine:

Don't know me? I'm:
Robert Klara, Features Editor
Brandweek magazine
(and the rest of his contact information)

Rob chooses not to take himself too seriously and was looking for a way to be "less-corporatey." His playful signature acts as an ice-breaker and also as a cue to people that he prefers informality. He says he "was simply owning up to my modest place in the publishing world. There's something human and genuine about it—a clear lack of ego, I suppose." It's a refreshing self-definition and definitely stands out in a sea of over-the-top rhetoric.

Find out company policy before tweaking your signature, and be playful and creative only when and if it's appropriate. Clear your new signature with your supervisor first, and check with friends and coworkers to make sure that it works for you and that you haven't included too much information.

Other e-mail tips:

- It may be helpful to find out the cultural background of your target, as they might not welcome a note addressed to their first name.
- Don't send attachments unless you know the recipient or have told them to expect it.
- Don't jazz up your note with complicated color patterns or background. Basic black or blue text in a clear, easy to read font works best.
- Sign your note by following the cue of the recipient, if possible. The following are always acceptable: "Best," "Regards," "Best regards," "Warmly," "Warmest regards," "Kindest regards," and "Sincerely."
- Mind your X's and O's. While sending a virtual hug and kiss to a close friend is not only acceptable but expected, salivating at strangers can sometimes be frowned on.

CAREER

You've chosen your vocation based on a number of personal preferences and passions. Hopefully the balance sheet favors the overall gestalt of your company and allows you to shine without compromising your personal mission statement.

CORPORATE

There are days when you'll feel just part of the wallpaper, and it will seem almost impossible to express yourself and your individual contribution to your company. On days like those you can use a quirky writing style, or end an e-mail with your favorite quote or flourish.

COOL

Two words: big picture. It can sometimes feel challenging to keep your individuality while abiding by all of the miscellaneous corporate rules and regulations. In the grand scheme of things, you are more than what you do for a living. In the United Kingdom it's almost considered rude to ask someone what they do for a living, while in the States so much of who you are is dependent on what you do. Author Max Barry poked fun at this concept in his book *Jennifer Government* (New York: Vintage, 2004), in which people were quite literally identified by the corporation that they worked for. In other words, I'd be Rachel GTK.

Chapter 4

Career-O-Rama

*How to Dress, Act, and Interact Whether You're a
Fortune 500 Company Executive or a Junior Manager at
an Ad Agency*

> *If you cannot work with love but only with distaste,
> it is better that you should leave your work.*
>
> —Kahlil Gibran

Taking Stock

Okay, it's time for the proverbial bracing cold water to be splashed in
your face. It's time to divest yourself of all clothing, attitudes, expressions, and other accessories that drag your professional persona down
and don't allow you to soar. Over the next six weeks (did you think
I'd make you do all of this at once?), take two hours each weekend to
really evaluate who you are, how you became this person, where you
want to be, and what you have to do to get there.

And now, without further ado, and for your entertainment pleasure (and mine if you want to e-mail the results to me), a quiz to help
you to determine which element of your life needs the most work.
And yes, there are trick questions!

SECURE, SOARING, OR STUCK IN A RUT—WHICH ONE ARE YOU?

1. When you get out of bed in the morning you:
   A. Wake up refreshed and ready for the exciting day ahead of you!
   B. Panic—you have no idea what to wear.
   C. Wish you could catch a couple more Z's, but know that people depend on you. Feed the cat. Feed the kids. Head to work.
   D. Curse the irritatingly perfect blue skies and those damn perky birds for chirping too loud.
   E. Trip over Brad Pitt on your way to the shower.
2. Your favored method of transportation to and from work is:
   A. By foot when possible. You love to see as much of your world as you can and exercise at the same time!
   B. The same bus or train every day, and hopefully time enough to gossip while en route. Get distracted by a juicy story and get to work late.
   C. The route that passes the kid's school and grocery store— lots to do before you get to the office.
   D. Car, cab, rickshaw—whichever one keeps you away from as many annoying people as possible.
   E. Vespa, tube, or gondola, depending on whether you're at the apartment in Paris, London, or Venice.
3. Your before-work morning indulgence includes:
   A. You don't really need anything, but you'll buy something tasty or cute if it catches your fancy.
   B. Hot yoga on Monday and Friday; gym on Tuesday, Wednesday, and Thursday—you have to work off that morning muffin.
   C. Those three minutes right after you drop off the carpool and before you pick up your coworker.
   D. A scratch-off lottery ticket. If you win those millions you'll never have to go into the office at all!
   E. A dip in your private pool and having a facial and massage.

4. When you get to the office you immediately:
   A. Check your date book because every day is different—you could be at a breakfast meeting or hosting an event for a client, or on a conference call with the London team.
   B. Say good morning to your work friends and turn on your computer—you're ready for the day.
   C. Look through your to-do list for the week. Realize that you still haven't caught up with last month's to-do lists.
   D. Pop two Tylenols and guzzle some water—that hangover is a killer.
   E. Read the cards that came along with the bouquets of flowers from your admiring fans.

5. Every single thing that could possibly go wrong has gone wrong. The phone rings. It is your boss or client wanting a full status report. You:
   A. Take a deep breath and figure out a crisis management plan. Leave the office if you have to. Talk to a friend, do whatever it takes to get through.
   B. Schedule some face time with your fellow team members or supervisor before meeting your boss. Try to assess and minimize the long-term damage to your reputation.
   C. Burst into tears. Wash your face. Walk into your boss's office with no clear plan.
   D. Quit. Who needs this nonsense day after day? Hollywood awaits!
   E. Call Page Six with an "anonymous" tip about Johnny Depp picking you up after work. Hope that the paparazzi block the entrance to your office long enough for you to make a clean getaway.

6. You hear a really juicy piece of gossip about your evil nemesis. You immediately:
   A. Analyze the details to figure out what the real story is. Figure out a way to improve your own performance to really shine in the next few weeks.

    B. Confirm that it's true. Wrestle with your conscience for a while before deciding not to tell anyone but your sister. After all, who needs that kind of bad karma?

    C. Figure out a way to get a coworker to spread the word. While you would never be the one to talk, it can't hurt for people to know what your enemy has done.

    D. Cackle madly. Update your blog. Send out a press release. Gloat.

    E. Ha! Hear a rumor? Your publicist planted that story.

7. It is your last day at work. Just before you leave for the very last time, you:

    A. Take a fond last look at your old, smaller work space. Know you've made the right decision in securing a larger space, but feel apprehensive and excited at the same time.

    B. Make sure that you've left your new contact information with your former coworkers. Hug everyone goodbye and promise to be in touch after you get settled into your new position.

    C. Triple-check that your health insurance will carry over until you find a new job.

    D. Tell each and every one of your former coworkers and bosses exactly what you think of them. Use-four letter words in combinations and permutations that would shock the cast of *Deadwood*.

    E. Make sure that your personal assistant's personal assistant doesn't scuff your Birkin bag as she slams the door behind you.

ANSWER KEY:

Mostly A's   You're frightfully *cool*—so cool, in fact, that you might just be in danger of freezing over. Enjoy the fact that you're in a good place in your life both personally and professionally. Know that you can cut yourself some slack at this point, maybe become more playful in your wardrobe or even e-mail interaction. People know and respect you, and are eager to see what you can do next—why not show them? Invest in a few key pieces, maybe a fantastic signature handbag or laptop case. Develop your own personal slogans and mottos, whether you share them with others or not. It might be time for you to become more of a name to know or watch.

Mostly B's You're fairly secure. You've made mistakes in the past, but for the most part you have a clear understanding of how to play the game to get what you want. Your wardrobe might lack a spark that sets you apart. Try taking a few more chances with your accessories, buy fun boots for fall, get an updated haircut. Take baby steps toward updating and modernizing your look. Browse through old documents that you've written, presentations that you've coordinated. Has your style evolved in the past few years? Is it better or worse? Take a good look at the materials that you use to present yourself. If the language feels old, stuffy, or dry, you might want to consider updating your communication style as well. Take a class or subscribe to trade magazines. Start exploring competitors' web sites to educate yourself as to their strengths and weaknesses.

Mostly C's You're in danger of falling into a rut. You need to find more balance in your life between family and work. You don't have to do everything on your own. Learning to delegate would give you more time to concentrate on building your brand at work, and also allow you to spend more time with friends or loved ones. You don't have to solve everyone's problems—concentrate on your own for now. Make a three-month projection of where you are now in your career, and put in soft and hard targets. Spend some time at the end of each week, either alone or with a life coach or mentor, considering how you have or have not moved toward your goal.

Mostly D's You're mad as hell and you're not going to take it anymore. It's time for you to reevaluate every decision that you've made that has led you to this place. Sure, these answers were tongue-in-cheek, but if you feel like you have no more joy in your life, it's time to consider a career switch and life makeover. Take a vacation, volunteer to help out with a nonprofit organization, lose the bad friends in your life. Even bad decisions aren't permanent, and it's time to let go of whatever is holding you back and keeping you unhappy.

Mostly E's   Either you're a character in a chick lit novel or your last name is Lauder, Hilton, or Kennedy.

Cool Classic Style Has Nothing to Do With Your Career

Drum roll, please. This is the moment when I finally tell you what to wear each and every day of your work life. First a caveat—you might not like this. I cannot tell you exactly what clothes to wear tomorrow, the day after, or even the week after that—only you can figure that out for yourself.

Why? Because jobs are subjective, trends change quickly, and climates, corporate culture, and even office atmosphere say more about a dress code than any companywide literature ever could. Because if you can afford Chanel and your boss can't, you'd be ill advised to wear couture every day. Because only you know deep down when you look really great or when you look really ridiculous. Because looking great is really a matter of feeling great and dressing well for where you are exactly in your life at this very moment. Because what might have looked great 10 years ago might still be the best style for you. Because thong panties may eliminate visible panty lines, but they might feel more than a bit uncomfortable if you're trying to negotiate tough terms. Because, let's face it, you've got quirks and style habits that are already cool—you just need to fine-tune them. Because individuality even in the most minimal way is a lot cooler than overall conformity. Because the only true keys to Career and Corporate Cool style are learning from your past mistakes, feeling comfortable and in control, and moving forward to become a better version of yourself.

Wardrobe Building Pieces

Now, that being said, there are always classic and cool wardrobe basics to incorporate into your closet that work whether you're in your 20s, 30s, 40s, 50s, 60s, or beyond. I've broken down clothing for most careers into mood more than by industry or for a specific reason. You might be a banker in Boston while your best friend is in finance in 'Frisco—what works for you will definitely not work for her. The mood or feel of the office or environment might be a better gauge than simply career choice.

ICONIC STYLE

Here's a conundrum. I searched high and low for well-known, power-ful, successful women to include as examples of the perfectly cool and classic look. I called friends, colleagues, publicists, and well-known personalities to submit their picks. Sadly, though, aside from a handful of well-known women, I came up with mostly actresses, who usually don't figure out their looks without the help of stylists, but who for bet-ter or worse are the most visibly well- or ill-dressed women around.

Why are famous women afraid to look great? (Hello, Hillary Clin-ton and Margaret Thatcher!) Do they fear being painted (or tainted) with the brush of frivolity if they are perfectly coiffed or accessorized? I've never found smart and pretty to be mutually exclusive, though in our society extremely beautiful women aren't encouraged to develop their mental prowess if their physical prowess is deemed to be pleas-ing enough.

Wanting to express yourself through beauty or fashion doesn't make you frivolous. You are your own canvas. Knowing your style helps you to dress in a way that you favor, keeping your personal hall-marks and quirks while refining what doesn't work. Whether you're famous or unknown, beautiful on the outside or inside, you've likely adopted a certain style, and while I would never presume to catego-rize you, you might just fit into one of the following cool groups:

Classic Cool You're an executive or in an upper management posi-tion. You follow the traditional mold from your suits to your separates but understand the importance of a well-placed pin or killer time-piece. You are addicted to your weekly blow-dry and manicure. *Clas-sic cool style icons*: Grace Kelly, Catherine Zeta-Jones, Jennifer Aniston.

Trendy Cool Words like *fabulous* and *fashionista* are frequently used to describe you. You shop at exotic locations and favor designers with difficult to pronounce names. You know that a great fit and inter-esting details (think stitching or linings) mean more to your overall style than simply the designer du jour. You're this close to becoming a fashion victim, but usually err on the side of chic. *Trendy cool style icons*: Mischa Barton, Sarah Jessica Parker, Rachel Bilson.

Evolving Cool   You may not have been born with a silver spoon in your mouth (or a Gucci purse in your hand), but you know and celebrate the person you are and are becoming. You take chances; you test-drive different looks, colors, tailoring, and textures. You mostly look gorgeous even when you really shouldn't. *Evolving cool style icons*: Oprah Winfrey, Jennifer Love Hewitt, Beyoncé.

Ka-Ching Cool   You're *so* money—literally. You work in a rarified air, and people's future security depends on your investment ideas or input. You favor muted tones and rich fabrics. Your clothes speak volumes, yet never louder than you, and they always command respect. *Ka-ching cool style icons*: Martha Stewart, Meredith Vieira, Carly Fiorina.

Creative Cool   You're an artist by word or deed. You entertain, delight, and engage those around you. Your clothing tends to shimmer or sway, and often floats behind you in a cloud of indefinable perfume. You love shocking people with your playful color combinations. You aren't afraid to make mistakes—you just wish you wouldn't be photographed during those times. *Creative cool style icons*: Anjelica Huston, Patti Smith, Bjork.

Retro Cool   You've found your muse, only she lives in a different era. Be it antebellum corsets or Rockabilly hair, you don't fit a modern mold—well, not externally at least. You understand that sometimes it can be liberating to celebrate your femininity and unique body shape or features by wearing updated styles from a bygone era. *Retro cool style icons*: Dita Von Teese, Salma Hayek, Gwen Stefani.

Cool at Any Age or Size   You've worked too hard for people to classify you by a number, be it age, weight, or height. You don't mind looking sexy or silly—sometimes at the same time. You aren't afraid to use your feminine wiles—both brains and beauty. *Ageless, sizeless cool style icons*: Queen Latifa, Dame Judi Dench, Helen Mirren, Jada Pinkett Smith.

Know What Works for You—And Work It!

There's an old saying about asking people for advice: You ask everyone for advice, and then do what you think is best. It's the same with personal style. You need to find the style that works best for your looks, lifestyle, and budget, and then make that your signature look. Carrie Foster, vice president at a boutique agency in Washington, D.C., sums it up this way: "Style is confidence interpreted through fashion. Seemingly style has limitations according to one's home, place of work, budget, and so on, but a Parisian designer can make a Wal-Mart outfit work if she needs to, because style is more about the comfort and the confidence of the look, rather than the label."

Don't try to be something that you aren't. Dressing the part doesn't mean pretending to be something or someone that you are not—it means incorporating all of the best elements of your own style and then cranking it up a notch or two. The key is in enjoying the process. Shopping isn't torture if you choose clothing that enhances your shape, clothing that will never pinch or dig, clothing that garners compliments or subtle admiring glances. Susan Safier, vice president of product placement for Twentieth Century Fox, considers her style to be casual, comfortable, and professional, and admits that "I love heels, but I can't deal with being in pain." Smart woman. Timeless and modern are not a contradiction in terms. Work your classic style and update it with trendy pieces and accessories.

Build Your Classic Wardrobe

While your taste may subtly evolve from season to season, it's always a great idea to stock your wardrobe with some basic and classic pieces. Bear in mind that *basic* and *classic* can mean very different things, depending on your location, income, age group, body type, and particular fashion likes or dislikes.

Some women consider twinsets to be de rigueur for everything from the PTA to an appearance on television; others would feel frumpy in a sweater set and pearls. Happy mediums abound, though—while a traditional pastel twinset might not scream "chic" in a major city, a bold print, unusual detailing, or of-the-minute color just might work. The key is to know your own classic choices and to let your taste evolve as you outgrow certain looks or find too many of one style in your wardrobe.

Kate Nobelius, founder of Billion Dollar Babes, knows a thing or two about shopping and about building a fantastic wardrobe. Nobelius says that "When it comes to shopping and particularly when it comes to sales, stick to what you know will look best on you. Always buy a size larger—easier to get things altered than to lose 10 pounds." Ann Watson, vice president and fashion director of Henri Bendel, says that "Wardrobe evaluation is essential to ensure that your closet has items that will last many seasons while still looking fashionable. Invest in seasonless, well-made pieces: a great black coat, a cashmere sweater in your favorite color, a leather or suede jacket, a tailored pant and skirt. All of these are well worth their price and will last you for years to come."

Here are some ideas for key wardrobe building pieces for women of all ages:

Work
- A solid-toned pencil skirt. Stick to a length that hits somewhere just above or just below the knee, and fabrics like lightweight wools or knits. Black always works best, or deep charcoal tones, white, or camel for less formal wear.
- Classic button-front shirt. Crisp white cotton is always classic, but try experimenting with shades that flatter your hair and skin tone.
- Cashmere knits. While traditional sweater sets run the risk of looking frumpy, a classic solid cashmere sweater set can easily take the place of a jacket at a meeting. Black is best, then opt for classic or jewel tones.
- White short-sleeve T-shirt. A crewneck is always classic; V-neck works best for bustier women.
- Camisoles. White, black, and navy are classic, but you can add some color to your wardrobe with punchier shades as well.
- Classic flat-front trousers. Style expert Sean Krebs explains that the leg opening depends on your body type. A slight boot-cut is most universally flattering. Look for lightweight wools in solid black, camel, and charcoal.
- Fitted blazers. The age of wearing a suit to work or meetings is just about over. Instead invest in well-cut jackets that can pull together skirts or pants and a top.

- Black shoes. Your needs might range from a classic pair of stiletto leather pumps, to a mid-heel sling-back or ballet flats.
- Pearls, gold hoop earrings, gold bangles. Choose any style of jewelry that clearly stands the test of time and keeps coming back season after season.
- Chic leather tote bag (as briefcase or laptop holder).
- A classic coat—be it wool or a long trench, the right cut and color can complete any outfit.
- Black sleeveless shift dress. Choose wool crepe, silk, or a fine cotton/lycra blend.

Weekend

- Jeans. Choose a cut that fits your body type perfectly, in several different lengths (to wear with heels and flats) and washes (dark denim, faded).
- Knit sweater. Choose one in your signature color, and find the look that flatters your figure, whether chunky turtleneck or sleek boatneck.
- Khakis, colored jeans. These are one step up from casual.
- Tennis sneakers or ultra comfortable Mary Janes. Dansko, Keen, Birkenstock, and Clark's offer cute and comfy styles.

Whatever

- Two little black dresses (LBDs) to see you through last-minute weddings and cocktails. Choose a seasonless fabric for one with a backup in velvet or some other luxurious fabric.
- One sexy dress in your signature color (for when LBDs are frowned on).
- A stylish shawl or wrap to cover up or accent your LBDs.
- A perfectly tailored pair of black pants to be worn with everything from a tuxedo jacket to a corset.
- Something sumptuous—maybe an ornately beaded jacket or a wrap top of the heaviest silk charmeuse, something that makes you feel bathed in luxury.
- A killer pair of boots to dress up your jeans or tone down your dress.
- A suede or leather jacket in an unexpected color.

Fashion Designer Cynthia Steffe suggests that layering your wardrobe basics provides the most versatility. She also believes that these versatile pieces make a great foundation for your suitcase essentials.

CAREER

While you might bemoan the lack of exciting pieces in your wardrobe, or be tempted to copy looks straight out of magazines, your best bet is a combination of the two. Start to weed through the elements in your professional and personal life that are holding you back. Eliminate poorly fitting or outdated clothing and attitudes, and make room for the new and improved you.

CORPORATE

Just because you're trained to do one job doesn't mean that you can't flex your creative muscles. Explore different aspects of your career. For instance, see if there's room for more or less interaction with clients, depending on which way you want to go. Ask if you can sit in on planning meetings. Take stock of the way that people perceive you both in and out of the office, and plan on taking baby steps to become a more confident professional.

COOL

Tighten up your personal brand, become more like yourself. Figure out the hallmarks that you are known for and try to enhance the best ones, while slowly eliminating or playing down the others.

Chapter 5

Attitude Adjustment

Quick Fixes for Common Mistakes to Help You Fit in Anywhere—
Or Fake It Till You Make It

> *Our attitudes control our lives. Attitudes are a secret*
> *power working twenty-four hours a day, for good or bad.*
> *It is of paramount importance that we know how to*
> *harness and control this great force.*
>
> —Irving Berlin

In the Beginning

In Chapter 2 we looked at some fabulous women who, much like modern-day Athenas, appear to have been sprung perfectly poised and polished onto the catwalk of life, but whose long-buried fashion faux pas are clearly visible in early films or photos. Now I feel it's time for me to share with you a tragic tale of fashion calamities and ultimate redemption—but one that hits a lot closer to home. I warn you, it isn't pretty, though it does have a happy ending.

A long, long time ago (in a time most of us pretend to have forgotten, an era commonly known as the late 1980s), in an outer borough far, far away (that would be Brooklyn before Caroline Kennedy, Heath Ledger, Michelle Williams, and most of Minnesota laid claim to it), lived a teenager named Rachel. Rachel ruled the bridge-and-tunnel roost with her feathered mane of lacquered locks, winged black eyeliner, and her jeans. Her jeans were the stuff of legend. The denim was more than scandalously skin-tight or distressed—these denims were simply devastated. When young Rachel (as you've correctly surmised, this was my younger self) wasn't clad thus, she could be spotted in too short, too tight miniskirts, tights that were decorated with all the colors of the rainbow, sweaters emblazoned with creatures and patterns impossible to describe, and accessories that jangled, clanged, and were frequently mistaken for frisbees or doorknockers, including a memorable pair of earrings that resembled miniature Tonka trucks. And while young Rachel didn't quite speak with the immediately recognizable nasal twang of Queens girl Fran Drescher or Bronx native Rosie Perez, she did present a credible aural impersonation of Eliza Doolittle crossed with the cast of *Saturday Night Fever* as she *wawked* and *tawked* (walked and talked) her way through her young life.

Okay, so neither my wardrobe nor my accent was ever quite that torturous, and no one ever mistook me for Melanie Griffith in *Working Girl*. But as my burgeoning sense of self fluctuated from day to day, my sense of style was definitely far from polished. In fact it occurs to me that my current, mostly unerring sense of style was developed through years of trial and error. It also occurs to me that to protect my reputation for all-around fabulosity I should break out a Sharpie and draw a black bar over my eyes in old and incriminating photos. Hi, my name is Rachel, and I am a former teen fashion victim. Worse still, I won't pretend that I outgrew that excess in my 20s. Most tragic yet? There are times when I still yearn for the freedom to wear whatever I want, without a thought as to whether others might care or what they might expect me to wear.

Live and Learn and Look Like You Did

So did I really change all that much? Yes and no, but most important, I learned how to incorporate my own personal style and quirks into classic looks and to use trend in moderation only. Even in those days, I had an all-consuming obsession for fashion and trends, but back then my ability to filter the good from the bad was not quite as refined as it is now. Back then I also copied trends instead of setting or, at the very least, filtering them. Back in the day, as fast as you could say "asymmetrical haircut," "argyle sweater," or "Naf Naf jumpsuit," this karma chameleon was almost instantaneously kitted out in despairingly trendy attire.

My impeccably clad mother would beseech me to wear the tailored suits or dresses that she favored or to at least limit my multihued, layered fishnet stockings to classic black (and to limit my multihued, layered hair to my natural brunette shade). But to become comfortable with who I am now, I had to make my own mistakes then. I had to figure out what did or didn't work for me. (Beer-cap barrettes and studded leather collars were definitely not a good look for my high school self.)

I always have and always will relish both dressing up and dressing down. For me fashion is, first and foremost, about feeling great and having fun with your looks. For better or worse, I've always been my own Barbie doll. If I didn't like the way a skirt fit, I'd rip the seams apart and sew it back together, only this time it might have a plaid taffeta bustle or a layer of tulle. Instead of fitting in as a teenager, I wanted to stand out; I wanted my clothing to express the external version of my inner turmoil and voyage of discovery, even if it meant looking really silly on occasion.

For some teens or 20-somethings, this experimentation can frequently take the form of extreme fashion or lifestyle experimentation. For the luckiest or most secure ones it can mean dressing up or dressing down, identifying with and emulating the look of athletic surfers like Kelly Slater or tennis player Maria Sharapova, while for others it might mean imitating the shock-value lifestyle of frenetic partiers like Lindsay Lohan or apathetic socialites like the Hilton sisters. Others affect the modern equivalent of tribal rites of passage in the form of extreme body modifications, tattoos, or piercing. But what might look vaguely appealing in an amphitheater and under klieg lights can have a completely different effect in the boardroom. I feel the same way about plastic surgery—take it too far and you've gone from looking vaguely refreshed to Jocelyn Wildenstein territory.

As a culture we celebrate youth and vilify aging. Wouldn't it be amazing if we could embrace the silly, ignorant people that we once were, and simply appreciate the way we've evolved to become who we are today? Wouldn't it be liberating to forgive and forget our past mistakes and instead celebrate the wisdom that we've earned—usually and especially the hard way? Wouldn't it be more amazing yet if, as a society, we would acknowledge instead of fighting the fact that this hard-earned wisdom, experience, and charm might show up in our faces and forms and voices and actions?

Don't Become Mired in Your Past Image

Crosby, Stills, Nash, and Young said it best (in "Suite Judy Blue Eyes") when they advised not letting your past remind you of what you are no longer. In other words, forgive your past self for saying, doing, dressing, or being the person that you felt best represented you at that moment in time. People change. Styles change. Careers change. Tastes change. Your exteriors change, but your core values generally stay the same even if the details fluctuate. Never stagnate, but always strive to respect and refine the core ideals that are uniquely yours, and allow yourself to evolve as necessary.

It can be painful to change. The people in your life might fight you on it, because sometimes they are comfortable only with the version of you that they know and already love. Your coworkers might not become automatically enamored with the supercharged version of you because it might make them look pale in comparison. It isn't easy to become a better version of yourself, which is why so many people settle for a one-size-fits-all approach to life and career. Be different. Give yourself permission to grow, to soar. And more than anything, if it feels wrong for you now, don't hold on to it just because it once was right.

Been There, Done That, Inspired the T-Shirt

At this point in my game, I certainly know what works best on and for me. While I'm always open to new experiences, I'm aware of which designers I favor, the shade of hair that suits me best, the tiny minutiae and personality trademarks that are practically impossible to pinpoint on their own but which collectively make up the brand known as

Rachel C. Weingarten. Like most people, I've learned the hard way; I've evolved by taking risks and having fun, and by not being afraid to look ridiculous as long as it led me to the path of becoming a better me. Even in my wildest moments, it was the exterior accoutrements that changed. I never made overwhelming or life-changing commitments in the name of style.

There are two categories of people: those who wear T-shirts with clever sayings written by clever people, and those whose lives inspire said clever T-shirts. (And before you throw rotten fruit in my direction, I do in fact have a drawer full of T-shirts with clever sayings—this is a fairly brilliant metaphor, you know.) When you sport a statement-making T-shirt, you sport more than just a designer name or label. In many ways you become a living, breathing billboard for yourself, announcing your theology, your idols, or your warped sense of humor.

Statement T-shirts allow anyone from a ninth-grade slacker to a midlife crisis sufferer to appear to be as witty as Dorothy Parker, as prolific as John Grisham, or as connected as Bill Clinton. T-shirts are the great American equalizer. Can't think of something clever to say? Wear this magic garment and be instantly transformed to a pundit, sex kitten, or activist. Too apathetic to take action? Buy and wear the limited edition T-shirt and instantly appear to give a damn! Rude, graphic, or obscene t-shirts allow every sleaze, frat boy, or enraged person to tell anyone who's looking just what they do or do not think. They aren't gifted comedic orators like Richard Pryor, as shocking as Lenny Bruce, or as expressive as Henry Miller. Instead they catch our attention visually and make us notice their awful sense of humor or barely concealed hostility.

But it doesn't take words on a T-shirt to give the wrong or right impression. It can be conveyed by the way you look, talk, speak, sneer, smile, or simply try to blend into the woodwork.

Brand You: When Appearance and Actions Do the Talking

Quick—sneak a peek at yourself in a mirror. What are some things that you automatically notice? Perfect hair? gleaming skin? confident smile? Or raggedy nails, bags under your eyes, scuffed shoes, dog hair on your pants?

You don't have to be wearing a statement T-shirt for total strangers to take one look at you and know more about you than you thought they could. Everything about you, from your slouched or perfect posture to your vaguely indefinable accent, to the way that you chew your food, chew out an employee, or tip or treat a waitress, sends a loud and clear signal to the person that you're with. How much you care about your appearance tells the world how much you do or do not value their opinion and invites them either to get to know you or to avoid you like the plague.

Whether you realize it or not, you've spent a good portion of your waking hours choosing to become the person you are now. For better or worse, every decision or even indecision transforms or cements your personal brand or lack thereof. While each interaction isn't necessarily the definitive or make-or-break situation, sometimes the most important relationships can be lost based on a gesture, a giggle at an inopportune moment, the wrong response to a no-brainer, or whether you know how to keep your cool in a tough situation.

No one expects you to be perfect all of the time. In art or pottery, for example, I always try to collect a piece that is somehow imperfect. A pot with the artist's fingerprint shows me that a greatly talented human being formed this, and the imperfection only sets off the exquisite detail of the rest of the object. I've heard that the artisans who craft the exquisite handmade rugs in much of the Middle East always leave a tiny section in which the stitches are imperfect or the color doesn't quite match, as a sign of their deference to a greater Being. In other words, they don't presume to attempt perfection, since they believe only their Creator is perfect. Many observant Jews leave a tiny section of their homes unpainted or unfinished for a similar reason—they consider their worldly happiness to be incomplete as long as they are in the diaspora.

Aspiring to be always perfect can be a double-edged sword because it doesn't give you wiggle room, not only to fail on occasion but also to become even better. Or as Todd Leopold, the entertainment producer at CNN.com, puts it, "You run the risk of becoming boxed into your own image." He continues: "What one person calls an image another might call a brand—and if you stray from the brand you might not become salable."

A healthier balance would probably be to strive to become better with each experience and to at least be able to assess a situation before taking action, hoping that the action you choose to take is appropriate and can move you forward to the next level.

Lose Your Cool or Keep Your Cool

The worst has happened. The biggest, baddest, scariest work or life crisis has transpired and you're frozen like the proverbial deer in the headlights (or like a tipsy, half-naked celebrity caught in the unflattering glare of the paparazzi's camera lens). You have only two options at this point:

1. *Lose your cool.* You have a full nuclear meltdown that involves tears, veiled threats, and curses that would make a sailor blush. You subsequently become the object of office urban legend and are hereafter used in corporate literature for decades to come as a prime example of what never to do.
2. *Keep your cool.* You realize that it doesn't matter if your heart is beating like a jackhammer and your mouth is as dry as Jon Stewart's wit. You will quickly assess the situation, act accordingly, and keep both your cool and your job.

Let's look at some specific situations in which you can either play the fool, stay cool, or "chill out"—forestall the problem by planning ahead.

Fool: You're running late. Instead of taking an extra minute or two to make contact with your client, you hop on the subway—which then gets stuck for an hour and a half.

Cool: You've left yourself more than enough time to reach your destination, choosing to arrive 10 minutes early rather than keep the person you're meeting waiting. You have all of your colleague's contact information handy, including office phone number, cell phone number, and e-mail address. As soon as you realize that you might be late, you phone your contact to inform them of your new estimated time of arrival. If you're even later than expected, you apologize profusely and then dazzle them during your meeting.

Chill out: Send them an e-mail the night before your meeting confirming the time and place of your appointment along with all of your contact information.

Fool: You've sent an e-mail to the wrong person or to too many people. Whoops, you've done it again, and no simple Nigerian letter of assistance or celebrity gossip this time—you've humiliated yourself or a supervisor or colleague in an e-mail to the masses.

Cool: Like it or not, you must apologize personally to the offended party, and to the entire group who received said e-mail. If the subject is too personal or painful, then leave out the salient details (and for God's sake don't include specifics in the apology, and by no means include the earlier e-mail content for people to view). Send out a short note explaining the error, but not its intent. It's okay to say, "I am writing to apologize for my earlier e-mail, which I inadvertently forwarded to your e-mail account. Kindly delete it from your inbox." It is *not* okay to say, "I apologize for my earlier e-mail, in which I referred to my boss as 'the trouser snake who bases his wardrobe on Seinfeld reruns and most resembles the love child of Medusa and Homer Simpson,' which I inadvertently forwarded to your e-mail account. Kindly delete it from your inbox."

Chill out: Three letters: BCC. Use the "blind carbon copy" function when sending out mass e-mailings so that people aren't always immediately aware of who is on your mailing list and who else has been privy to the public humiliation. Also, be vigilant about sending out e-mails or responses to groups. Double-check each e-mail before you hit "send," not only for typos but also to make sure that it is addressed to its intended recipient.

Fool: Your nemesis has achieved your dreams. Whether it's the corner office or a byline in the *New York Times*, he or she has beat you to it!

Cool: Oh please, we all seem to have assigned ourselves a nemesis on our road to success. Less dramatic than Lex Luthor and Superman, it can be a person in your high school class, your annoying coworker, or even a columnist in the local newspaper. While it's smart to challenge yourself by gauging the success level of others, it can be detrimental to your own success to obsess over each gain they rack up.

Chill out: The next time a not so well-meaning friend tells you about the success of your dastardly archenemy, take the opportunity to toot your own horn—to yourself, that is. Keep your own success list and write up a point-counterpoint. Instead of moping around the office, you'll realize just how far you've come toward reaching your own goals and dreams.

Fool: You're asked for a last-minute proposal for a gig you just know you're never going to get. It's specific, it's annoying, and you know you're going to research and write it anyway.

Cool: Instead of handing in a carelessly written or poorly researched document, you decide to dazzle them anyway, because even if they don't hire you for this project, they'll definitely keep you in the mind for the future. Also, you never know when the information will help you in your own career. I spent a few months on a minor consulting job for a male grooming line in the hopes of working on their launch—a launch that never happened because they ran out of funding. Instead of being aggravated (well, at least not for an extended period of time), I used all of my updated information to provide keynote remarks for a major advertising conference sponsored by a top men's magazine—and got three new clients out of the experience.

Chill out: It can be hard to walk away from a request for a proposal, even if your gut tells you that it isn't a good fit. When given a request for proposal (RFP), be sure to weigh the situation and all sides of the equation before responding or writing a proposal. It can sometimes be worse to hand in shoddy work, since word of mouth can be so powerful and you don't want to become known for handing in poor proposals. The second time this company requests more information, however, is a good time to ask very specific questions about their plans, budgeting, and implementation strategies.

Fool: You lose all of your contacts' information and e-mail addresses, or your computer is down. You've upgraded your system and now you're a blank slate—literally, since you can't find any of your contacts or documents.

Cool: In today's computer-dominated business world it's imperative to have several systems for keeping track of your urgent data. Back up your computer daily, both to an external hard drive and also to a remote server. If you can't access your backup information, try to search through old group e-mails that you might have sent out. While you won't be able to immediately view e-mail lists, clicking into the e-mail properties and details should give you a list of recipients.

Chill out: When you have some extra time in your day (I heard that snort!) weed out old contacts from your address book. Keep a mini flash drive with all of your current projects and contacts.

Fool: You and your assigned team partner don't see eye to eye on a subject. Who are we kidding? It drives you nuts when he says *catsup*—it's *ketchup*, dammit! Okay, tomatoey goodness aside, it can be torture to work with him and you find yourself bickering with each other all day to the detriment of your work and project.

Cool: You know how Mom always told you to play nicely with others? It doesn't matter whether you actually get along with the coworker from hell—what matters is that your combined work takes your career to the next level and satisfies your boss. Words like *compromise* and *negotiation* come into play, but it's more about having a blended agenda: As long as the end result satisfies your boss or client, it doesn't matter how the results are achieved. Unlike math class where you have to show your work to get extra credit, in this case be willing to compromise on the details that aren't as important to you, and fight for only the make-or-break details. As for negotiation, Anthony Elia, a publishing attorney in New York, explains that for the most part negotiation involves "getting the parties' expectations out in the open, and forcing them to think about contingencies that they hadn't thought about, helping to avoid surprises later on." Elia believes that it's much easier to talk about a difficult situation before it's happened.

Chill out: If your überannoying colleague is predictable, try to always be one step ahead of him in the project. You'll have a better idea of your own nonnegotiables and be able to work around his annoying habits. You might even try to prepare an informal written contract or agreement between the two of you, detailing the process and the responsibilities of each party.

CAREER

The most interesting people have the most interesting backgrounds and stories. Picture the best cocktail party: At the center of a group of raucous laughter is the person telling the story of their greatest past foibles—not the one sharing tales of past perfection. It's okay to have a stylistic skeleton or two in your closet—just let that become the yardstick by which you measure your current brilliant and perfectly cool self.

CORPORATE

No one expects perfection—that much has been established. But if you're going to screw up, try not to do it at work. If and when you feel a tense situation is about to get even more tense, try to assess the potential for long-term damage to your job and/or reputation and the reputation of your company, and act accordingly. It may feel weird initially to go into full crisis mode, but as you become more comfortable with dealing with work emergencies it will become second nature to take responsibility not only for your successes but also for potential failure.

COOL

It isn't easy to become a well-respected, brilliant _____ (insert your own job title here)—but it can be done. You can't control life, you can't control your boss or coworker or even clients, but you *can* control the way that you choose to react to potential disasters.

Chapter 6

Personality Plus

Etiquette, Social Rules, and Tools to Help You Climb the Corporate Ladder

> *Always do right. This will gratify some people and astonish the rest.*
> —Mark Twain

An Accelerated Trip Down Memory Lane

Okay, think back for a minute—no, further back than that. Past your recent promotion, past your last vacation, past your first day at work, past your college graduation or even high school orientation, past middle school, maybe even past elementary school. Okay stop—you're there.

Picture this: You're somewhere in the first decade of your existence, and you've learned a thing or two about life. You've got a newly minted set of likes and dislikes, you have a group of friends, favorite books, school subjects that make you cringe, and TV shows that you don't want to miss. Heck, by now you might even be able to walk and chew gum at the same time.

But here's what you can't do: You can't seem to set your own rules. Everywhere you go, it seems like some authority figure is trying to mold you into an idea of who they think you should be. Your mother is obsessed with you washing your hands, not talking with your mouth full or talking to strangers (and heaven forfend talking to strangers with your mouth full), being polite to your elders. It seems that for each thing you do right, she's correcting you for two you messed up on. School doesn't seem to be any different; you're constantly faced with new concepts, new dichotomies, new relationships, and worst of all, new hierarchies.

If you stop to think about it, you've likely spent much of your young life being chastised for your slipups or reminded of what you must or must never do. This doesn't make the adults in your life bad people—on the contrary, this is likely what turned you into a viable citizen of the world. But as you've grown you've also learned that some rules were made to be broken. Author and educator Linda Formichelli is a self-described renegade both in deed and action. Her advice is, "Know the rules, then decide on a case-by-case basis whether those rules work for you. If a rule doesn't make sense to you, break it and see what happens. If the results are positive, you now have a new way to work."

The Need for Speed

We live in an accelerated universe, with what feels like a daily onslaught of new communications devices, news and entertainment delivery mechanisms, and technology innovations. These brave new gadgets promise to make our lives easier, but frequently leave us feeling more confused and less in touch with ourselves and our loved ones. Add to that a constant barrage of news and information, with information popping up at us almost instantaneously from our computers and phones.

It's been said that a century ago the average person had as much information available to them in an entire lifetime as is contained in the Sunday version of the *New York Times*. To this information overload, add social and business networking, speed dating, new and improved antisocial behaviors like road rage and incessant cell phone chatter, and it can frequently feel as though we live in very confusing or hostile times. Caryl Chinn, an events marketing specialist in New York, says that she "mourns the general decline of good manners everywhere." And she isn't referring to complicated social mores and gestures, but rather "the simple things like holding open a door for someone, or saying excuse me when you bump into someone."

It's Nothing Personal, Just Bad Business Practices

It's one thing to have bad manners on a personal level. People from other cultures can find the subtle nuances of Western behavior to be overwhelming or insincere, and it isn't necessarily your job to educate them. When you encounter someone who is misguided, rude, or over-bearing, you can choose to walk away from a potential future relationship. If the person seems unaware of their behavior, or worth keeping in your life, you might want to subtly inform them of the correct system or way things are done. On the business level, however, poor behavior can make or break a future relationship on many levels. If you inadvertently insult a potential client, mispronounce their name, or seem not to be paying attention, they may shy away from working with you.

At a recent pitch meeting, I was trying to win over the marketing team at a major cultural cornerstone of New York City. I was quite thrilled about the potential project and gave an impromptu and impassioned speech detailing what my company, GTK Marketing Group, might bring to the table. I also explained that as a born New Yorker, it would be a dream for me to work with . . . and then I accidentally named their neighbor and greatest nemesis. I quickly realized my faux pas and apologized repeatedly, imagining that I'd blown the pitch. I was told that it was a source of great aggravation for them to constantly be mistaken for their competitor.

However, I was able to turn the situation around, because I immediately realized that instead of simply launching a new project, this iconic cultural institution was also in need of some immediate and intense rebranding to distinguish them from their competitor. After all, if *I* had made the mistake after weeks of research and during a pitch with all collateral clearly in front of me, there was obviously a need to rework their branding and recognizability.

I was lucky—I'm able to think on my feet and to recognize opportunity. I'm also cognizant of the most basic business etiquette, which, in my goof, I momentarily lost: Never call your client by the wrong name—and if you do, you'd better figure out a way to make it up to them.

Mind Your P's and Q's

So is it even possible to keep cool, calm, and polite in today's immediate-gratification universe? Ultimately, it's even easier than one would think. Think back to what your parents taught you. In business as in life, it's always imperative to remember the ethics of reciprocity, or the golden rule. Every great religious icon or major philosopher has advised treating others as you would be treated.

Does it annoy you to hear endless cell phone conversations? Make sure to keep yours short and private. Do you hate it when your coworker nukes particularly pungent food in the office microwave? Limit your own kimchi consumption to home only. Does it set your teeth on end when someone wallpapers a networking event with their business cards? Hand yours out only when asked. In other words, think before you act, and think even harder before you act with impatience or outright rudeness.

While every industry has its own set of insider rules, there are a few basics to keep in mind. One "do" that came up time and time again is do take the time to thank people if they've helped you out. A handwritten note is a classic way to show appreciation, but in a pinch a heartfelt e-mail will do the trick. Always remember to acknowledge the kind things that others have done for you.

Basic Business Manners

You're the consummate professional—there's no doubt about it. But sometimes those crunch times and deadlines can cause you to be a little sloppy with your manners, or a little overfamiliar with your supervisor or client. Sometimes it can be even more subtle or confusing. For that reason, try to always keep these basic behavior guidelines in mind.

Good Customer Service Can Never Be Too Good

Believe it or not, Craig Newmark is as familiar to most people as better known mono-monikered celebrities like Cher or Madonna. In fact, I'm guessing that at some time or another you've spent some time on his list—Craigslist, that is.

Craig is obsessive about good or, in his words, "Serious customer service," and told me that he spends several hours each day attending to the details that some might find too annoying to tackle. Craig does everything from dealing with misbehaving apartment brokers in New York City, to lightly moderating the message boards, to personally answering e-mails to dealing with the occasional bad guys. Much like a restaurant owner who will roll up his sleeves and wash the dishes if his staff is short-handed, Craig is completely at ease working in any capacity that he's needed. His priority is consistent and superior customer service.

Jane Wagman, a graphic designer in New York refers to it this way: "Hug your client."

Too Much Information Is Simply Too Much Information

Sure, you exchange polite chatter with your coworkers, and maybe even complain about clients, projects, or your boyfriend—but save the really gory details for your friends outside of the office. Bottom line: The workplace is not a place for idle chatter. Be polite, express interest in the most basic elements of a coworker's life, but never share yours and never, ever pry. Not only is it bad practice to spill the details about your latest conquest, but you never know when that particular bit of shared titillation might be used against you.

Keep Your Workspace Clean and Uncluttered

Heidi Anne-Noel, senior director of publicity for Virgin Records, credits her spartan desktop as one of her best business tools. She sets aside time every morning before her work day begins to sort through and prioritize the day's commitments. In this way she's sure that she never misses crucial information and is never bogged down by less important detail work.

If you're one of the nearly 70 percent of all Americans who eat lunch at their desks, you might want to pay attention to the findings of Dr. Charles Gerba, a microbiologist at the University of Arizona. Dr. Gerba discovered that the average desk has 400 times more bacteria than a toilet seat, with the desk, phone, mouse, and keyboard containing the highest concentration of bacteria. So if clarity and control don't motivate you to clean up your workspace, those germy tidbits just might do the trick.

PRIORITIZE

An informal poll of friends and colleagues revealed that the average professional receives about 50 e-mail correspondences each day. Add to that the constant ringing of the phone, with requests from the ridiculous to the sublime to the benign, and a huge chunk of your day might be spent just getting back to people. Because we live in an immediate-gratification society, it can be tough to know when to dismiss a request or when to move it to the top of your list.

Set up a system for answering phone calls and e-mail. In my inbox I've set up close to a dozen inbox subcategories ranging from a box marked "Answer" to one named "Urgent" to one labeled "Think About." I also set up new mailboxes by project. For instance, if I have a project coming up, all correspondence related to it would be routed that way, with subcategories for team players involved in all moving parts.

Additionally, don't become a slave to your inbox. Designate a time to regularly respond to correspondence, to return phone calls, or simply to file and delete older messages.

PLAY NICE

At some point in late August of election years, the candidate endorsement TV commercials start to trickle in, and by November our televisions are packed with back-to-back mudslinging, where candidate X publicly reviles candidate Y, and vice versa. Instead of regaling us with their own list of good deeds, they cast aspersions on the reputations of their nemesis. And instead of making me want to vote for either party, it usually causes me to instead muse about the pettiness of politicians.

Every celebrity tends to have adoring fans and irked detractors, and dozens of celebrity gossip blogs have sprung up, no doubt inspired by the proliferation of celebrity gossip magazines. It can be okay to obsess or gossip about celebrities, since they have no actual impact on your life, other than as benevolent objects of affection or loathing. But in the case of organizations such as the Rachael Ray Sucks Community, a Web-based group devoted to slagging the über-perky chef, the overall feeling is of spite.

On the complete opposite end of that spectrum, a few months back I was standing in a packed New York subway car, loaded down with presentation materials, and feeling miserable after the day from hell. A total stranger offered me her seat (and if you've ever been on a rush hour commute on the subway, you'll know just how kind this gesture was). The stranger turned out to be Erin Cox, book publishing director for the *New Yorker*. When I later followed up by e-mail to thank her for her kindness, she said, "I saw it in your face that you were having one of those days, and that was an easy thing for me to do to help out. . . . I always try to smile or share some joy. Can't hurt to do such things, right?" Absolutely not. I was so moved by Cox's good deed that I went home and committed some random acts of kindness of my own.

If given the chance, don't badmouth a competitor, and certainly don't do it in a public or open forum. Whether you're a politician, a celebrity chef, a dog walker, or a landscape artist, your best work speaks louder and more clearly than your competitor's negativity ever could. And whenever you can, try committing a random act of kindness.

FOLLOW UP

I'm always vaguely amused when people are surprised to hear from me after an initial meeting. I've never been shy about making the first move either personally or professionally, and I really don't know why most people are hesitant to initiate a follow-up conversation. After all, few pitches, meetings, or meet-and-greet opportunities are strong enough to stand on their own merit.

Bringing in new business and strengthening existing ties means nurturing a new or burgeoning professional relationship. Following up is the natural progression to any professional interaction, whether by phone, via snail mail, or with a simple e-mail acknowledging the meeting, the points covered, and your enthusiasm to move forward. If someone doesn't seem as keen to work with you, then it's time to move on.

Follow up even when you're sure that you haven't won someone over, or when you think their business is going elsewhere. You never know when your professionalism and moxie will at least encourage someone to give you another try or even a small piece of a larger project—just enough to get your foot in the door.

Howard Lieb, an entertainment and intellectual property lawyer, brings members of the children's entertainment industry together in an intimate yearly conference called BrainCamp. To ensure that attendees aren't spending more time exchanging business cards than ideas, Lieb immediately follows up each conference with an updated file containing all participants' contact information. In this way, he ensures both participation and followup.

One more thought: Acknowledge someone else's efforts at followup. Whether you intend to do business with someone or not, it's common courtesy just to let them know that you appreciated their e-mail, and to state that you do or do not think that you will be able to work together in the future. Being polite leaves the door wide open to future opportunities, and you never know which door opportunity will choose to knock on.

Mean What You Say and Say What You Mean

At some point or another we've all noticed a particularly annoying and somewhat smug type known as a yes man. A yes man doesn't really have an opinion on things, but rather tells people—clients and supervisors alike—what he thinks they want to hear. His thoughts are never original; rather, this sycophantic scourge of the cubicle world will promise a lot and deliver less, thereby giving his business a bad reputation in the long run.

Before you open your mouth at a pitch meeting, make sure that you not only *can* deliver on your promise but that you *intend* to. Before you offer up flowery language or complicated, animated audiovisual components, make sure that you are clearly explaining what you mean. It's great to dream, but it's even better to deliver. Your clients and coworkers will appreciate you more if you are someone who can be depended on for results.

Being the go-to guy or girl depends on a lot more than simply saying the right thing. It's more important to keep your word than to use the most popular jargon of the day. Be confident enough in your talents and abilities to make them dazzling instead of disappointing.

Give Credit Where Credit Is Due

We've all sat through long-winded and painful awards ceremony speeches where the recipient spends several minutes thanking everyone from her personal assistant and manager to God, her facialist, and the guy who works at the bagel store. While listing everyone that you've ever met as influencing your business life might seem a bit excessive, acknowledging the hard work of your coworkers not only makes them feel appreciated but also shows that you are gracious and secure in your own abilities.

Millie Martini Bratten, the editor in chief of *Brides* magazine, has been at her coveted post for close to three decades now, a nearly Herculean task in the competitive magazine industry. When we spoke, she was full of enthusiasm for her readers and projects, but more than anything she constantly made sure to credit her editorial staff for their fresh ideas and ingenuity. It's unlikely that the magazine could have enjoyed such consistent and evolving levels of success without Bratten at the helm, and yet she is sure to list off and include her talented staff as an irreplaceable source of her inspiration.

Say You're Sorry, and Don't Hold a Grudge

You goofed up. We all have. But it's how you deal with the aftermath that sets you apart from the pack. Before you go bemoaning your screwup to all and sundry, create an immediate action plan. Assess the situation: Is there any permanent damage? Can the relationship or project be salvaged? Is a written apology or small gift of flowers necessary? If you don't know, consult with a more experienced friend or mentor.

You know what comes next. Your next move should be to apologize to your boss—in person if possible. You don't want to hide behind your mistake, but rather to express your remorse face to face. Call your client, and only when you must, put it in writing. You don't want a paper trail of this faux pas to haunt you for the rest of your professional life.

Conversely, if someone has unintentionally hurt you or your business and is genuinely apologetic, it's probably in your best interests to accept their apology and move on. Do you question their sincerity, or has long-term damage occurred as a result of their actions? Hear them out, create a crisis management plan, and limit contact with them as soon as the issue is cleared up.

Don't Always Stand on Ceremony

Poor Prince Charles, he's got a list of protocol dos and don'ts that have been centuries in the making. Chances are that unless you're the long-lost relative of European royalty, you've got a little more leeway with your own daily dos and don'ts. For that reason, try to personalize your own way of doing things.

Georgette Mosbacher is known as both a socialite and a CEO, and when people come to her office, not only does she personally hang up their coats, but she also makes them a cup of coffee. Some might see this as beneath them, but Mosbacher's intention is to be as welcoming in her place of business as she is at one of her fabulous dinner parties. And above all . . .

Keep Your Sense of Humor

You know how you have the urge to laugh at the most inappropriate moments? Well, there are times when nothing breaks the tension like a fit of the giggles. Try not to laugh when tempers are flaring, but in a tense situation, sometimes pointing out the little absurdities can bond you with a potential nemesis and add a sense of camaraderie to a crunch time.

Evan Blaustein, CEO of Boston-based Mimoco, puts it this way: "Humor is an important part of style, so don't trap yourself into a caricature of yourself."

CAREER

You are the ambassador for your own career. You might have an Ivy League pedigree, but if your manners are lacking, or if you don't treat people in an appropriate fashion, chances are they're not going to want to work with you—or with your company, by association. Trust your gut on sticky issues—you've probably got a strong base of manners and ethics to build on.

CORPORATE

Whether you're self-employed or work for a Fortune 500 company, you're likely to have a guiding set of rules and regulations to follow. If you're unsure of company protocol, ask a trusted colleague or mentor.

COOL

Fabulous manners never go out of style. If people remember one thing about you, let it be your impeccable manners, sense of grace under pressure, and ability to rise above bad situations with your sense of humor intact. For more of my advice on business manners and etiquette visit www.msbizmanners.com.

Chapter 7

Accessorize!

From Earrings to Laptop Case,
What Your Add-Ons Say about You

> *Take care of the luxuries and the necessities*
> *will take care of themselves.*
> —Dorothy Parker

Accessories Make the Woman

It's been said in many different ways that clothes make the man. For women, though, getting just the right look can often involve many more moving pieces and attention to detail. If you're like most women, you've got a wardrobe full of jeans and another containing black pants and skirts. Your black-tie appropriate outfits might include several variations of the ubiquitous little black dress or sexy strapless number.

What sets your little black dress apart from my little black dress, however, is the way in which we each choose to accessorize it. While I might opt for an armful of bangles and matching hoop earrings, you might choose tiny sparkly studs and a velvet headband. While your best friend might choose to drape a cashmere shawl over her bare shoulders, you might be showing off your biceps or layering your strapless dress over a ribbed T-shirt. In fact, if you take 100 women and give them the identical dress to wear, you'll likely find that they have accessorized it 100 different ways.

Karen Giberson is the president of the Accessories Council, a not-for-profit, national trade association committed to increasing consumer use and awareness of accessories. Giberson (whom I like to refer to as the empress of accessories) says that when accessorizing you should "Pick personality pieces that you feel comfortable with, and that you fall in love with—because at the core it always has to reflect you."

It's All In The Details...

Accessories That Work for You

As a woman in business, you've got a lot on your mind. Not only do you want to distinguish yourself professionally, but you want to figure out a way to balance your personal and professional lives. Not only do you want to do the kind of work that gets you kudos and moves your career in the right direction, but you want to look great doing it.

Here's the tricky part—you want to look great but you also don't want people to be distracted by what you wear. You want to balance chic with capable, style with efficiency, and whimsy with practicality. Make no mistake about it, from the height of your heels, to the size of your handbag, from the photos hanging over your desk to the cool or incredibly dated gadgets that you favor, your accessories speak volumes about you.

When trying to figure out if that perfect purse is worth the investment, take into account the advice of Ann Watson, vice president and fashion director of Henri Bendel: "Each season, refresh your wardrobe with trend based items at a price point that is comfortable for you, knowing that next season those pieces might feel dated. My rule of thumb, when shopping for trend pieces, is 'I must love it!' because, as with all trends, these items have an expiration date."

Take Inventory

I'm not sure which famous doyenne of fashion set the 11-item rule, which goes something like this: To be considered perfectly accessorized, you should never be wearing more than eleven items. So while Coco Chanel might famously have draped herself in pearls and gold chains, you're going to have to be more vigilant about how you ornament yourself. Keep in mind that each earring counts as one accessory (as opposed to a pair counting as one item). One other famous fashionista always advocated removing one accessory just before you leave the house. In that way, she surmised, you could always be just coolly underaccessorized instead of over the top.

To give you a better idea of iconic women and their signature accessories consider Paloma Picasso and her signature bold gold pieces. She turned her penchant for bold and dramatic jewelry into a career.

Carrie Donovan was a famed fashionista and editor of *Vogue*, *Bazaar*, and the *New York Times Magazine*, but to many she was best known for her huge, round, black eyeglass frames (and commercials for Old Navy). Queen Elizabeth II is rarely seen without a handbag, though as monarch of Great Britain for over 40 years there isn't much that she actually has to carry with her (keys to the kingdom, perhaps?). It's rumored that the only things she keeps in her purse are dog treats for her many beloved corgis. Wonder Woman's trademark gold bracelets were not only chic—they also deflected bullets, thus helping her to be a safe and stylish superheroine!

24-Karat Style

What's that they say about diamonds being a girl's best friend? I'm not that finicky. I equally favor emeralds, rubies, and sapphires. If it sparkles, I'm ready to cozy up to it. To be honest, though, I'm always cognizant of my coloring even before my outfit, and I try to wear jewelry that highlights my best features. For instance, my hair is usually a deep mahogany or warm auburn, and my eyes are kind of hard to describe—sometimes golden, sometimes green, sometimes amber. I collect tigereye pieces and tend to favor yellow gold and citrine or topaz to set off my uniquely colored eyes. I'm known for my trademark collection of unusual earrings, and they usually present an easy topic of conversation with clients or colleagues.

When meeting a prospective client for the first time, I generally treat the situation as a job interview, which in essence it is. So while, as the founder and president of my own company, I can generally take liberties with my attire and rock some really bold accessories, when meeting new people I try to tailor my look to what they will accept and understand. I also try to always abide by the no-noise jewelry rule. If it clanks or is distracting it has no place in the workplace—end of story (and if anyone ever tries to tell you that they've seen me wear miniature truck or razor blade earrings, I shall chalk that up to a universally accepted get-out-of-jail-free concept, more commonly explained as the heinous taste exhibited in extreme youth).

As for choosing between costume jewelry and genuine pieces, as with everything else, budget plays a huge part in the decision, as does your career. There are lots of companies that make great fakes, almost better than the real thing. Don't use this as an excuse to purchase huge faux diamond rings. Draping yourself with large faux jewels is far from fabulous. Take your cue from your boss or coworkers and accessorize accordingly, while still letting your unique personality show through.

People in creative fields ranging from art gallery directors to interior designers can carry off a bit more creativity with their choice of adornment, but you never want people to pay more attention to your accessories than they do to you. Here are some rules of thumb:

- Don't overdo the rings. If married, wear your wedding rings and one other ring, tops. Try to save rings with large stones for special occasions.
- Necklaces are fun, but not when they are overlong, overly bulky, and can get caught in your belt or desk drawers. When in doubt, go for a test run and try bending over and reaching into drawers while wearing the necklace. If it gets caught in closet doors or drawers, don't wear it to work.
- Bracelets are timeless, but noisy ones are just plain inappropriate. Try to wear one thick one in a bold color instead of an armful of jangly ones. There is nothing quite as annoying as shaking hands with someone who provides their own sound effects. If you favor chains or gold, opt for an unusual pattern or color gradation.
- Try not to wear earrings that overpower your face, but rather a pair that enhances your features and attracts light to your face. If in doubt, save the really blingy stuff for your time off.
- Just for fun, sometimes accessories can be completely unexpected, like Swarovski crystal bra straps from Margarita Couture, which can take your LBD from typical to sensational.

You're Such a Shoe Off!

From Cinderella and her glass slippers to Imelda and her thousands of pairs, shoes have always had an almost mythical allure to a majority of women. Whether you're petite, plus-size, or pregnant, you can almost always find a pair of shoes to make you look and feel perfect.

Along with the lust for the perfect pair comes some general silly and sometimes dangerous behavior. Naomi Campbell once fell spectacularly on her face while walking down the catwalk at a Vivienne Westwood fashion show. Former Spice Girl Emma Bunton, aka Baby Spice, was known to totter around in dangerously high platform heels. And in Japan, extreme platforms were banned after several driving accidents and even a platform shoe–related death were reported.

In 2005, what was probably the first politically related flip-flop flap of our decade, much was made over the fact that the Northwestern University Women's lacrosse team wore flimsy flip-flops to the White House to meet President George W. Bush (who himself favors custom-made cowboy boots).

Shoe designer Nancy Geist of Cynthia Rowley, NancyNancy, and Nancy Geist shoes offers these tips:

♦ "Absolutely don't buy shoes that are too small! There is always a way to pad a shoe that's a half size too big, but tight shoes will wreck your tootsies!"

♦ Nancy also declares the peep-toe style to be flattering to every foot, with just one or two toes showing. Nancy believes that peep-toes can "fem up jeans and deformalize business suits" and make "even yucky feet, manicured of course, look cute."

♦ As for heels, Nancy has some great advice: "Go with the highest heel you can gracefully walk in." She adds that two- to three-inch heels work best for most women.

♦ Nancy's pick for a classic look would be "the timeless, casual elegance of a two-piece shoe on a kitten heel." Having the sides of the shoe open, and also possibly the back if it is a string tie or sling back, really accentuates the curve of the arch.

The Great Hose Debate

Time was a well-dressed woman couldn't be seen in public without her hat, gloves, and hose. These days things aren't quite as clear. The only way to really know your company policy is to ask and observe. If policy dictates that it's okay to go sans stockings, but everyone else in your office always has nylon-clad legs, you might want to err on the side of caution and wear hose or at least knee-highs to the office. As for winter looks, while fashionistas might love the look of spike-heel sandals worn with bare legs and heavy winter coats, to the rest of the world it's just plain silly. Don't just cover your legs to get it done; match hose or tights to your skirt or shoes. Find out if your office frowns on open toes before you wear sandals to the office, and if you do show your toes make sure that they're perfectly polished at all times. You might be too busy working to go for a much-needed pedicure, but chipped and manky-looking toes really drag down an outfit and make you look sloppy and unprofessional. Stick with lighter or neutral tones, though, since you don't want your cherry red tootsies to be the focus of attention in the conference room.

Handbags

What do Grace Kelly, Jane Birkin, and Hello Kitty have in common? They're all iconic female characters who have inspired frenzied devotion and handbag addiction. When Grace Kelly first used her oversized Hermes alligator bag to disguise her rounded pregnant tummy, little did she know that she'd be inspiring the ensuing cult of the Kelly. The waiting list for a Birkin bag is said to be a shade under six years. Hello Kitty products are generally less pricy than the Hermes versions, but they inspire equally intense loyalty.

While it might seem more than a bit over the top to spend several thousand dollars on a handbag, some women allow the price tag and exclusivity factor to determine their preferences. When considering an investment piece, Karen Giberson advises: "If you're going to splurge on a brand, you want to own a statement piece, be it your bag or sunglasses or shoes, because a piece like that is always going to be in style." Most of us rely on a variety of factors that might include fluctuating fashions, value, price, durability, size, comfort, and practicality.

For working women especially it can be cumbersome to lug

around not only a handbag but a separate laptop and PDA case or gym case. FranklinCovey.com has an impressive array of totes, luggage, and accessories created especially for women, with clever pockets for phone and more; former contestant on *The Apprentice* Tammy Trenta has created a couture-worthy collection of business bags for women with incredible details like unusual fabric linings and even a case for sunglasses or business cards.

Tech Toys: PDA, Phone, Laptop

Oh admit it—you're as much of a tech toy junkie as your boyfriend is, maybe even more. You covet the latest, teeniest, tiniest phone with not only a camera but maybe even a food processor as well. The fact of the matter is that as technology evolves, so do our tastes and passion for newer, smaller, faster. While a standard iPod was once the ultimate MP3 player, the next generation has evolved to smaller size, longer battery power, and improved capabilities. And as soon as you buy your new computer it's likely obsolete.

So how to keep on top of the trends? Research before you buy, and don't be seduced by features that you don't need and will never use. Ask your friends for their recommendations and favorites, and be sure to find out return policies. You don't need to get the hottest model, but rather the one that best suits your needs.

Robert McGarvey researches and writes about the newest technology products, though he isn't bothered by having the latest or greatest tech toys: "Technology comes, it goes. Don't worry about being right—focus on what works." Technology also changes so quickly that by the time you research and invest in something, it's likely obsolete. For that reason, try to forget about buyer's remorse and instead focus on how your life has been simplified.

One of my favorite tech toys is by a company called Mimoco. "Ramona," my Rockabilly-inspired flash drive, may not hold as much information as my Seagate pocket drive, but she's ridiculously adorable, complete with a personality and provenance, and always a conversation piece.

Business Cards, Card Case, and Personalized Stationery

For the most part your work accoutrements don't have much to do with you. All of your work collateral will likely have your company's logo and address, and your business card is less about you and more about your place in the company.

That being said, there are small ways to make your name stand out. Find out from your supervisor if there is any leeway with your card—perhaps you can make the wording more playful or have your name in a different color or font. If there's no room for play on the card, then make your personal style show up with a customized card case. Express yourself in the tiny details. Your business card holder not only protects your cards but also shows the world what you think of your job and position. You can choose anything from retro design to a clever theme that highlights your career, capabilities, or hobbies.

The GTK in my company name, GTK Marketing Group, stands for "Good To Know," and all of our collateral is built around that theme. My business card highlights my first name, while my last name is in a much smaller font. Directly under my name in our logoed bracket it says "She's Good To Know!" which not only injects a bit of humor into my card design but also lets people know that I work hard to become someone worth knowing, and that if you engage my company's services I will put my network of contacts and creativity to work for you as well. The back of my card is a playful bit of self-promotion. It advises you to "Read My Books" and has a photo of my book covers. I use my card as a 2.5-inch billboard—it gets people to laugh and ask questions and also to realize that I think and act differently than most people do.

It seems a shame to waste the potential impact of a business card by simply stamping some information on it. Make it work for you and your company. If you can, let your business card remind people of who you are and what sets you apart from others in your field. Your card also tells the world that you have an existence and presence outside of the office that is as stylish and professional as your work persona. Besides your standard corporate letterhead you should also invest in a set of personalized stationery and use it for thank-you notes, follow-up, and more personalized interaction. Be sure to always keep your information lists updated. Use your signature at the bottom of your e-mail as well. Why not give people links to recent work, press, and your web site? Include your company slogan and contact information. Many times I have the urge to pick up the phone and explore business opportunities or potential partnerships. If I can easily find your contact information, it's much more likely that I will approach and not forget about you and your goods or services.

Desk Set

Depending on your work environment—smallish cubicle or glass-encased corner office—you might have more or less room to make things personal. Depending on your company policy, you may also require permission just to hang up a postcard or photo. Let's face it, you spend upwards of eight hours a day at your desk, and it makes sense to personalize this home away from home. What doesn't make sense, however, is to create the image of being anything other than a complete professional.

- ◆ Limit pictures of loved ones. One or two close family members (spouse, child) in a low-key frame should suffice.
- ◆ Inspirational sayings or words are great, but try not to get too religious or potentially inflammatory. Sayings by philosophers and historical figures generally work well. Sayings by saints or controversial religious figures complete with gory imagery does not.
- ◆ Cute works—cutesy does not. While displaying a few fun postcards or decorative elements (like my Jane Austen action figure complete with quill) is almost highbrow kitsch, setting out your troll collection will not likely impress your boss.

CAREER

Just because you're a professional doesn't mean you can't be a really well accessorized one. The key is in moderation. If it's noisy, overly big, or overly cute, you're probably best off avoiding it. Don't skimp on handbag or shoes, and be vigilant about scuffs, tears, or tarnishing.

CORPORATE

It isn't only yourself that can be well accessorized but your workspace as well. While recent studies state that a neat desk doesn't indicate a better work style, for your own peace of mind and sense of style, keep project work organized and color-coded if possible. Keep your desk accessorized and let it make the right kind of impression—whether you're sitting there or not!

COOL

Even if you have to wear a uniform to work, your accessories can distinguish your quirks and sense of style—just make sure that your company policy allows it.

Chapter 8

Extracurricular Activities

How to Dress and Act Away from the Office—At Company Retreats, Holiday Parties, or Networking Events

> *Learn to value yourself, which means:*
> *to fight for your happiness.*
> —Ayn Rand

Hope for the Misanthrope

Not everyone is cut out for life as a social butterfly—far from it. Some people obsessively pore over the gossip and party pages, salivating over glossy images of the privileged few flitting from fabulous cocktail party to fashionable premier, clad in fierce Fendi frocks paired with chic Jimmy Choo shoes. Some women would rather face a WMD than be forced to don an LBD. For others, even a business lunch can be torturous—they'd much prefer sitting at their desk munching on a BLT and limiting their interactions to electronic exchanges.

For the majority of us, business-related socializing is a crucial part of our day-to-day process. Industries ranging from public relations to fashion, beauty, entertainment, and publishing are practically built on the concept of the highly evolved power lunch. Sharing a high-profile and well-thought-out meal or social evening with a colleague or client can make or break a deal. Introductions are made, deals are discussed, partnerships explored, and relationships cemented. It is crucial that not only the venue is appropriate, but also the choice of wardrobe, table mates, timing, and small talk.

It's important to know your socializing strengths and weaknesses and whether mixing and mingling is your thing. While Casey Gillespie, managing editor of *Zink* magazine, admits to having her "*Sex and the City* moments," including "traveling luxuriously to the most fabulous places around the globe" and being "invited to glamorous parties and meeting fascinating men," others view even work-related events as torturous. Rob Walker, who writes the "Consumed" column for the *New York Times Magazine*, is an admittedly low-key person who prefers to remain behind the scenes and mostly anonymous. He opines that, "Some people go into a room and the whole room changes. I'm not that guy." Walker also says that perhaps if he were more charismatic he'd feel differently and enjoy the schmoozing and networking. In his case, self-perception is more of a deciding factor than public perception.

Socializing with your colleagues is as important to your career process as everything else in your professional relationship repertoire. It gives you a chance to relax to a degree and share a more personal side of yourself. It also gives you and your colleagues or clients time together to form more of a bond, a feeling of unity, or to nurture a burgeoning team or approach. Some people hate their work personalities and find that taking the time to socialize with coworkers can help them highlight a completely different aspect of themselves.

Sticky Social Situations

Ask anyone for their worst work memory and there will probably be far too many tragic tales of layoffs. But usually there will also be sheepish grins as people recount cringe-inducing details of drunken excess at the company holiday party. This points to a hazardous roadblock to successful work/leisure crossover: becoming far too relaxed and saying or doing really stupid things. Of course there's a lot more fun to be had and a lot more boundaries that have yet to be tested, but there are also a lot more ways to get into serious trouble that can have a long-term negative impact on your career.

I suppose the most important thing to keep in mind when socializing with coworkers, employers, or clients is that, as friendly as things seem, these people are not your friends. Certain protocol and elements of good taste must always be respected and only breached if you feel willing to risk losing your job.

All Work and No Play

Before you start pouting and swear off these situations forever, keep in mind the tangible benefits of socializing with your work colleagues:

- Being perceived as a team player. The expression does in fact have very real roots and merit. You might not be a fan of softball, but playing a game with your coworkers can successfully show your boss that you not only can shine on your own but are also supportive of and enthusiastic about the company as a whole.

- Showing off another facet of your personality. Perhaps you're known around the office as the quiet one, the one who waits to speak until everyone else has had their say. In a social situation you might be able to show off more of yourself—your love of trivia, your ability to mesmerize a group with a ghost story, your perfect memory for names and details. In other words, it's always good to remind the decision makers that you might in many ways be an untapped internal resource with even more to offer if needed.

- Having some quality time with your boss. It can be hard to both manage a company and have face time with all of your employees. Bonding with your boss in a social situation can ensure that you're on her mind for future projects and promotions. In other words, if you had to promote someone and both candidates had the exact same skill set, who would you choose—the office recluse, or the charming and witty woman you just had cocktails with?

- Get to know your clients. A couple of years ago I was less than thrilled when a client invited me to a stuffy charity event.

However, I had no choice but to accept since I had advised him on becoming active with said good cause. He had reserved an entire table, and while I can't say that it was the most exciting night of my life, it was certainly an eye-opener. I saw that my client was not just a very savvy businessman, but was also beloved by his employees. There was an air of ease and genuine caring that just couldn't be faked. Seeing my client in this light helped me to reformulate the company's brand strategy to incorporate the very warm and dedicated CEO almost as the father of his brand instead of just a figurehead.

Retreat and Advance Your Career

More and more companies are inviting their core management teams on corporate retreats or weekends spent with coworkers outside of the office at rustic or luxury locations. Sometimes corny, sometimes torturous, these weekends or even weeks away are meant to boost morale, improve relationships between employees, foster new interagency relationships, and keep all of this happiness active when you come back to your cubicle.

To be honest, I feel that many of these team-building exercises, which can involve anything from sports to treasure hunts, can feel forced or unnatural, but when done right a corporate retreat can prove to be an invaluable bonding tool. The key to a successful corporate retreat experience is in matching your goals with your destination and selected team members.

If you are invited on a retreat, it's probably in your best interests to attend. The invitation can either mean that your boss thinks you need to learn how to play well with others, or that she is grooming you for a more active role within the team. In either case you'll likely come out of the experience having a better idea of what she expects from you.

Before you go:

◆ Research the venue/destination. Where are you going? Is it a high-tech spa or rustic cabin? Shop accordingly, buying everything from mosquito repellent to thick socks or thermal under-wear. Show your boss or colleagues that you're a person who doesn't need to overpack to be prepared for every eventuality.

◆ Find out who else will be on the trip. Is it your closest work friend or your evil nemesis? Try to speak not only to the one or two people that you generally socialize with at work, but rather make an effort to get to know the extended group.

◆ Wrap your head around it. It's okay to ask your boss or supervisor what the purpose of the trip is. It's even better to try to get into the mind-set, whether it's competitive, relaxing, or fun. Don't strive to win if the point is just to have fun. Follow the lead (as you would at the office) of your supervisor or employer.

Party Hardly

You're not quite sure where the year went, but suddenly it's December and the full-fledged party season is nearly upon you. You'll likely be invited to the office do, and depending on your relationship with clients and friends, you might be heading to their work parties as well. While the word *party* is definitely bandied about this time of year, it's the emphasis and placement that you need to take into account. In other words, when looking at the expression *office party*, you should definitely place the emphasis on the word *office* and respect all the boundaries that exist within your physical place of employment.

Two things to keep in mind:

1. *Your outfit.* Little black dress or formal ball gown? Invitations can seem unbearably tricky these days, but they always provide clues as to what you should or shouldn't wear. If you receive a formal invitation sent to your home, you can likely assume that this will be a dress-to-impress event. Check the venue, but also check the time of day—a posh restaurant at 12:30 P.M. will not likely be a black-tie affair. Don't be afraid to ask the person coordinating the event what she suggests you wear. While you might have the urge to really go nuts with your outfit, keep in mind that you will be facing these same

people day after day for as long as you stay at your current job. Avoid anything too short, too low-cut, or too revealing. This isn't the Oscars, but rather a night for your employer to show you their appreciation in the form of a night on the town. Fashion Week mainstay and style writer Faran Krentcil advises investing in a great-looking cover-up: "Coats are amazing for party hopping. If you arrive in a great coat, no matter what's underneath, you automatically look great."

2. *Your attitude.* Many people seem to think that the company party is the night to really let loose. It isn't. While it's fine to have a cocktail, try to stretch one drink out for the entire evening, or supplement it with fruit juice or cola. It's fairly annoying when overly inebriated coworkers are trying to get you to drink as much as they are, or to act as idiotic as they're act-

Mingle 'Til You Tingle...

ing. Always keep in mind your bottom line and agenda: Fun is what you do with friends, work is what you do so that you can pay your rent or mortgage and keep food on your table (and cookies in the pantry). Everything else in that confusing gray area must be vigilantly and diligently protected. You are your reputation at work, and while your work may be stellar, you really don't want to be remembered as the girl who flashed the boss and then barfed in her shoes. And if all else fails? Bribe people with sweets. Krentcil admits that "Sometimes during Fashion Week, I also feed people candy."

Networking Is Still Working

Okay, remember how this chapter started? With me talking about how some people shun the party circuit and hate hanging out and socializing and would rather chew on glass than make small talk? I am definitely not one of those people—well, maybe some of the time. While I spend a good deal of my day huddled over a computer or creating strategies for clients, I also spend a portion of my workday networking with people within my sphere and with total strangers. I've always loved connecting people with other brands, products, or people, but only when I believe that each has something exciting to offer the other. So dedicated am I to networking and expanding people's personal and business circles, that I've helped to launch an entrepreneurial network in the United Kingdom and also regularly run networking events here in New York City.

People are constantly asking me about the value of networking. They seem to have only negative experiences to report, tales of people aggressively pitching business or forcing business cards on any hapless soul who has the misfortune of crossing their path. But when done well, networking can create a relationship, partnership, or brand-new collaboration that creates opportunity and sparks creativity and ideas.

I believe a common misconception in networking is that immediate results are even remotely an option. Relationships require constant care and nurturing. While I can make it look deceptively easy when I simply pick up a phone and almost immediately produce results, in actuality I have likely proven myself to the person that I am calling, either through a long-term relationship or by having produced results in the past. Much of my business (about 95 percent) is through word of mouth and referral. In other words, I am my company, and my reputation is my strongest selling point. When I meet new people, I am not only meeting them for myself, but also for my clients. My mind is always racing to figure out not only how to get the most out of someone else, but also how to give them the most exciting and fulfilling business proposition possible.

When done right, networking is like the symbol of infinity. As you evolve, so does your circle and sphere of influence. As your level of success grows, so does that of your friends. As you meet new people, you have more to offer them and can expect more in return.

There is no one right way to network. Think about the other relationships in your life for a minute (and not the ones where there's shared DNA). How did you meet? There's your oldest friend from grade school, your college boyfriend, your friends from your first job, acquaintances from your building, that cute guy that you met on an airplane, and the woman who sat next to you at a recent seminar. Then there are your work colleagues, mentors, supervisors, trainees, former interns, dozens of people from different walks of life who allow you to enhance your day-to-day experiences. You don't have to meet someone at a formal networking event to network with them; even lunch with colleagues can be a form of networking, where you check in with others, update each other on projects and clients, and figure out common ground and possibilities for future collaborative or supportive efforts.

Expanding Your Circle

Okay, so you've trolled through your existing resources and realize that you need an infusion of new blood. The key isn't to attend as many networking events as possible; the key is to put yourself in a position where you can meet the right kinds of people. If you're feeling brave you can organize your own networking event, but it's probably best to start out by attending professional events.

Depending on your vocation, a quick search on the Internet will likely give you a great starting point. Are you most at ease online? Then consider joining a social networking group, message board, listserv, or support group. You can log in only when you have time and get to know the rhythm and give-and-take required. If you're looking to drum up new business, you might consider joining your local chamber of commerce. If you want to educate yourself about new developments in your field, consider attending conferences and conventions. If you'd prefer to combine socializing with your networking, then look for listings of events being held in your field. You'll be able to find everything from wine tastings to speed networking. Keep in mind, though, the point isn't to rush your way through and meet as many people as possible in as short a time as possible. The point is to meet the right kind of people and see if the spark is there to keep pursuing and exploring.

Networking Tips and Tricks
WHAT NOT TO WEAR

As a single woman I will admit that I find smart, successful men very attractive. I'll also further confess to the fact that at many of the networking events that I've hosted or attended, there has definitely been a surfeit of guy candy of exactly the kind that I favor. While in theory this might seem like the perfect recipe for dating success, it can sometimes backfire if you act too available or treat networking events like simply another venue to meet a potential date. I've attended events where some of the women were so skimpily clad that they became something of a joke to a lot of the other attendees. While love (or at least lust) can blossom anywhere, you never want to look, dress, or act in a way that casts aspersions on your professional self. Flirting on occasion is fine; over-the-top behavior or dress at a professional event is just plain tacky and highly inappropriate.

While it's flattering to have someone ask you out to dinner when at a networking event, you must always balance your personal and professional reputation and choose carefully—is that risotto really worth it? Chelsea Rippy, the CEO and founder of Shade Clothing, a company specializing in modest attire, feels that words like *sexy* and *modest* are frequently misused. "I believe the term *sexy* is frequently misused. That word should not be reserved exclusively for when you're showing cleavage or too much leg. Instead, sexy should be used about attitude. Sexy is anything or anyone that is appealing and/or attractive. . . . Women feel sexy in our clothing because they are confident in our clothing." Jennifer Brown, a recent college graduate and intern for some very trend-conscious companies, has her own take: "I will never wear an outfit, piece of clothing, or accessory that I do not like, no matter who else is wearing it. I also have to be physically and mentally comfortable with my outfit choices."

So, to ensure that you're sexy by any definition, confident, and comfortable, again, check out the venue and timing of the event. Instead of wearing a typical suit, try wearing a silk dress with a jacket and slightly more playful accessories (dangling earrings, sexy boots) than you might wear to work. Play with textures and proportions so that you aren't wearing an uptight, strictly work outfit, but rather a more relaxed evening ensemble. Halter tops under jackets are also a great option since the neckline adds interest and, whether you take off your jacket or not, there's always the illusion of wearing something slightly flirtier.

BE SINCERE

When I started working on this section, my instinct was to call a friend who has a reputation for being a networker extraordinaire for his advice and input. So committed is this guy to meeting new people that he regularly travels to other countries just to attend networking events, and he's in the midst of forming his own networking group. And yet I didn't call him and don't intend to.

Here's why. Networking Guy is a networker in name only. He's most definitely a *player* in the professional sense of the word. When presented with the opportunity to meet new people, he immediately turns on the charm full throttle. Over-the-top is subtle to this character. When you meet him for the first time, he attentively listens to all of your professional grief and makes the right soothing noises.

But here's what he does not do, ever: This guy does not follow up.

Not by phone, not by e-mail, not by instant message or even telepathy. When you are out of his orbit you cease to exist—until he needs something, and then it's back to the corporate wooing.

We all know people like this, and while they might be great fun to hang around with, they are generally not great people to do business with. Networking adrenaline junkies seem to relish the prospect of prospects, but can never quite figure out how to carry this over into real-world results.

FOLLOW UP AND BE OPEN TO OPPORTUNITIES

Last year I attended a networking event and broke my own rules (and yes, I'm hanging my head in shame). I ended up dating a guy that I met there, the CMO of a major news distribution service. We only went out a handful of times, but on our dates we both kept referring back to the event. He couldn't seem to get past the fact that he hadn't made one viable business contact, while I had found not only a potential client but also a new friend and potential boyfriend.

When I asked him if he had followed up with even one person that he'd met there, he replied no. When I asked him if he had done some research into the companies of the people we had met that night, to see if there could be a future connection, he again answered no. When I asked him if he would consider having his company host or sponsor future networking events, so that he could control the invitees and event, he refused to see the potential brand exposure for his company and again his answer was an emphatic no. When he asked me if I would go out with him again, I responded simply—no.

This guy had so much going for him, and knew in theory that while his company's reputation was stellar, he needed to create growth opportunities. What he did not see was the fact that sometimes one has to create opportunities where there are none to begin with.

CAREER

Sometimes being great at your job doesn't involve your job at all. Sometimes it's the little extras that can actually make or break a career. Much the way a fine meal is enhanced with subtle, almost indiscernible seasonings, the high points of your career don't always occur in the office.

Corporate

You can have the best relationship with your boss, employees or coworkers, but you should always be cognizant of the fact that you have a *working* relationship. While cocktails, office parties, and lunches with your work friends can be fun, and a great way to unwind and catch up on office gossip, don't ever indulge to the extent that you're in danger of putting your career in jeopardy.

Cool

If you're the one who chooses the venue for business lunches, spend some extra time choosing the perfect spot. If your client is a jazz aficionado, try to find a neighborhood joint that features live jazz; if your boss is addicted to Italian food, opt for a spot with homemade linguini. In other words, being considerate and taking care of the extra details can do wonders for your career and reputation as being the coolest person in the office. Carrie Foster, vice president of a boutique agency in Washington, D.C., adds: "Cool is saying 'nice to see you' when the person you've met a dozen times doesn't remember your name." Cooler is reminding them when you met last (with the most sincere of smiles).

Chapter 9

Entrepreneurial Extras

Working from Home Shouldn't Mean Sweats and Fuzzy Slippers—How to Clean Up for Any Occasion

> *Prosperity is only an instrument to be used,*
> *not a deity to be worshipped.*
> —Calvin Coolidge

That Was Then

Once upon a time there was a serfdom known as the Land before Telecommuting. In this archaic land, industrious women and men labored exclusively in giant hives known simply as "office buildings." On rare occasions these hardworking souls would call in sick (and then only when necessary bodily functions such as breathing were compromised and/or high doses of antibiotics were involved), or they would take time off to attend quaint family functions like parent-teacher conferences, destination weddings, or bar mitzvahs. Vacations were few and far between, and mental health days were all but unheard of.

Back in those dark days, these anxious escapees from the traditional grind would fretfully phone their work colleagues several times each day. Each rushed phone call was meant to convey a sense of calm, a sense of responsibility, and an urgency to remain relevant even while ill or dancing the hora with someone's aunt Millie. Both participants in said phone calls were left feeling uneasy—the missing workers wondered if this precious time off had proven them to be dispensable, while their colleagues were frustrated at the extra workload and irregular communications.

This Is Now

In other words, in the not too distant past, one's work reach was hampered by limited options and even more limited accessibility. The personal computer and desktop publishing ushered in the era of mass telecommuting. Then cellular phones, PDAs, the advent of the Internet with its online communication methods from instant messaging to e-mail, and an addictive handheld device known as the BlackBerry, decimated what was left of the old rules of work, commuting, and communicating. A traditional desk job once exclusively meant nine to five in the same office tower with the same coworkers and two weeks off for good behavior; our new work styles are defined or limited only by our capabilities and talents.

These new communication methods also ushered in a new era of entrepreneurship, from the initial wave of dot-com pioneers taking Silicon Alley by storm, to freelance artists, computer programmers, and others, taking advantage of the brave new medium to create successful e-commerce enabled cottage industries specializing in everything from handmade body lotions or wedding favors to baked goods or sex toys.

According to the U.S. Small Business Administration web site (http://www.sba.gov/), over 600,000 new businesses are started in the United States each year. Many of these are businesses that might never have existed five years ago, and their principals include refugees from the corporate world, new mothers, recent college grads, and retirees. This new generation of entrepreneurs and sole proprietors have working styles and skill sets that are best served by a nontraditional work environment. Their corporate headquarters might actually be housed in a spare bedroom or garage.

Tools of the Trade

So what are the tools of the trade for this brave new generation of impresarios? A pared-down work existence might include a regularly revised business plan, which small business expert Gwen Moran considers crucial to any business because "If you don't have a plan and a set of objectives for your plan, it's easy to get distracted and follow up on leads that aren't critical for your business and can divert attention away from your business and what you want to do." In her opinion, "The setting of goals is the thought process that is the answer to the question, what do I want to achieve?"

As a college student, Dain Lewis won the Yale Entrepreneurial Society's $50,000 business plan competition twice consecutively, in 2005 and 2006—the first time as part of a team, the second time as team leader. Lewis is a firm believer in trusting his gut and then creating the business plan to clarify and map out his vision. "When I hear a new idea and think about it for a long time, I feel that I can determine whether or not it is a good, sound idea that has real potential. If I'm sold on the idea I make sure that I do all the other things in business right—research, presentation, recruiting a good team, and so on. There are general things in business that you can apply to any industry, any idea, any product."

When you have an idea of what you'd like to achieve, and have clearly mapped out your intended goals, progress, and benchmarks, it's time to invest in some office accoutrements. Don't skimp on your day-to-day necessities, like a top-model computer with some groovy extras like a color printer, all-in-one fax/scanning device, external backup, the fastest and most reliable Internet connection, a phone headset, and a mobile PDA device (so that leaving the home office actually becomes a viable option). For businesses that involve fulfillment options as opposed to intellectual or consulting models, warehousing and shipping options are also a must. Above all, carry an unshakable sense of determination.

If you're having a hard time figuring out how to balance your finances, Emma Johnson, a multimedia correspondent for MSN Money, says, "You've heard it before, but keep track of your spending. . . . Many people are amazed how money slips through their fingers without much thought. Imagine if you found you blew through $300 on a weekend for drinks, dinner, a trip to the makeup counter, music store, and a movie or two. Now ask yourself to name a meaningful way to spend $300. Perhaps it is a plane ticket to visit your family, or a piece of furniture you've had an eye on for a long time. That $300 can be spent in a meaningful, intentional way, or not."

Tightened belt aside, the at-home entrepreneur's life is filled with the obvious perks that many in the corporate world can only dream of: working for yourself and setting your own hours, not having to commute, and generally living *la vida loca*. Well, at least that's the perception of being self-employed. The reality can be quite different—quite lonely and financially insecure, though some freelancers wouldn't have it any other way.

Freelance writer and author Wayne Curtis says that "If everyone is heading in one direction, I'd like to look in the other direction if not head there myself." As for corporate life, it's not for Curtis: " I had only one job where I had to wear a tie and had about two weeks vacation. I was about 25 and quit after reading a memo about dirty coffee cups and looking down the barrel of a future of a lifetime of such memos." It isn't that he has problems with set rules or roles, but rather "I like the flexibility; if I find the rules to be not good, I like to be allowed to walk away."

So the isolation of at-home entrepreneurship can be balanced by the ability to make your own rules. Self-employment can also mean having to navigate the new complications of business setups, health insurance, and the expectations of family and friends. The rate of success to failure in any business launch is brutal, with a large percentage of businesses failing. The data on the success rate of privately held businesses is hazy at best, though estimates say that less than half of businesses launched will earn a profit while a third just break even. And yet the American dream is built on the concept of boldly going where no others have gone (or is that *Star Trek*?—no matter), of creating something out of nothing, and of leaving a legacy for future generations.

Since this book isn't a guide to starting your own business, I won't presume to detail the minutiae involved in the process of setting up a business. Instead, a good place to start is the U.S. Small Business Administration (SBA) web site, specifically the online small business planner (http://www.sba.gov/smallbusinessplanner/index.html), which will help give you an idea of each step involved in the lifespan of a small business. For the purposes of Career and Corporate Cool, though, I'm

The Power Of One

more interested in discussing the ways in which you present yourself to the outside world—the way that you put on your game face and become the ambassador of your small business while at meetings and interacting with others.

Home Advantage

Admit it, whenever you've heard about your friends or colleagues working from home or starting their own businesses (or writing a hybrid business/style guide such as this one), you've pictured them working from home in their pajamas, listening to loud music, and flirting with the UPS guy (yes, I've been guilty of all three—and no, I have no intentions of telling you what I'm wearing at this very moment). For the most part, though, self-employed people work longer and more intensive hours, since it's not only their reputation at stake but also their dreams and sense of self-worth.

Designer Joanna Alberti has created her own line of greeting cards called philoSophie's Stylish Stationery and Greetings. While she has some revolving staff, she's mostly a one-woman show. So how does she keep motivated? She defines herself first and foremost as a dreamer and says that "When faced with challenges or the stresses of running my own business, I take a step back and let myself look beyond the day to what I envision for the future of the company and concept."

While many entrepreneurs will invest in their businesses, chances are they've been cutting corners on the rest of life's little luxuries and work necessities. If you don't interact with or even see others on a daily basis, it seems unimportant to have a closetful of work clothes—until the dreaded specter of a last-minute meeting rears its ugly head, and you're suddenly faced with a cornucopia of outdated or poorly fitting pantsuits, scuffed tennis shoes, and a freebie briefcase from a long-forgotten conference.

Be Prepared

The key to looking good at a moment's notice is to have a backup plan—and a seasonally perfect emergency outfit. First impressions in business can be critical. It's easy for someone like Bill Gates to get away with that "Aw shucks, I'm a brilliant billionaire and careless dresser" attitude. For the rest of us, though, first impressions can make or break a potential business relationship.

When meeting someone for the first time, it's important to take into account the other person's expectations, the corporate aesthetic, and the venue, but most of all the hope of a potential future relationship—and then to dress accordingly. While it isn't practical or even necessary to have a perfect manicure or blowdry if you're setting up a business as a caterer or a florist, it is crucial if you're in the fashion industry, because you will be judged not only on the job that you can do but on the way that you have packaged yourself as a business commodity. If you're a graphic artist or greeting card designer, your ink-smudged hands or paint-flecked jeans might usually add an air of authenticity, but if you're meeting the president of Hallmark Cards, your sloppy appearance might appear disrespectful of their time and position.

So for the purposes of meetings, be it with a potential client, agent, or editor, adopt the Boy Scout motto and always be prepared. And never, ever assume that because you've been working from home for three years, you're never going to have another meeting again. As each season changes and you switch from your summer to fall wardrobe and then back again, do a critical analysis of the contents of your closet. Try things on and if they don't fit or they look outdated, give them away. At this point in your life your mind needs to be cluttered only with thoughts of growing your business, not with the too-tight waistband of your designer jeans. Spend some time putting together an entire outfit, so if someone calls you the night before for a last-minute meeting you can set it up without a moment's panic or hesitation.

One Perfect Outfit

It could be a sweater and skirt, it could be a pantsuit, but make sure you've got all of it: the handbag, the shoes, the makeup, the hair. The last thing you want to do is run around like a crazy person that morning. It doesn't take much work to be prepared. If you're a person who always wears pantyhose, make sure you have a pair of hose with no runs. If you're a person who wears black pumps, make sure you have a pair that isn't scuffed. Do everything in your power to make sure that you have one outfit that makes you feel your professional best. Almost like Superman transitioning from Clark Kent to Man of Steel, your super outfit gives you pause and allows you to say to yourself, "Wow, I'm a super professional. I am a serious talent and force to be reckoned with."

Or Three

On the flip side of the occasionally gregarious entrepreneur and formerly friendly freelancers are entrepreneurs who seem to be in a perpetual state of meet and greet. For these professional networkers, their very bread and butter depends on how many power lunches, charismatic cocktails, dynamic dinners, and loquacious launches they can rack up. For this sociable set, seeing and being seen is a key element to their business model. Entrepreneurs who work within the entertainment, public relations, or style-related industries not only have to be seen at fabulous events, but they have to out-fabulous the well-dressed competition, which can be tough to do on an irregular paycheck.

For this more social group, it's important to have at least three great daytime outfits, since frequent meetings mean frequent opportunities for face-to-face appraisal, and repeating outfits in high-profile industries isn't always the best idea. A good rule of thumb would be a killer black suit (either pants or skirt), one of-the-moment color ensemble, and one day-to-night option.

For the chic business set a little black suit can say more than a little black dress, since black is and will always be the new black. For a chic variation on basic black, though, look for unusual detailing (great buttons, unusual lapels, or colorful stitching), a great fit, a fashionable cut, and different options for accessorizing—which means that different shirts, jewelry, or scarves can become outfit focal points. For color, consider these statement options: the color of the season, which shows that you are professional but also up to the minute; the hue that suits you best or your signature color, which becomes a color that people associate with you and your personal brand (mine is a coppery brown that sets off my eyes and hair); or a power color like red, which ensures that all eyes will be on you.

A day-to-night outfit is always great for when a languorous lunch turns to dinner or cocktails, or even a last-minute event. A day-to-night look might be a wrap dress worn with a jacket (jacket removed for evening), a quirky suit that can be as cocktail as it is Career and Corporate Cool, or even a sleeveless dress worn with a cardigan by day and more formally for a last-minute party. In other words, what might not feel appropriate for a meeting in an office tower might be ideal or de rigueur in a more personal and low-key setting like a bar or restaurant.

The Art of the Sale

Whether building your business by word of mouth or proactive networking and prospecting, it's crucial to know where you are in the sales cycle. The most elegant sales are those that are not made but rather occur through the natural progression of an ongoing dialogue.

Michael Main, a managing partner at ChapterHouse, a Chicago-based health care strategy consultancy, finds that "new business relationships most often occur at the confluence of buying authority, an addressable issue, and trust and credibility." Main emphasizes the importance of talking with the right audience and building chemistry through trust and credibility first; only then can the relationship progress toward a more formal analysis of the situation and solution design. "After consulting with hundreds of sales organizations, I can honestly report that a salesperson's own enthusiasm can backfire by skipping over important early development steps," says Main.

Read All about It

When possible, try to find out as much information as you can about your lunch/dinner/meeting partner and chosen venue. If you're heading for a low-key kitschy diner that's a client favorite, it might not be appropriate to wear a severely cut überchic suit, while a restaurant opening calls for a bit more dazzle. The last thing that you want is to look out of touch with your client's preferences and local or style trends.

In other words, do your research. Googling prospective dates is almost a given; doing background research on your meeting partner can prepare you to avoid potential minefields or congratulate them on well-publicized successes. You should also try to read up as much as possible on their industry in general—you don't want to congratulate someone who might be worried about industry wide shake-ups.

Even if you feel as though you've been living under a rock for the past few years, you never want to convey that to a potential employer or client. Read the day's newspapers, brush up on nonoffensive gossip—the latest TV shows, wardrobe malfunctions, or awards ceremonies. You might not be exchanging tidbits about Dr. McDreamy and the staff at Seattle Grace, but you want to be able to pick up on nuance, inside jokes, and pop culture references.

Accessorize Wisely

When working from home it can also be tough to keep track of hair, makeup, and accessories; after all, when is the last time that you worried about matching your clogs to your sweatpants? An easy rule of thumb is to wear your daily signature pieces, and if they include engagement/wedding ring, a treasured locket, or signature watch, they do not necessarily have to match your outfit. However, you might want to reconsider an armful of your signature bangle bracelets; while you may no longer notice their pleasant jingle, your lunch partner might find them to be noisy and distracting and leave, remembering later your jewelry more than your brilliant concepts.

Location, Location, Location

A whole new generation of entrepreneurs have laid claim to their local coffeehouse as an extension of their office and also a meeting place. Coffee and tea experts Travis Arndorfer and Kristine Hansen have noticed that "for self-employed people, cafés are an extension of the office and very valuable when a conference room is not available." Instead of just hitting the local java joint, though, they recommend researching your location to suit your intention.

Show and Tell

So your family and friends are sick and tired of hearing about your celebrated new book, your appearance on network television, or your latest press clipping where you and Giorgio Armani are the only experts quoted. Well spare them the gory details, but make sure that your potential clients know what you've been up to. Take them a copy of your book, mention your latest successes and coups. Your client is relying on you to bring attention to them, through your art, through your input, or through your media contacts. They don't want a wallflower to represent their best interests, and it's actually flattering to them to have in their employ a respected and recognized professional. So feel free to share your successes with a prospective client, but always remember that the bottom line is all about them—their needs, their business, their project. You are there to look your best and to represent their best interests.

CAREER

Whether or not you have the luxury of inviting a prospective client or employer into your office, your appearance has to convey all of the style, talent, and reliability of your business. Your clothing has to tell your client in no uncertain terms that you are smart, capable, and always perfectly able to handle whatever comes your way.

CORPORATE

You are always cognizant and respectful of your client's corporate needs and expectations. You will make them proud to have hired you, and while your work will always speak for itself, your appearance at meetings also instills your clients with confidence in your abilities and your understanding of their needs.

COOL

You might roll out of bed and into your desk chair on a daily basis, but you should always be prepared for an unexpected last-minute meeting. Clean your closet seasonally and weed out unchic or worn-looking garments. Assemble one to three perfect outfits, including everything from a great handbag to the perfect clean suit, underthings, and shoes. Make like a Boy Scout and always be prepared! Take it that one step further by always personalizing whatever you wear with signature style—your favorite woven leather belt, hipper-than-thou boots, or designer sunglasses. These little extras tell the outside world that you might know how to play the game, but you're also an innovator and tastemaker in your own right.

Chapter 10

Hello Gorgeous!

*A Perfectly Polished Face, Subtly Gleaming Hair,
and a Nonoffensive Cloud of Perfume
Can Make You More Professional*

> *There is no excellent beauty that hath not some
> strangeness in the proportion.*
> —Sir Francis Bacon

Beauty through the Generations

Try, if you will, to describe the definitive classic beauty, the one perfect ideal of female splendor that would satisfy every taste or aesthetic. Would you opt for Egyptian Queen Cleopatra's exotic olive-colored skin, exaggerated kohl-rimmed eyes, and sharply cut wigs? Or would you perhaps think of Helen of Troy, whose face was said to launch a thousand ships in the form of the epic battles between Sparta and Troy during the Trojan War?

Would you trace the trajectory of beauty in great art, from the half-smile of DaVinci's *Mona Lisa* to John Singer Sargent's exquisitely rendered but coolly detached *Madame X*, to Pablo Picasso's cubist lovelies—none of them beautiful, all of them startling? Or is it the works of Peter Paul Rubens that you find depict true female beauty, in all of their sensual yet distinctively rounded glory?

In more modern times, is it the sophisticated yet decidedly boyish-looking flapper of the early twentieth century that you deem to be perfect? Do you deify the curvy goddesses of the mid-era, from Bettie Page, Dorothy Dandridge, and Jane Russell to Marilyn Monroe (who would all have definitely burst the seams of the size 00 jeans worn by a majority of today's frail-looking skeletal celebrity set)? Or perhaps you've been swayed by our own era's obsession with self and scalpel. One wonders what might come next after this period in which women actually buy into the cult of insecurity that deems implanting silicon into their bodies necessary to be rendered attractive, or listen to dire media warnings against the horrors of "toc-besity" in which the shame of having pudgy piggies might keep you from wearing your favorite Manolos.

Perfectly Imperfect Beauty

Forgive me for a moment while I pontificate on one of my favorite expressions and concepts: *jolie/laide*, which translates exactly as *pretty/ugly*. The French, who famously celebrate "women of a certain age" for their grace, wisdom, evolving beauty, and sexuality, have also coined this clever phrase to describe women whose quirky features or less than perfect attributes come together to form true beauty.

In 1989, a French film called *Trop Belle pour Toi* ("Too Beautiful for You") detailed the struggle of a less than spectacular-looking man, played by Gerard Depardieu, struggling with marriage to the picture-perfect but emotionally unavailable Carole Bouquet, while being in love with the passionate but plain-looking Josiane Blasko. Along those lines, unlike Hollywood films, which tend to favor a certain look or body type that usually include line free-faces (no matter their age), bee-stung lips, endless legs, and bosoms of Amazonian proportions, the films of Spanish director Pedro Almodóvar, tend to lovingly highlight the uneven features and Technicolor personalities of women who most resemble cubist art.

As for our own perceptions of beauty and imperfection, one need only look at the likes of Jennifer Aniston, Minnie Driver, Madonna, Sarah Jessica Parker, and Reese Witherspoon. True, these beauties may have subtly enhanced their looks over the years (whether or not they'll admit it on the record), but they've left their signature pronounced jaws, gapped teeth, large noses, and pointy chins mostly intact. We love these gorgeous and gutsy women more than the tiny Audrey Hepburn wannabes or golden goddesses, because their imperfect beauty reminds us that while we may be far from perfect by Hollywood standards, we are all perfectly beautiful in our own way.

Bring on the Beauty Tips

But I digress. It's tough enough at the best of times to become comfortable enough in your own skin, or self-confident enough to know what works or doesn't work for you no matter what the glossy magazines declare. It can be even trickier to navigate the balance between work professionalism and fashion and trends or looking outdated.

Over the years, while applying makeup to faces famous, infamous, and nearly unrecognizable (due to excessive cosmetic surgery), I've picked up or invented some cool beauty tricks. Fast-forward to my business life, where I've learned to strike a balance between over-the-top theatrical looks and a perfectly polished career look. (But who am I kidding? There are times where I feel compelled to combine the two.) The main thing that I've learned over the years? (Say it with me now.) There is no such thing as one definition of beauty. There is also no way to try to embrace every aspect of popular beauty, lifestyle, fashion, or physical aesthetic. It's too hard, and it's too much work, and it hurts too much to try to compare yourself to something that isn't and has never been real, and to feel that you are in some way lacking when you aren't.

My best advice then? As with your wardrobe, figure out what works for you, subtly enhance those features, and evolve as new formulations and textures are developed. In other words, if your eyes are your knockout feature, have your brows professionally shaped to best frame them. Choose and use the best mascara to play up your peepers. Don't overwhelm them with color or shading, but rather keep practicing eye makeup application until you've created the perfect look for you—and then keep practicing until you can create this ocular masterpiece in five minutes flat. The same goes for lips, cheekbones, and a swanlike neck—find what works for you and really work it.

Don't Look Dated!

While you're at it, consider your overall look. Are your eyeglasses fabulous or merely functional? Is your hair classic or outdated? Celebrity colorist Rita Hazan has artfully tinted the tresses of notables including Jennifer Lopez, Jessica Simpson, and Brooke Shields (and has also given me the most beautiful highlights of my entire fine-haired life). Hazan advises changing your hair seasonally to reflect the more muted shades of winter and the brighter or lighter effect that summer might have on your hair. In this way, you won't risk falling into a hair color rut.

A great rule of thumb is to subtly change the small things. Cutting your fringe choppy or feathered while leaving your overall hairstyle the same, or wearing different eyeglasses to match or contrast with your clothing, can keep you looking chic and in control.

Lights Please—And Other Potential Office Face Flops

Did you ever happen to notice just how luminous Oprah Winfrey looks on her TV show or on the cover of her magazine? Not only is her hair and makeup perfect, but her skin positively glows and seems lit from within. If you see Ms. O on other shows or venues, though, she doesn't always look quite as stunning because she's subject to the whims of the sometimes unflattering lighting and camera angles.

Did you ever notice just how great your makeup looks when you leave your house, but how you can end up looking positively peaked at work? Most offices contain painfully unflattering fluorescent lighting, which can tinge even the rosiest skins greenish and add an unattractive tint to even the most expensive highlights. It isn't vain to want to look great at work; it's actually an investment in your career equity. Why look tired or sluggish when you aren't?

When you're going to be stuck under harsh and unflattering lights, you have to actually apply your makeup differently. If possible, try applying your makeup under similar lighting until you can combat the effects of the dark shadows and unkind effects of office lighting.

Pay special attention to:

- Concealer. You might actually have to go a shade lighter for your office face, or try using a creamier consistency. Office lighting can make even the most perfectly matched cover-up look too beige or patchy.
- Foundation. Again, play around with the shades. Office lighting often makes even base on darker skins look too pale or ashy. Experiment with shades with a bit more warmth to counterbalance the cool effect of the fluorescents.
- Blush. Powder blush is great for oilier skins but can have a striped effect under office lighting. Try cream or gel blush for a more gentle glow. Also consider playing with peachier shades, which are for the most part universally flattering as a blush color (though rarely as an evening gown).
- Lipstick and lip liner. Eight or more hours of recycled air can leave your lips looking parched and accentuate fine lines around your mouth. Try a lip gloss or sheerer formula and reapply throughout the day (but not so often that when coworkers ask where you are, they are told you're in the ladies room doing your face!).
- Translucent powder. Again, your skin might look flawless at home but papery at work. Try to find a formulation that has the tiniest bit of shimmer in it, but not so much that it's noticeable, to add a little lift to your daytime face. Be vigilant about avoiding a shiny nose, which only looks worse with the reflected glow of overhead or desk lighting.
- Dated details. Dark lip liner with pale lipstick, blood-red lips with an otherwise bare face, two-tone hair with dark roots and overprocessed ends, chipped or ragged nails—you get the idea. While rock stars may purposefully affect an artfully dishevelled

look, it rarely works in the business world. Don't convince yourself that your boss will think you're working too hard to have time to primp; you'll probably look like you just you don't care or don't respect your work environment.

♦ Unruly eyebrows. While there's not one perfect method for shaping brows, some basic tips include plucking away the uni-brow (for both men and women) and enhancing your arch. Where you place it depends on your natural brow line, but gen-erally it should start at the outer edge of the iris, not the center. Use a stiff eyebrow brush to brush brows in an upward direc-tion, until you reach the top of the brow. Hold the brush steady and trim any stray hairs that stick out. When using color on brows, match it to your eyebrows and not to your hair. Use short gentle strokes to fill in any sparse patches. Eye shadow applied with a stiff brush works equally well, especially during sweaty summer weather.

Desk Set

So you've figured out what works best under less than flattering office lights. Be sure to keep extra mini versions of your makeup around for unexpected emergencies, to touch up your face during the day and also to get ready for unexpected dinner dates or meetings.

While at the drugstore, pick up travel-size versions of your favorite products. Keep the following in your desk: breath mints or mouth-wash; a mini sewing kit; an extra pair of shoes; tampons; pantyhose and underwear; contact lens solution and case; protein bars; Tylenol; hand cream; a nail file; hairspray and assorted ponytail holders, hair bands, or barrettes for hair emergencies; velcro tape for fallen hems; and these cosmetic extras:

♦ Tiny lipsticks and glosses. Companies like Elf, Bourjois, Stila, Cargo, and others have created these in their most popular colors.
♦ Eye drops to soothe computer-irritated eyes.
♦ Deodorant.

◆ Towelettes containing everything from eye makeup and nail polish remover to scent. Keep some leak-proof samples around for touch-ups.

Beauty Emergencies

You're mostly prepared, but sometimes the unexpected occurs. In those situations try these:

◆ Missing an earring back? Cut a wedge from a pencil eraser to replace it.

◆ Broken nail? Use the striking strip on a matchbook to buff away the ragged edges.

◆ Ripped pantyhose? Brush on some clear nail polish to prevent the run from growing.

◆ Garlic breath from lunch? Chew on the parsley garnish to freshen up.

◆ Shoes scuffed? Use a matching Sharpie to touch up the bare areas.

◆ French manicure chipped? Use Wite-Out to touch it up.

◆ Hair oily? Sprinkle in some baby powder at the roots (be sure to use it sparingly) and brush well.

◆ Zit from hell? Use eye drops to take the red out.

◆ Nose shiny? Empty a teabag and use the bag itself to blot away shine.

Day to Night

Most of us have crazy weeks where grueling days are followed by nights out for enforced merriment with clients or a hot date, or a night out with the girls. After a tough day, the last thing that most of us want to do is head home and start from scratch. For those days here are some easy ways to get glam in minutes.

If you know about your plans in advance, try to figure out your look before leaving home in the morning. Wear a sexy sleeveless shift topped with a jacket and lose the cover-up at night, or take along a sexy pair of sling-backs to replace your practical shoes. Prepare a touch-up kit that will let you deepen and intensify your daytime look and pump up the volume in your hair.

If you have only five minutes:

- Repair any melted makeup.
- Apply a tinted moisturizer, or dot a luminizing product on cheekbones and under the arch of your brows.
- Spritz on some perfume.
- Dab a sheer gloss on your lips.

If you have 10 minutes:

- Fix your foundation, hide any blemishes or discoloration.
- Blend cream or gel blush on the apples of your cheeks for a bit of flush.
- Smudge eyeliner on your top lids.
- Add an extra coat of mascara.
- Stain lips and then add a tiny bit of gloss.

If you have 15 minutes:

- Freshen your hair with velcro rollers or a portable hair straighter or curling iron (make sure to shut it off before you go). Or, for extra volume, bend from the waist and spritz the roots of your hair with hair spray.
- Spend more time on your foundation to really perk up your complexion.
- Work on defining cheekbones, or use a bronzer for some night-time sizzle.
- Apply a deep midnight blue, gray, black, or even taupe shadow to top eyelid and along bottom lash line. Use a thick pencil or liquid eyeliner to line both top and bottom lash lines. Smudge gently for a subtle version of an evening eye. Follow with two coats of mascara.
- Go for a more playful lip shade—maybe a shocking pink blotted and then topped with clear gloss or a sheer baby pink.

- Take off your jacket or cardigan, undo an extra button or two on your blouse, and, depending on the occasion, sweep some bronzer on cleavage to deepen your décolletage.
- Use a perfume oil in key pulse points for a subtle bit of scent.

Look your best in and out of the office with some of my favorite easy-to-use products:

- Crest Whitestrips. Apply after work to brighten up your smile before an event. Put on Whitestrips, fix hair and makeup, remove Whitestrips, apply lipstick.
- ModelCo minis like Skin Drink Airbrush Moisturizer, Tan Airbrush in a can, or Shimmer Airbrush Illuminiser can perk up work-sluggish parts. Spritz Skin Drink on tired complexion, use the Illuminiser on décolletage or legs. Be vigilant about any kind of tanning product, though, if you're short on time since you could end up with uneven application or streaks.
- Matrix Biolage Bodifying Creme Gel will perk up even lank locks. Use a tiny bit at the roots and massage through hair. Velcro rollers are great for instant body. Maxius AdjustaCurl ionic adjustable rollers are the coolest yet since you can adjust the size to create as much volume or curl as desired. Remington Wet 2 Dry hair straightener adds polish to hair; use one of 16 settings to defrizz or even add a stylish flip.
- Wash the day off your face with Olay Daily Facials Express Wet Cleansing Cloths, or just dab on Bourjois Retouche Express to remove melted mascara or wayward lipstick.
- Too much Purell leave your hands dry and irritated? It's a toss-up for best hand cream between Bliss Glamour Glove Gel and Borghese Splendide Mani Smoothing Hand Creme. Both actually heal and repair ragged cuticles and ashy, dry skin.
- Sephora has too many brilliant private label products to list. The concealer kit has four different shades to correct everything from redness to sallowness; the highlighting bronzing powder has three shades that blend together perfectly to perk up your face; the tinted moisturizer with vitamin E evens out

your complexion and leaves you less pale or tired looking. Lierac Skin Care from France is available in drugstores but is as effective as pricier skin care products.

◆ Blot your shiny spots with Lancôme Matte Finish Shine-Control Blotting Sheets, follow with Lancôme Dual Finish powder makeup applied over moisturizer for a flawless finish.

◆ Smashbox Photo Finish Foundation Primer applied first thing in the morning will plump up tired-looking skin and keep foundation from drying into wrinkles or smile lines.

◆ Much of the Sue Devitt line is plant- or sea-based, such as Triple C-Weed Whipped Foundation; or try Maybelline Dream Matte Mousse. Both are workplace miracles—light and airy foundations that can be applied in a matter of seconds and last all day. Touch up your cheekbones with Maybelline Dream Mousse Blush; Peach Satin is one of the most universally flattering colors.

◆ It's nearly impossible for me to narrow down my favorite Tarte or Bourjois cosmetics products since they're almost all intuitive, dummy-proof, and supercool. Tarte Rest Assured Brightening Wand is a two-step tool to wake up tired eyes and face. Tarte Cheek Stain in Flush adds a glow of color to any complexion. Bourjois Effet 3D in Rose Symphonic is my all-time favorite lip gloss (I even have a miniature Bourjois lip gloss cell phone charm).

◆ Moisturizers that will nurture and replenish even the most exhausted skin include Elemis Pro-Collagen Marine Cream, Darphin Hydraskin Light, and Shiseido Bio-Performance Super Restoring Cream.

◆ Fresh In-Flight Kit contains cleansing towelettes, an in-flight mask, and post-flight serum.

◆ No time for a facial? Dr. Brandt Pores No More minimizes the appearance of large pores (especially on the T-zone).

◆ No time for a manicure? Essie Shine-E Polish Refresher makes your polished nails look shinier and fresher.

◆ Can't live without your favorite products that only come in full-size packaging? Bobbi Brown Empties are tiny travel-size jars, bottles, spatulas, and labels to create your own mini versions of your favorites to help keep you organized and beautiful on the go. (Bobbi Brown products are brilliant for the office as well since their neutral shades blend work well under fluorescent lights).

◆ Hall-of-famers in the beauty department include Guerlain Lip Lift, which smoothes out lines, deflakes lips, and keeps your lipstick on for hours longer. Yves Saint Laurent Touche Éclat radiant highlighter inspired an army of imitators, but nothing quite brightens up tired eyes so well. Darphin Instantly Radiant eye-brightening stick moisturizes and wakes up tired eyes. I recommend anything Phyto (I have a crush on this all-natural plant-based line), but especially Phytophanère dietary supplements, which make my hair shinier and more lustrous, and Phytovolume Actif Volumizer Spray with keratin amino acids, which instantly perks up even tired and droopy hair.

CAREER

Unless you've got a professional makeup artist on your payroll (along with your stylist, colorist, tailor, and virtual assistant), chances are that you're going to have to perfect your beauty-in-a-hurry regime, and likely under less than flattering circumstances and lighting. Don't assume that your usual look will work at the office, but practice your makeup for other lighting as well.

CORPORATE

There's a fine line between applying subtle, professional makeup and looking like you've spent far too much time on your face and not enough on your workload. Part of a polished professional look involves a subtle makeup technique. Unless you work in a fashionable industry you don't want to attract comments on your cosmetics, but rather want them to highlight your best features.

COOL

Face it (literally)—as much as you grumble about having to put on your face before leaving the house, the right kind of cosmetics can provide an extra business tool. Pull an all-nighter completing a project? While the rest of your team looks exhausted and out of sorts, you can at least look as fresh as the proverbial daisy.

Chapter 11

He Said, She Said

Understand and Navigate the Differences between Masculine and Feminine Work Styles

> *I have yet to hear a man ask for advice on how to combine marriage and a career.*
>
> —Gloria Steinem

> *It's different for girls.*
>
> —Joe Jackson

Il A Dit, Elle A Dit

In many foreign languages it's fairly simple to figure out whether a man or a woman has written a certain text, or whether said text refers to one of the sexes, since the language is automatically separated into the masculine or feminine. In English, aside from a few grammatical blips like ships being referred to in the feminine, or your school as your *alma mater*, we're mostly gender-neutral unless specifically using the "he said, she said" variables. In other words, simply reading this sentence, you have no idea if it was written by a man or by a woman.

To further delve into the concept of definitive linguistic locatives, one might employ analytic programs that actually break down paragraphs and sentence patterns to determine whether the speaker or author is actually a man or a woman. One might also expand on that concept to include the actual skill of typing—once considered the

His Style/Her Style

domain of professional secretaries or other traditionally female vocations, typing (or its bastard cousin, the hunt-and-peck) is now a necessary and almost mandatory skill for anyone ever hoping to work with a computer.

Say It with a Smile

It would be overly naive and somewhat utopian-minded to infer that the disparity between women's and men's business communications is limited to the actual ways in which they communicate, interact, or are perceived by the opposite sex. One must also take into account the concentration of communication, follow-up, and very noticeable ways that their business styles are received or rewarded simply by virtue of their gender. Countless studies have presented the notion of women being instinctively more sociable and nurturing and of carrying this through to the workplace. Conversely, the stereotypes of men being stubborn, more aggressive, or instinctive problem solvers are also said to come into play in the business arena.

Susan Silver, a New York–based comedy writer, played up some of those more over-the-top gender-attributed traits in classic episodes of television shows including *Maude*, *The Bob Newhart Show*, and *The Mary Tyler Moore Show*. "My writing for Mary Tyler Moore was very much my own life—I never made up a story," she said. "I always write about my own experiences honestly and amusingly. Of course in comedy you exaggerate." While the clothes may seem dated, several decades after these shows first aired, their distinct "he said, she said" gestalt and differing work styles and gender perceptions frequently still hold true.

The Old Boys' Club versus the New Girls' Network

Depending on who you speak to, the old boys' club, that proverbial society that not only excludes women from its ranks but rather reaches out to ally, employ, and promote well-connected males within its ranks, is either alive and well or an archaic concept that is rapidly wending its way towards extinction.

Georgette Mosbacher, who famously wears the title of socialite as comfortably as that of CEO, nonetheless believes, "It's still very much a man's world and any woman who doesn't understand that is at a disadvantage." She further suggests that for women and men to effectively communicate with each other in business, women must understand that the "women's movement lied to women by saying that women could have it all. Women were told that they could have it all as long as they behaved like a man." Mosbacher suggests that a majority of women are fighting the wrong battles by pretending that the very real differences between the sexes do not exist. She prefers doing what she does well, in her own way and as a woman, rather than fighting to prove that she can do things in a way that a man might.

Mosbacher believes that the biggest obstacles to women reaching the corner office are not men but rather other women. "We don't help each other; women at the top like being at the top of the boys' club instead of bringing other women along." She also offers the concept of women's inclination to carrying grudges being equally ill suited to a place of employment. She offers the example of two men arguing over a drink at a dinner party. "If a deal came along the next day, they would chat amiably and make that deal happen." Mosbacher believes that would never happen with two women: "A woman might not talk to another woman over a perceived slight for the rest of their lives. That's where the guys have it over us."

What about powerful and successful women? Mosbacher believes that society considers these words to be "synonymous with being tough or a bitch—and we're scared of being labeled these things." She continues, "We haven't gotten past not having to apologize for success. You can aspire to make a lot of money and it doesn't make you a bad person." She does acknowledge, however, that it might be somewhat off-putting to a majority of men: "Men are afraid because it transfers a traditional sense of power. They believe that their number one asset is that they can take care of you and they don't think they'll be attractive if that shifts."

For the record, the old boys' network isn't even exclusive to boys—it can sometimes include daughters of old boys as well, or can also include companies with a *miraculous* story. Sometimes you have to do a little digging to find out that one of the unknown founders of an overnight $50 billion sensation is actually the son-in-law of an Internet pioneer.

Put Your Money Where Your (Lipstick–Wearing) Mouth Is

There's no denying the very real wage gap that still exists between men and women. Arin Greenwood, an attorney who has relocated from New York City to Saipan, comments on "a really enormous number of young women from the Philippines and China who are supporting their whole families on jobs that pay $3.05 an hour here." She also refers to the "funky gender dynamics." Equally prevalent is the "glass ceiling" effect, so called because women can ostensibly reach the highest levels of success only to be blocked by an invisible gender-based barrier.

My sister Kiki is one of the millions of women who have transitioned through several careers. She's currently a career coach, but worked in New York City government and began her career as an educator and teacher trainer. She regularly recounts the way in which she taught grade school children about the inequality of pay in the market place. She would assign two children, a boy and girl, the exact same task, perhaps each erasing half of the blackboard. She would then "pay" them for their work. The boy might earn one dollar salary while the girl would only be given 75 cents. When the children would complain, my sister would say, "But you're a girl—girls don't earn as much as boys." The children were perplexed and would continue to complain, and a dialogue about inequality in wages paid to the sexes would rage.

The wage disparity has been blamed on educated women leaving the workforce to care for their children, and also on the belief that women are not as competitive as men and are therefore content with earning a smaller income. On the other end of that wage-earning spectrum are Chicago-based Camille Noe Pagan and her husband, both of whom work in the publishing industry. At this point in their respective careers, she earns significantly more than he does. While this might be a major issue in many relationships, Pagan and her husband "have a very solid relationship and have always communicated really well," so fighting about money is for the most part a nonissue. Pagan admits though, "The guilt factor, on his part, is there occasionally, and I sometimes have to remind him that if it was the other way around—if he was the one earning more—he would be as okay with it as I am."I once took a career aptitude test, and the career recommended to me was benevolent despot to my own island nation (a vocation that most people who know me would agree I'd be well suited for). So are women less competitive than men? I think not. I think that we just manage our egos, their egos, and the feelings of those around us more carefully—because we usually have to.

All in the Family

According to family legend, my grandmother Mindy was known for having something of a peppery personality; her flame-colored hair matched her notoriously fiery temperament. While attending school was unheard of for the majority of the boys in her village, Grandma Mindy was the first girl to attend and graduate both elementary and high school—no mean feat in Hungary in the early decades of the twentieth century. My father was clearly influenced by his mother's dedication to learning, and he always encouraged my siblings and me to rabidly pursue knowledge and seek out higher and ever-evolving forms of education. My mother is equally enamored with the quest for culture, is a voracious reader, and jokes that she has an accent in seven languages.

Growing up in my family, we discussed current events, pop culture, and literature around the dinner table. I was never aware of being treated like a junior citizen; even though I was the youngest, my thoughts and opinions were as viable and open for discussion as those of my older siblings, parents, or other relatives. As a very little girl I remember my parents' reward system in which I would

have the choice between a doll and a book as a prize for good behavior—and books always won. At the age of four, I had my own
subscription to a magazine, and while I didn't quite get the concept
of a monthly delivery, I remember the incredible pride I felt seeing
my name on the address label. Since my father was a teacher and
then a school administrator, education became play for us. While
other kids played with Barbie dolls, I played with an educator's version of SRA (a school-based reading mastery resource) and was
reading at an eighth grade level when I was still in the second
grade.

I Don't Know How I Do It—I Just Do It!

Earlier this year, I had a chat with Mrs. Shirley Sokol, my second grade
teacher, someone I hadn't had contact with since elementary school.
Mrs. Sokol told me that when she tries to stress the concept of thinking differently than the pack to her college students, she tells them a
story about me. The story goes that Mrs. Sokol asked my second grade
class if any of us knew what a vowel was and was met by a roomful
of blank faces. She then tried to give us a hint by explaining that vow-
els have to do with reading. I raised my hand and said, "I don't know
what a vowel is. I just read." I didn't need to know how something
was done correctly to do it—I simply started doing it until I was doing
it right.

When I heard my second grade teacher recount this story, I was
stunned—she had just succinctly and retroactively summed up my
adult personality and work style. To this day, I do not wait to hear the
whys, hows, or parameters of a project or major task. For better or
worse, I simply take the tools that I already have and work at a problem until I have succeeded in figuring out how to do whatever needs
to be done. I loathe complicated diagrams or instructions, I detest in-
struction manuals, and I avoid training sessions like the plague. As
you may have surmised, my work style can drive colleagues, both
male and female, to distraction.

I'm certain that behavior specialists would have much to say about my personal work style—perhaps they would find it to be inherently masculine, while others would argue the feminine traits. The bottom line is that I have found a style, for better or worse, that works for me as a woman in business. I have not only tapped into my own abilities but have also drawn on the legacy of learning and independent women that are the hallmarks of my family. I imagine that many of us have pure, unadulterated talents, skills, quirks, and abilities that have either lain dormant for decades or clearly make up our individual styles. Some of these hallmarks are clearly masculine while others borrow from the feminine side. One hopes that the bottom line is getting a job done well, in the way that takes full advantage of our unique talents.

Back to Basics

My friend Ryan recently shared the great news that his pitch had been accepted by a major television network, and that his concept and outline were in development and would be turned into a new sitcom. After congratulating him, I immediately asked him about his relationship with his writing partner, someone whom I had heard about often as being an intransigent and sometimes difficult individual. I queried Ryan on the formal or informal nature of their relationship, asked if there was a legally defined relationship, and advised him on hiring legal counsel for himself alone and a separate lawyer to represent him and his partner as a team. Since he had been writing with his partner for well over a decade, I advised him to be diplomatic in his approach, to invite his colleague out for an informal meeting, perhaps over coffee, and to broach the subject delicately—to draw on their history, to talk about future success, and also to explain that his wish for legal representation was to ensure that their long-term friendship and partnership would remain intact and uncompromised.

His reply? "Nah. I'll just call him and tell him that I'm hiring a lawyer. We're close enough that I don't have to sugarcoat anything." He marveled at my suggested approach, appreciating my instinct toward diplomacy, while I marveled at his laid-back approach. Both approaches would have been viable, but would of course depend on the existing relationships, work styles, and yes, gender approach. As a woman in business, my instinct is always to protect the long-term relationship in any interaction. In my business I create a lot of partnerships and develop strategies that sometimes take years to implement and integrate. I carefully assess the long-term goals and effects and always work to protect the egos and best interests of all involved parties, though I have to wonder if my overprotective instincts might, in some cases, be somewhat based on my gender.

My Hobbies Include World Domination, Contact Sports, and Sweating Profusely

It's a well-known fact that one of the worst things any job seeker can do on their resume is lie about their skills, experience, or history. What you may not realize is that often when job seeking, you don't even have to include your name or even vital statistics for your potential employer to figure out if you're a man or woman.

Whenever I peruse the resume of a prospective employee, I have an immediate and clear idea of their age, skills, and gender. Younger and more inexperienced women, usually straight out of college, tend to add filler to their resumes that includes their volunteer work and group memberships, love for cooking, and even aerobics or tennis. Education is often a badge worn a bit too proudly by women who pursued a designer degree with little backup skill or initiative. Many of the resumes submitted by young men, by contrast, stress fraternities, group sports, and team activities—if I hold these resumes close enough to my ear, I swear can almost hear the grunts.

The bottom line? Once you're out of college, your alma mater is mostly just an indicator of your social status or scholarship. It tells people if you overpaid for your tuition or went to a party school. In other words, your college degree does not and should not act as your sole defining characteristic. (Unless of course you belonged to some secret society that boasts secret handshakes, indiscernible tribal tattoos, and former presidents.)

She Stoops to Conquer

Whether it's a misguided attempt not to outshine their male counterparts or a calculated move to have people underestimate them, you'll frequently find women underplaying their skills, experience, opinions, and other outstanding abilities. In negotiation in particular, many women adopt an almost poker-playing tactic, in not revealing their hand but rather allowing or encouraging others to relax around them and let down their guard.

I admit to having employed this tactic in the past, much to the chagrin of a former mentor. As an übersuccessful charter member of the old boys' network, my former mentor was tickled pink (as it were) at how many people would seek me out for business partnerships and projects. In his world, pedigree was frequently a major deciding factor over talent, skill, network, and abilities. Because I was still a fledgling negotiator I would sometimes feign weakness, much to his dismay. Inevitably, though, I would get our negotiation partners to reveal their hand or strategy.

In retrospect I can't say that I would advise anyone to specifically pretend to be less able than they are. I would, however, strongly recommend taking full advantage of any potential partner or colleague who isn't smart enough to realize the full extent of your talents and business prowess.

But Don't Ever "Shtup" to Conquer

We've all read or repeated the whispered rumors of coworkers or well-known actresses sleeping their way to the top, or sadly in some cases sleeping their way to middle management or further career mediocrity. I can't stress this enough: There is never a time when it's okay to use your body or sexuality as a method of moving your career forward. While clever banter between colleagues may sometimes verge on inappropriate, you'll always know when the line has been crossed. You don't need to make excuses to get out of an awkward situation—just go. There are few actions that can be deemed career suicide, but trading sex for any level of employment would top that list.

Bart and Lisa or Full-Blown Bullying?

Loads of offices have a family feeling to them, especially when you work for a family business. Employees take on the role of siblings or cousins, joking, teasing, tormenting—in other words, sometimes taking the company ethos of informality way too far. Know that you don't ever have to assume the family role or part that is thrust upon you. Know also that if you are uncomfortable with the way that a male or female colleague seems to be taking advantage of your close-knit work situation, or seeing how far they can push you, it is okay and perhaps necessary to confront them on their bad behavior, or to keep track of any inappropriate or threatening comments and then report them to your supervisor. Don't be surprised if you are accused of hypersensitivity.

The good news is that in work, unlike in family situations, you do not have to and should not accept teasing that makes you feel bad about yourself, your looks, or your skill set. Informality can be useful in many work environments, but teasing that takes on hostile overtones is simply harassment under the guise of friendship.

Hogging the Limelight

For the record, writing about the really irritating work habits of some men does not mean that all men in business possess these quirks. We're just trying to figure out how to make our individual foibles mesh for the best possible professional outcome.

A good friend of mine frequently sits in on pitch meetings at work—at a male-dominated advertising agency. She has great ideas, which are frequently poached and then restructured and presented to her boss as having been thought up by her male colleagues, who then go on to receive kudos and awards and other incentives. Instead of sitting idly by and letting someone take credit for your ideas, keep an idea log—preferably on your computer, with a time and date stamp as proof of concept. If a poacher attempts to hijack your concept, speak up for yourself.

My friend is an only child, and when I reminded her that she'd grown up without brothers, she realized that she wasn't used to having to speak up for herself and demanding equal time to voice her thoughts and opinions. So before meetings, she started imagining that the idea-poaching guys at work were more like unruly siblings than back-stabbing nemeses, and she has since been able to stand up for herself, claim credit, and demand recognition for her concepts and ideas.

CAREER

Let's face it, men and women are different in just about every way possible, so it certainly stands to reason that their work styles will differ as well. Contrary to what Professor Higgins thought, the key isn't for a woman to be more like a man, or vice versa, but rather for us to try to understand and work with our natural tendencies.

CORPORATE

It's a sad fact that while countries like Israel, India, the United Kingdom, and most European countries have had women as leaders, the United States still considers the very concept of a female president to be controversial. We feel comfortable paying silicon- and collagen-enhanced actresses upwards of $20 million dollars per film to portray celluloid politicians, but we won't pay a female leader to rule our nation. One almost wonders if, when elected she would be paid the same three-quarter salary that most working women are subject to. We shouldn't be surprised then at the dearth of female CEOs or other well-paid women in positions of extreme power and influence. It's time for an updated and ongoing dialogue on across-the-board maternity leave laws and other family-friendly initiatives that don't force women to choose between motherhood and a career. (We're one of the few nations whose government doesn't regulate or even factor childcare and maternity leave into our workplaces—similar only to some Third World nations.)

COOL

Whether you want to admit it or not, there's something fun about learning a different way of doing things, or about figuring out how not to be so hypersensitive or critical. The best part about working with the opposite sex is having a unique insight into some of their distinctive behaviors—on some level, learning to work with those quirks, and in some instances incorporating them into your own professional repertoire.

Chapter 12

Eat to Live

Healthy Nutrition, Fitness, and On-the-Go Snacking Tips for Maximum Productivity

> *The secret of staying young is to live honestly,*
> *eat slowly, and lie about your age.*
> —Lucille Ball

Food For Thought

I am willing to wager that no matter how old you are, no matter where you were born or raised, at some point or another (perhaps even at this very moment) you've been on a fad diet. Whether or not you feel comfortable with your body size and weight in theory, in practice I'll bet that you've given serious thought to the South Beach Diet—and Atkins, and the Abs Diet. You've probably eaten too much cabbage soup, grimaced through a regimen of grapefruit, floated through protein shakes. No fruit, all fruit, red fruit but no blue fruit—you've tried them all.

I'm also willing to bet that there have been dozens, nay, hundreds of times when you compared yourself to a model or actress and ended up feeling depressed, fat, or ugly—or a combination of the three. Now, I know you've heard this all before, but seriously, would you even want to look like a model or actress? Let's break it down for a minute. Most models are freakishly tall and required to keep their bodies at a weight that is significantly less than enough to support their larger than average frames. The body weight of the average model would probably not be enough to support a preteen girl, much less a grown woman.

Is Beauty Even Skin Deep?

Before a fashion show, photo shoot, or other appearance, women who make a living based on their looks have to further beautify themselves and rid their flesh of poochy tummies, pockmarks, or pimples. Anything from juice fasts to high colonics becomes de rigueur in the days leading up to the grand event. Can you even imagine a job that required you to have a Brazilian bikini wax in your contract? And if that's not bad enough, consider the average actress going out on a publicity junket. Imagine every element of your personal life scrutinized before the salivating masses, from your love life or lack thereof to your choice of clothing, mates, and movies. Eat too much over the weekend? Well, you might just have *Star* magazine and *US Weekly* speculating that you're showing early signs of a baby bump. Fight with your husband? Divorce rumors might become cover stories.

And that's all based just on the way that you *look*. Your professional life would also provide endless amounts of speculation as you were judged on your last successful film and not on a lifetime of hard work and commitment. While a handful of actresses are paid obscene amounts of money to pretend to be other people in front of the camera, their popularity depends on the fickle tastes of the public, and in many cases on favors from friends in extremely high places. The next time you sneak out to the grocery store looking like you need a scrubbing, imagine heading home to find myriad images of your whiffy self posted on every gossip web site. In other words, as the salaries are magnified so are public scrutiny, adulation, and pillorying. While the entertainment-craving public can utterly adore its heroes, it is a notoriously capricious lot. For the rest of us, keeping an eye on our waistline can sometimes feel like a full-time job in and of itself.

If you find that you need help with your weight management consider visiting a nutritionist or dietitian. While the newspapers abound with weight loss success stories as a result of quick-fix surgery or medical procedures, the sad fact is that they do not print the stories of negative complications, permanent internal damage, or disfigurement. The following information is provided in part by some of the top nutrition and fitness experts around, but don't take this as medical advice or information, and be sure to consult with your own doctor before starting any kind of new eating plan or workout.

SMARTER SNACKING

Many working women either grab a bite on the go, are prone to stress eating, eat irregular meals, or drink too much coffee or wine. So many women simply don't have time to plan out their meals, and they end up skipping some meals while overindulging at others. Some of the worst crimes against nutrition that women commit include consuming too much alcohol and eating bottom-heavy diets.

Too Much Alcohol While Americans as a rule do not drink as much as many other Westernized societies, we still spend far too much time socializing and drinking. How many of your recent nights out involved cocktails with clients or friends? Can you even think of the last time that you had a nice meal at a restaurant that wasn't paired with wine for nearly every course? How many times have you heard a coworker yearn for the end of the day so that she could curl up with a glass of wine and a sympathetic friend? And who hasn't felt that way?

New York City–based dietitian Martha McKittrick, RD, CDN, CDE, offers some great tips on eating healthfully without being deprived. In her opinion, "alcohol adds empty calories, can decrease willpower, and [can] potentially affect energy levels and food intake the next day." She advises drinking less and trying to find activities that don't revolve around alcohol. McKittrick suggests allotting yourself a certain number of drinks a week (she suggests four) and keeping to this amount. If you feel that you must indulge, opt for a lighter white or heart-healthy red wine in place of rich liqueurs like Bailey's Irish Cream.

Bottom Heavy Diets While your day might start out calmly enough, or at the very least in a relatively organized fashion, work schedules and deadlines can be notoriously unpredictable. How many times have you found yourself forgetting to eat or, worse, grabbing sugary snacks throughout the day and then stuffing your face when you finally get home after a stressful day at work?

McKittrick advises never skipping breakfast or lunch and when at all possible planning meals that include a light afternoon snack. You know how your mom always said that too few calories a day can slow your metabolism? Well, it's true. Not eating during the day can lead to snack attacks at night, and skipping meals leads to greater hunger pangs and food festivals—c'mon, you know exactly what I'm talking about. Consider keeping an energy-boosting emergency snack pack in your desk to keep from becoming too hungry

Or consider these hunger pang fillers that provide an energy boost:

- Baby carrots.
- Raisins.
- Melba toast and peanut butter.
- Protein or nutrition bars (check calorie content in these—it can be higher than you'd expect).
- String cheese (or portion-controlled cheese).
- Bananas.
- Yogurt.
- Almonds.
- Mini cottage cheese.
- Fresh fruit.
- Dried apricots.
- Mini packs of whole wheat crackers.
- Mini bag of microwave popcorn.

While there are so many miniature snack options out there, McKittrick advises being vigilant on portion control. It can be tempting to overdo the minis!

Supplement Your Meals

While in theory we all wish we'd eat the required amount of fruits and veggies, most of us miss out on the most basic daily necessary vitamins and minerals. McKittrick prefers to customize her supplement recommendations to each individual, but as a rule recommends the following dietary supplements:

- ◆ A multivitamin to add more balance to your daily diet. Bear in mind though, that while the multi will help provide what you're lacking, it is not a get-out-of-jail-free card for poor food choices or junk-food-heavy diets. Consider it a backup plan and not a substitute for healthful eating!
- ◆ A fish oil supplement. In a perfect world you'd be consuming fatty fish three or more times per week (and according to Dr. Nicholas Perricone, your weekly or daily salmon infusion would leave you with glowing skin). Omega 3 fats found in fatty fish are not only said to contain antiinflammatory properties, but are also being researched as treatments for many chronic conditions, including heart disease, depression, skin conditions, hypertension, inflammatory bowel disease, and rheumatoid arthritis. You can also increase the Omega 3 in your diet by sprinkling flax seeds on your breakfast cereal or by snacking on walnuts.
- ◆ A calcium supplement. Hopefully, you're consuming at least 1,200 milligrams of calcium daily in the form of milk, yogurt, or cheese. Calcium will help prevent osteoporosis, a disease that can cause bones to become brittle and prone to fracture and which, according to the National Osteoporosis Foundation, plagues over 50 percent of people over the age of 50. Another great benefit of calcium and vitamin D supplements, according to the Archives of Internal Medicine, is the alleviation of a lot of the worst symptoms of PMS.

I become lazy when faced with a choice of vitamin bottles and tend to prefer having things are already figured out for me. I love Olay vitamins, particularly Total Effects Beautiful Skin & Wellness supplements, which come packaged in 30 daily packets and include a multivitamin along with three other skin-loving supplements.

McKittrick also offers a basic eating plan that includes smarter choices like eggs or peanut butter for your protein, or whole wheat bread or pasta. While the optimal daily caloric intake depends on the individual's needs, McKittrick advises 1,200 calories for weight loss and 1,600 calories for weight maintenance.

A sample daily weight loss menu might include:

- Breakfast: egg whites and a slice of whole wheat toast or a fruit.
- Lunch: salad with grilled chicken, two tablespoons vinaigrette dressing on the side.
- Dinner: grilled chicken with side salad, small potato with skin, fruit for dessert.
- Snacks: two to three healthy snacks during the day.

You'd Better Work Out

Okay, so you have a basic idea of what to eat to lose weight and what supplements to take to make up for missing nutrients. Now it's time to sweat and jump-start your nutrition/fitness regimen. Phil Black, the creator of FitDeck, an ingenious workout deck of cards that contain illustrated exercise options and instructions for every fitness level, is in great shape. Trust me when I tell you that this former Navy SEAL really knows just what does a body good. Black suggests entering a body transformation contest to challenge yourself to get back in shape after a sluggish couple of months as a desk jockey. He entered one of the most popular of these contests, the "Body for Life Challenge," along with about 500,000 other people over the years. While Black did not win, the results were absolutely incredible (yes, lucky me, I've seen the before and after pictures) and he admits that the experience has permanently changed his outlook on health and fitness.

A transformation contest generally consists of a 90-day program with a clear-cut guide to transform both your eating habits and exercise routine—or lack thereof. Black says that tremendous commitment is required and the competition is fierce, but that winning shouldn't be your motivation for change. He considers these contests to be "a great blueprint for success" that will help you develop the right kind of eating and fitness habits to last for your entire life.

Black offers this advice for anyone interested in replacing their unhealthy habits with healthier options:

♦ Baby steps. Say it with me now: Rome wasn't build in a day, and neither were the buffest of bodies. Change one small habit at a time, live with the results, and then move toward the next change.

♦ While you're at it, substitute water for coffee, juice, or soda for 30 days. It's only a month, and the added caffeine and calories can make a tremendous difference.

♦ As you're tottering toward your one-month goal, start waking up earlier every day. Black suggests getting up 30 minutes earlier every morning for 30 days and doing some kind of exercise or stretching routine—walking, five FitDeck cards, Pilates, yoga—anything that gets you moving.

♦ Slow down. It sounds contradictory, but consider living without a Mc-anything for 30 days, and avoid all fast food. Instead, prepare a healthful lunch and snack at home.

♦ Don't watch TV while eating. Avoid mindless munching with movies and television. You pay less attention to what you're stuffing in your mouth when you're involved in what's on the screen.

♦ Eat breakfast every morning—but no muffins, bagels, croissants, or scones. Instead, opt for whole wheat or light versions, a high-protein breakfast, or oatmeal, which is both filling and heart-friendly.

♦ Sign up for an organized race with a friend or coworker. You know how competitive you are with your cubicle mates? Well, imagine running them into the ground with your fastest time.

♦ Explore a new fitness activity. Try a 5K fun run, a mini triathlon, a half marathon (walk or run), a full marathon if you're really ambitious, Pilates, yoga (Black suggests Bikram yoga), tai chi, tennis, dance, surfing, golf, judo, martial arts—anything that sounds like fun to you and shakes you out of your do-nothing doldrums. Black advises choosing a sport or activity that is off the beaten track and one that takes you out of your comfort zone.

- Take "before" pictures—it will really make you work toward getting to the "after" pictures.
- Educate yourself. Take a class on nutrition, subscribe to a fitness or health magazine.
- Become a certified personal trainer for fun. Obviously, Black and I have very different ideas of fun, though who hasn't fantasized about being known as "the aerobics instructor." That would be fun.
- Subscribe to receive daily nutrition or fitness e-mails.
- Volunteer at a local fitness event or competition to help get inspired. My friend Darci coached a team of young girls through a race—I still don't know who was more excited on the day of the race.

Healthy on the Outside

Okay, so you've established a new and improved you. You run! You swim. Your body does all kinds of neat, flexible tricks that show off your buff arms and trim tummy—and then you're invited out and panic that your resolve will crumble in light of all of the yumminess.

If parties make you nervous, try to eat something before you leave the house so that you won't make a beeline for the hors d'oeuvre trays. Don't feel compelled to keep drinking, but rather try to see how long you can make one drink last, or alternate with sparkling water. If you're watching your waist, opt for the crudités or fruit and cheese and avoid the deep-fried soggy snacks. If you know that your host will only be serving high-calorie treats, consider bringing an edible gift to the party so that you'll at least have something that you can snack on.

Food and nutrition writer and recipe developer Bev Bennett was kind enough to share her delicious and dummy-proof recipe for spicy pecans. Bennett is convinced that one of her clients keeps her on his payroll "just so he can get a gift of these every holiday season." For a gift presentation she spoons a cup of the pecans into a mug that she buys at a craft fair, and then wraps the mug in colored plastic wrap. A great gift idea that will ensure you won't go hungry at the next party!

Spicy Pecans

1/4 cup (1/2 stick) unsalted butter

1 large garlic clove, smashed

1 tablespoon medium-heat chili powder

1/4 teaspoon ground cumin

1 pound raw pecan halves

Salt to taste

Preheat oven to 300 degrees. Line a baking sheet with aluminum foil for easy clean-up (optional). Melt butter in 12- to 14-inch skillet or large shallow pot. Add garlic, chili, and cumin. Cook over low heat for two minutes to infuse butter with garlic. Discard garlic. Stir in pecans. Sprinkle on 1/4 teaspoon salt and stir again.

Spread pecans on baking sheet. Bake for 25 to 30 minutes, stirring twice, or until nuts are aromatic and lightly browned. Remove from oven. Cool enough to taste. Adjust salt as desired. Allow pecans to cool on baking sheet. To serve, spoon into a large bowl. Makes 16 servings.

You can store leftovers (who are we kidding?) in a plastic container with a tight-fitting lid for a few days. Freeze for longer storage.

CAREER

It's hard enough to do a great job when you're in prime physical condition, and much harder when you're feeling sluggish or just plain out of shape. It can be difficult to eat healthfully while under so much pressure, but planning meals in advance and incorporating snacks, even treats, can keep your energy level stable and ensure that you won't pack on the pounds.

CORPORATE

Working out isn't easy (I suppose that's why it's called a *work*out and not a *play*out), and sneaking a workout into your busy day can sometimes feel like a Herculean task. While some people try to cram a workout into their lunch hour, it's probably a better idea to opt for an early-morning or post-workday exercise session instead, since at lunch you won't be able to unwind completely and the last thing you want is to come to the office smelling like you've just been to the gym.

Cool

If you are fortunate enough to be able to fit a workout into your busy day, be very cognizant of what you do or don't wear to the office. Form-fitting Lycra might be perfect at the gym, but do you really want your office mates to have a vision of you in bicycle shorts and a crop top permanently etched into their brain? Companies like Athleta, Title Nine, Sense, and Fit Couture create exercise clothes that are not only tailored for a real woman's body but also come in really chic styles, colors, and cuts.

Chapter 13

The Best Guest or Hostess with the Mostest

Be a Great Guest or Host a Perfect Event without Losing Your Sanity

> *At a dinner party one should eat wisely but not too well, and talk well but not too wisely.*
> —W. Somerset Maugham

You're Invited!

There are quite a few reasons why you might suddenly find yourself breaking bread or sipping schnapps with your boss's boss, her irritating assistant, or your least favorite cubicle mate. In addition to the more traditional rounds of holiday parties, business breakfasts, lunches, and dinners, over the course of your career you might have to attend, plan, or host any number of unexpected events. From casual networking or meet-and-greet evenings to chichi cocktail parties to over-the-top launch events, it isn't enough to blithely order some wine and cheese and hope for the best. In life and especially when important events are involved, if anything can go wrong it just might. The smoothest-running events are generally the ones that had the most meticulous advance planning.

Be My Guest

Okay, let's start with the easier of the two party options: You've just received an invitation to an event. Whether you're feeling festive or not, you should consider attending if:

- ◆ It's a work-related event.
- ◆ You boss or client is on the board or membership committee.
- ◆ You might have the opportunity to network and expand your professional or social circle.

Your responsibilities as a guest include the following:

- ◆ *RSVP.* Let your host know whether you plan to attend. If you are invited to bring a guest, inform your host whether you will be bringing someone. But if the host didn't mention it, it's generally not a great idea to ask if you can bring a a guest, since your host may have limited space or budget and might not be able to accommodate extra people.
- ◆ *Mark your calendar.* It sounds simple, but based on how many people completely forget about attending events, it's always a good idea to keep track of your commitments.
- ◆ *Dress appropriately.* Follow the cues on the invitation. If black tie is specified, then faded jeans are not an option. If you are unsure how to dress, ask the host for suggestions or even what they intend to wear.

BE A GOOD GUEST

Your host has gone to a lot of trouble planning the event, show your appreciation by:

- ◆ *Showing up at a decent time.* Every city, state, and country, or even industry, has its own unique perception of what is considered fashionably late. An easy rule of thumb is to show up about a half hour after the event is scheduled to begin—but of course, every case is different.

- *Bringing a gift.* If the event is in a private home, or if one specific person did the majority of the planning or is the evening's host, it's always nice to show your appreciation with a small gift. Flowers or wine are the most common hostess gifts, but if you know the host's quirks consider bringing a small token gift instead—a vintage apron or a rare baseball card for a collector will always be appreciated.

- *Helping out.* If your host looks busy, offer to help with the greeting or by directing people to the bar or coat-check area.

- *Enjoying yourself.* Georgette Mosbacher is known for hosting many fabulous events in New York City. She feels that it's the guests' responsibility to make sure that they have a fun evening. She suggests that they make conversation, enjoy the entertainment, and actually decide that they will enjoy themselves.

- *But not too much.* While a drink can calm your nerves, too many will likely affect your decision-making abilities and make it easier for potentially damaging behavior to slip through.

- *Saying thank you.* Before you leave, thank your host for inviting you. The next day be sure to send a handwritten note or personalized e-mail thanking your host for the evening. Mention one specific occurrence, decoration, or tasty morsel that made the night unique.

- *Reciprocate.* Turn those perfectly set tables and remember to be the one to do the inviting the next time around, which leads us to the next topic . . .

Hosting Services

I'm guessing that you never realized just how much work it is to be a great guest. Well, get ready for the really hard part—being the event planner, producer, and/or host!

I am one of the few, the proud, the demented individuals who love nothing more than to be working behind the scenes to coordinate, plan, and run a killer event. Over the years I've had my share of spectacular events—working on everything from launching networking communities both nationally and overseas; launches for new movies, cosmetics, products, books, celebrities, concerts, and charity events, to the Governor's Ball for the Academy Awards, events around the Grammies, the Golden Globes, Fashion Week, and some that I'm sure that I've forgotten. I've had spectacular highs and devastating lows and, of course, more awkward and hilarious situations than I care to remember. Since I worked for a number of years as a celebrity makeup artist, I've also been privy to backstage meltdowns of monumental proportions, and was somewhat prepared for the ego-driven disasters that can occur when working on even the most innocuous event—but I'll skip those stories for now and share some of the fun ones instead.

FAMOUS FAUX PAS

I remember working on a charity concert some years back for hip-hop performers Wyclef Jean and Coolio. I was in the green room, chatting with some of the guests, when a colleague shared some great news with me to which I replied (using one of my favorite slang expressions), "Coolio." One of Coolio's publicists rushed over to whisper to me that it was "Mr. Coolio" to me, though Mr. Coolio himself was sweet about it and said I could use his name any old time. Since that time, I'm always sure that while great events might inspire me to use the expression "coolio," the really spectacular ones rate a "*Mr.* Coolio."

I'm not much of a television person, though my company, GTK Marketing Group, frequently works on promotions supporting TV programs. One year when I was at one of the gifting suites for the Golden Globes, I was chatting with a very shy guy and his ridiculously cute friends. One of the female members of the group was obviously the celebrity and having the time of her life collecting freebies. It was only after they left that I realized that the group of hotties I'd been hanging out with were Dominic Purcell and the cast of *Prison Break*, and that the female "celebrity" was actually someone's publicist. Trust me, I'm still swooning retroactively.

I once embarrassed actor Oliver Platt by admitting to him my decade-long crush, I once embarrassed myself by asking Frank McCourt to hold my drink while I tended to a client. I was asked by the wife of a shamed politician to create a new makeup look for him that would make him look "more human." I've seen celebutantes make off with gifts earmarked for charity, Oscar-winning actors on mass amounts of recreational pharmaceuticals flirt with the table decorations, and the famous offspring of more famous parents try to use their famous last names to solicit an endless supply of freebies.

I've organized countless editorial events in New York City, and I can't forget the time that my client left her guests, a roomful of the top editorial names in the country, to go shopping for souvenirs; or the time that a client badmouthed his extremely high-profile publisher while she was standing right behind him; or still another time that the events director of a restaurant disappeared the night of a huge event without cluing in her staff to our event. We later found out that her father's nickname was "The Godfather" and that she was a part-time employee of the *family business*. Then, of course, there was the time when a client with a huge ego refused to include a charitable component to his launch event because he feared that attention to him might be diluted (his exact words: "But then it's not all about me anymore"). Oh, the list goes on.

But for all of the nightmares, for the most part, there is no rush like pulling together an event where everything goes spectacularly right, and where everyone goes home with a huge smile, great memories, and an even better gift bag.

Party Hearty (Smartie)

Before you can plan and host the perfect event, you have to lay the groundwork. Even if you choose to work with an event planner, you still need to be as hands-on as possible and always pay close attention to detail. The most important thing that you can do? Set a budget and stick to it. As with much of your business life, leave about 20 percent higher or lower wiggle room for tipping, gratuities, and unexpected extras like overtime.

Theme or Occasion   While you don't theoretically need a *reason* to have a party or event, you'll likely have an easier time filling the room with the right kind of people if you do in fact have a really cool reason to celebrate. New product launches, offbeat or unexpected holidays, and company milestones are all great reasons to celebrate. Or find ways to celebrate local events. For instance, add glamour to your sportswear line by celebrating the Oscars or Fashion Week. Better yet, have celebrities or famous faces on hand to add validity to your celebration.

Date and Time   It should be simple enough to schedule an event, right? Except for the time a client insisted that we have a champagne reception on Ash Wednesday. While we were nervous that we might appear disrespectful to our observant Catholic guests, they all took it in stride and showed up accessorized with smudged ash crosses. Another client wanted to have a gala dinner on Yom Kippur, the holiest day of the Jewish calendar, and in fact a fast day.

Check the date to ensure that it's not a major holiday. Summer in New York City is always a tricky time for events, since many people are away for long weekends. Trying to compete with major events can also leave you with a sparse guest list.

Publicity   If your event is newsworthy, then promote it—but first create an outstanding and newsworthy story. Court and invite key media and create individual pitches and stories for their particular publications. Follow up with details that make the story juicy, fun, or relevant. For instance, yet another party on Oscar night might not be newsworthy, but an event that boasts 12 celebrity chefs, with 12 major designers creating the table decor, and boasts such an übercool guest list that Jamie Foxx, the night's winner in the best actor category, gets turned away at the door along with throngs of celebrities—well, that's a great party story! The extremely pricy launch party for another luxury building in Manhattan? Not a thrill. The launch party for another luxury building in Manhattan, at which one attendee wins a multimillion-dollar penthouse apartment? Now *that's* a great party story!

Venue   Follow the real estate industry's credo and remember these three words: location, location, location. While there's no shame in not keeping up with all of the hottest restaurants, lounges and clubs, the last thing that you want is to have your event in a venue that's inappropriate because either it's yesterday's news or it doesn't offer superior menu, service, or a really gorgeous location.

Invitations/Guest List Nothing sets the mood like a creatively crafted and fabulously worded invitation. This is the first interaction that your guests will have with your event. If your party has a theme you can choose to send out a handcrafted invitation by messenger or an e-mailed save-the-date notice. The key is consistency. Be vigilant about spelling, spend time on the copy, add in interesting flourishes and as many enticing teasers as possible. Engage your invitees from the minute they know about your event until they're recounting details of it to their rapt friends and colleagues.

Create a well-padded primary and secondary guest list, making sure to overinvite since many people don't show up, and if needed designate an exclusive RSVP phone line or e-mail address. Don't wait until the last minute to tally your guest count. Don't expect everyone who has RSVPed to show up, and do expect extra guests as well. Be clear on whether you will be firm about the guest list and not allow others in.

Decor From lighting to furnishings, tablecloths to chair covers, flowers, balloons, gauze, chandeliers, and candles, you can set the party mood. Work with a trusted designer if needed and allow ample time for both setup and removal.

Menu Take into account everything from the theme of your event to your venue (is there an appropriate kitchen?) to special needs like vegetarians or diabetics. Create a menu that matches the mood of the event, including a signature cocktail and hors d'oeuvres.

Staffing Make sure that not only are there proper waitstaff and bussing services, but everything from bartenders to coat check and security (or even a separate entrance) if you will be having high-profile guests. Besides interns and employees, you should also have a close friend or relative there with you to help out if things get too crazy.

A close friend of mine plans and executes incredible events. I'm her "wing woman" at her events and she fills the same role at mine. My sister is also amazingly generous in showing up at most of my events and acting as a surrogate hostess. Lean on your close friends and family and ask them to lead people over to you and to the evening's hosts. Boyfriends or significant others never work quite as well in these situations, since people then start to speculate about your romantic life instead of concentrating on the event.

Transportation   Depending on your budget, there is no luxury like having a Town Car or other suitable luxury vehicle whisk your guests to and from your event. It's almost the only way to ensure that your VIPs will actually show up!

Program   Decide whether there's going to be a speech or presentation. Make sure that any necessary audiovisual equipment is close by and working. At every stage of your event, let your guests know what is coming next so that they never feel rushed or ill at ease.

Surprises and Entertainment   Let's face it, you've managed to get a roomful of people to come out of their cozy homes or busy offices to celebrate your achievements or allow themselves to learn more about you and your company. Dazzle them, delight them, spoil them silly so that when they see your name on an invitation they'll be sure to show up at your next event. Depending on the occasion, you can include anything from a massage or manicure station to a world-class hair stylist, to tarot card reading or kissing booths. Only you know what will become the talk of the water cooler. Have a great DJ and work with him to set the mood of the evening, or hire a live band—anything to really liven up the event.

Gift Bags   Send your guests home with not only a smile on their faces but also a tangible memory of you and your event. This isn't the time to pinch pennies, since many events are judged by their gift bags. Include the usual literature and some unexpected delights, anything from spirits to cosmetic products or truffles. Reach out to your clients and also showcase their products in front of this captive audience.

Be a Great Host   Trust me, I know just how exhausted you are after pulling together such a spectacular event, but now is the time to really work the room and remind everyone why they came out to support you and your brand. Have one of your interns or colleagues stand near the elevator or entrance to welcome people in, show them to the coat check, and then direct them toward you. Welcome your guests, remind them about the reason for the event, direct them to the bar and the food and entertainment. I always make sure that my guests have someone to talk to, so I'll introduce them to another guest as they enter, or later in the evening if they look lost.

About halfway through the event, you'll be able to leave your post and check in with all of your guests again (and yes, I make sure to greet each and every guest at least twice, even if it means glad-handing or air kissing 500 or more people two times in a night). Talk about the food, the entertainment, the great turnout. This is not the time for a hard sell for the product or launch—this is a time to pamper your guests. Save the business push for a follow-up call. Have several people monitor the gift bag table to ensure that a mass gift grab is avoided.

Follow-Up   Don't wait for the kudos to roll in. Send e-mails or handwritten notes, or make phone calls to thank people for coming. Then sleep for the next five days—you've earned it!

CAREER

No, being a social butterfly was not in your job description (unless of course you're an event planner, fashionista, or maitre d'), but over the course of your working life you will find that many a deal is born outside of the cubicle jungle or boardroom, be it on the golf course, in a posh restaurant, or at a jazz club. Polish up your small-talk skills, get to know a film noir from a pinot noir, and you should be fine.

CORPORATE

If you stop to think about it, working in a large corporation means that on some level you're socializing on a daily basis (only without the fluffy dress and canapés). Try to pay attention to any red flags that might go up before hosting an event—anything from a nonresponsive contact to a florist who can't seem to find any flowers in season should clue you in to the fact that you should probably find a different source or vendor.

COOL

Would it sound horribly clichéd of me to say that you work hard and you should play hard too? Okay, forgive me then. Socializing with your friends is purely for pleasure. Socializing with your colleagues can be a lot of fun, but don't ever let your guard down completely, and keep the juiciest parts of your private life private.

Chapter 14

On the Road

Protocol, Packing Tips, and Fashion Advice for Business Travel

> *Though we travel the world over to find the beautiful,*
> *we must carry it with us or we find it not.*
> —Ralph Waldo Emerson

Meet Me in St. Louis

You'd think, with the myriad new communication devices available, from teleconferencing systems to virtual offices and smart phones, that business travel was on the wane. Not so. According to the web site of the Travel Industry Association of America (www.tia.org), business travel for the purposes of consulting or client service or for attending conferences, conventions, or seminars makes up about 20 percent of all U.S. domestic travel. Depending on what you do for a living, you might find yourself spending a lot of your time on the road, sussing out new business opportunities, checking in with new clients, supervising projects, or managing remote team members.

With all of this travel comes a lot more emphasis on doing your job right, dressing correctly for each occasion, and making sure not to step on any toes along the way.

Taking Baby Steps

Many thousands of years ago (okay, only about a decade and a half) I was fortunate enough to land, as my first job out of high school, an ultra glamorous position as a receptionist for one of the largest diamond manufacturers in the world. Every day was an adventure for me, as I learned the subtleties not only of working in an office staffed with an international team of characters, but also accommodating the likes and dislikes, expectations, and obligations of my bosses, supervisors, and our incredibly colorful, quirky, and moody clients. As I worked my way up the ranks to a modified internal public relations position, I learned how to manage not only the expectations of our clients but also their considerable egos.

I also learned that there was never just one approach to handling problems that arose, since each client had a different cultural background and set of business beliefs. The faintly obsequious tone that I reserved for our Japanese clients was wholly inappropriate for dealing with Swiss clients who expected a certain level of sophistication. While our Israeli clients enjoyed verbal jousting, our clients from the American South expected a more refined, practically flirtatious interaction.

The one constant throughout my tenure in the diamond industry, however, was the concept of sealing a business deal not with a document, memo, or invoice, but rather with a handshake. No matter if the deal was for a tiny parcel worth thousands, or an important stone worth millions, when one person uttered the Hebrew word *mazal* (good fortune) and the other clasped his hand and said, "*Bracha*" (blessing), the deal was irrevocably sealed. There was no going back once you'd given *mazal*. It didn't matter if you were from Brooklyn or Mumbai, your word was now your reputation.

While things have changed somewhat in the diamond industry, the rules of the deal still frequently trump culture or nationality. Most industries, however, do not operate under the same stringent and international code of ethics and expectations—and that's never quite as clear as when you are out of your office and at the mercy of an existing or potential client's home team advantage.

Global Good Manners

While you can never predict every eventuality or the outcome of every deal or business engagement, it is possible and advisable to educate yourself about the customs and cultures of the people that you en-counter on a day-to-day basis. I think we can all name several annoy-ing celebrities who, after living abroad for a few years, start to mimic the speech patterns of their adopted homes. While it's never advisable or professional to copy the affectations of your colleagues, it's in your best interest to understand their way of doing things and to adapt to their customs when on their turf.

Steve Glauberman, CEO and founder of Enlighten, an Ann Arbor, Michigan–based interactive agency, is known for his quirky dress sense and fondness for red shoelaces. While in the confines of his own office space, he feels free to experiment with his wardrobe and encourages his staff to do the same. While visiting clients, however, he makes sure to tailor his attire to their particular dress code. So, if con-sulting for a banking client, while in their corporate space Glauber-man will always be attired in a business suit and tie, reserving his shorts and sandals for his own office.

While I was born and raised in Brooklyn, New York, I am also the child of immigrants, my mother having been born in Romania and my father in Hungary. Growing up, I heard and spoke smatterings of dif-ferent languages, and in fact I was a teenager before I knew that there was actually an English word for *hamburger*. In other words, while I am an American through and through, I am also very cognizant of the old-world European sensibilities, manners, and courtliness instilled in me by my parents. As such, I have a keen ear for language and am also tuned in to other ways of working, communicating, and interact-ing. When I meet people for the first time, they usually ask me where I'm from, and when I answer "Brooklyn," they try to figure out where I'm from *originally*, because it seems incongruous to them that a New Yorker can also have continental manners and behavior.

In the past few years, I've worked with a number of clients from the United Kingdom, a country whose inhabitants might seem cold or distant to Americans. As a fairly effusive and warm person, I fre-quently found myself tempering my enthusiasm and perky nature (and cutting down on the exclamation points in my correspon-dence) since it felt out of place and almost inappropriate. I held back on the quantity of my correspondence, limiting e-mails and

Pack It Up Baby!

phone calls and following my clients' lead, instead of charging forward. I didn't change my enthusiasm for the project, and I didn't slow down my energy or ideas—I simply learned how best to work within the parameters set by my clients.

Jim Edwards, a senior editor at *Brandweek* magazine, is British by birth, though he's lived in the States for over a decade. He believes that the key to working effectively within a new environment, be it a new company or a foreign country, is to make sure "when you enter a new environment that this is really what you want to do and that you're qualified to do it. If you don't, you'll find yourself in over your head and being asked to leave pretty quickly."

As for the age-old question of whether to make it a three-martini lunch, Edwards continues, "Apart from that, Europeans like to drink alcohol at lunchtime (and regard the American refusal to do so as some sort of infantilization of the culture), while Americans regard booze at lunch as a sign of alcoholism. There must be a happy compromise in there somewhere." Compromise, it would seem, is the most effective tool in business both at home and abroad.

While it's nearly impossible to offer solutions for working with every country and culture, there are a few tips that should work both nationally and internationally.

- ◆ *Follow the leader.* Follow your client or senior team member's lead in all things. Don't mimic them so much as allow them to set the pacing, and solicit input or feedback. If you feel close enough to your client, ask to have a company liaison assigned to you to explain protocol, introduce you to others, and give you a quick rundown as to the dos and don'ts.
- ◆ *When in Rome* . . . If you're traveling to a very conservative city or country, if there are strict dress codes in place either culturally or companywide, dress and act accordingly. It is a sign of respect, not weakness, to show that you have researched not only the customs of your host but also their dress code, and that you respect their established systems of interaction.

- ◆ *Shake? Kiss? Shake and kiss and hug?* Your handshake tells the world a lot about you and where you come from. Getting someone's hand in a death grip won't distinguish you as a powerful player, but rather as someone who is trying too hard. Different cultures maintain different methods of greeting, incorporating everything from a giant bear hug and two-cheeked kiss to barely touching palms. I remember trying to keep track of the level of intimacy of my French colleagues by counting the air kisses.

Pack It Up, Baby

Sometimes I travel for business at such a manic pace that I keep a series of packed overnight cases waiting for me at home. I recover for a night or two and then just reach for an already packed case and start the travel whirlwind again. (For an amazing array of travel and desk minis visit www.minimus.biz.)

Debbie Geiger, president of Geiger & Associates Public Relations, Inc., in Tallahassee, Florida, has in the past 25 years escorted hundreds of journalists on thousands of trips, and offers this advice on packing for a trip: "In these times of increased airport security I try to make the whole process as streamlined as possible. Everything I take coordinates with black. I use packing cubes to separate my clothes and waterproof containers for toiletries. I take two small travel alarm clocks (one in my hand luggage and one in my suitcase); *lots* of reading material (in case I am unexpectedly delayed); a small digital camera; preaddressed FedEx envelopes and a computer printout of FedEx drop boxes in the places I'll be going (since I frequently have to send materials back to my office before my next stop); maps of my destinations; and printouts of hotel and rental car confirmations. I am also a big fan of affinity and premium user programs for a few selected hotels, rental car companies, and airlines. Those cards can mean the difference between sleeping in the airport and getting out of there and on your way when problems arise." Great advice from someone whose business is travel.

Clint Brownfield, who for nearly three decades has written about exotic travel destinations for popular women's magazines, prepares for his trips by studying his itinerary and then mentally planning each day—from waking up in the morning and washing up, to dressing for the climate and changing for dinner. In this way, he can figure out how best to mix and match wardrobe staples, while also being prepared for every eventuality.

Make a List (Check It Twice)

Unless you're planning to hike the Himalayas, chances are very good that you will be able to find whatever it is that you need while on the go. Be that as it may, there's nothing quite as excruciating as forgetting your contact lenses at home, having your luggage burst, or being overcome with hunger pangs at 3:00 in the morning local time. Consider making a checklist of the everyday items you use that cannot be borrowed from a friend or found in a local department or drugstore. These may include:

- ◆ Contact lenses (take several extra disposable pairs), eyeglasses, eye drops, saline, and cleaning solution.
- ◆ Birth control or other prescription medications. Make sure to pay attention to how many days you'll be traveling and how many pills you'll need. Keep a list of all of the prescription drugs that you're taking.
- ◆ Batteries, rechargers, or electric current converters. There's no pain like an extended airplane journey with no juice on your iPod.

Also remember to:

- ◆ Buy travel insurance.
- ◆ Take a photocopy of your passport and all credit cards. Keep it separate from your original documents in case they are lost or stolen.
- ◆ Leave an itinerary or emergency contact list with friends or family members.

Safety First

If you do not feel safe in the room that is assigned to you, ask for a different room. Find out where the emergency exits are, and do a quick visual of your room before settling in (check under beds and in closets).

Carole Moore, a former police officer offers these safety tips when at home or on the road:

- Trust your instincts. If something seems wrong or you feel uneasy, listen to that little voice that's talking to you. Sometimes your senses pick up on things your brain has yet to process. That's the cardinal rule of survival. If someone tries to abduct you, fight back right there and then. Never, ever let anyone get you into a car and move you, because you won't come back. It's that simple. Make noise, fight, run like hell—it's better to take a chance that way. Personally, I'd rather go down fighting than bound with duct tape and tossed into a lake somewhere.

- At home, don't let strangers come inside. I don't care if he says he's the telephone repairman—call the company and ask if they sent anyone out. Deadbolt your doors when you lock them. Don't just push the little button on the doorknob—I can pop one of those in seconds, and if I can do it, you better believe criminals can. Call the crime prevention unit of your local law enforcement and ask for a home security survey. They'll take a look at your place and point out weaknesses and won't charge you a thing.

- While traveling, the same rules apply. Don't open your hotel room door to an employee without checking with the front desk. Always check to see where the stairs are in relation to your room in case there is a fire or you have to run.

- Don't haul your money, passport, and credit cards around in a purse. I have a passport holder I wear around my neck and under my clothes when traveling. Be careful with expensive camera equipment on subways and undergrounds. Don't carry these items during rush hour because that's when people can crowd you—it makes it easy to cut that camera strap.

♦ On the road, avoid getting into confrontations while driving. If someone wants the right-of-way, give it to him. Who cares if he's acting like a jerk? While you might be fully justified in giving him the finger, do you really want to run the risk he might be carrying a gun and in a bad mood? It's not worth it. If your car breaks down, stay inside with the doors locked and call for help on your cell phone. Be very leery of strangers stopping to help you, particularly in isolated areas.

CAREER

At some point or another, you will likely find yourself crying your eyes out under a strange blanket on a strange bed in a strange hotel in a strange city, after a particularly challenging meeting, presentation, or missed flight. At a moment like that you might be questioning every career move you've made up until that point. With every business success come great business challenges. While some people hate business travel, others relish it as a time to get to know their clients on their home turf. The key is to know yourself and your limits. If you're done in by jet lag, don't plan a huge presentation for your first day in town, but rather give your body clock time to adjust. Above all, be safe and aware.

CORPORATE

Many of us have a shameful, cringe-inducing work memory (sort of like Renée Zellweger as Bridget Jones, drunkenly crooning at the company Christmas party). Being away from home and office sometimes makes it tempting to relax or drink too much or flirt shamelessly with coworkers. But make no mistake, being out of the office does not give you free reign to disregard all company policy and sense of decorum. If you're traveling for business, you are still representing the business. Even if you're traveling to a tropical destination, try to keep your wardrobe professional. Enjoy the hotel amenities, but within reason. Don't raid the mini bar (which is notoriously overpriced)—you'll look not only cheesy but also unprofessional.

COOL

Reliability is a much-maligned and highly desirable quality. Acting in the same way while at the office or on the road will show your supervisors or clients that you are not only trustworthy and reliable but also the cool, consummate professional.

Chapter 15

Emergency! Don't Hide—
Learn to Accentuate the Negative

Fast Fixes—How to Gracefully Handle Family Emergencies, the Flu, Maternity Leave, and More

> *To establish oneself in the world, one has to do all one can to appear established.*
> —Francois de La Rochefoucauld

Lessons Learned from Reruns

I am sitting in the waiting area of a hospital emergency room, anxiously waiting for news about a loved one. I could conceivably pace around (and blithely ignore the Almond Joy bar cruelly taunting me from the candy machine). I suppose I could also look at the communal television and try to figure out how and why the raucous laugh track comes into play in this desperately unfunny sitcom. Instead, I choose to fret about things that I should be doing—something I'm quite adept at—while also scribbling madly into a notepad. A million anxious thoughts are going through my addled brain, the majority of them concerning the looming deadline for this book.

It's been a particularly grueling year, one filled with both great successes and monumental lows, capped off with nearly six weeks spent battling a mystery bug. In the last month and a half I've suffered from one part cold, one part flu, one part scary and really icky eye symptoms that made me look like an extra in a zombie movie, one part hacking cough, and the mostly benign by comparison laryngitis that kept me from even using the phone. In all, it's been a completely debilitating few weeks—and now, yet another family emergency.

Career and Corporate Triage

As my sister Kiki and I wait for news, we play yet another round of "Spot the cute doctor." While there's clearly no Dr. McDreamy on staff (this is Community Hospital, after all, not Seattle Grace), my sister and I do manage to distract ourselves with sizing up the white coat–clad talent. As we follow the general flurry of activity, beeping monitors, belabored breathing, and anguished sighs all around us, Kiki almost offhandedly observes that "one person's emergency is another person's livelihood." To be fair (caution: nepotism alert), I say *almost* offhandedly because being a trained psychoanalyst, career and executive coach, and co-founder of DailyLifeConsulting.com, a coaching company, there is precious little that my sister does say that is ever offhanded, and she is maddingly nearly always spot-on with her assessments. (Incidentally, for those of you who don't have life coaches as sisters, I highly recommend it.) I suddenly zero in on the "Triage" sign near the emergency room door and reflect on Kiki's comment, and that's when I have my aha moment, which goes something like this. True *emergencies* mean one thing—life and death situations. True emergencies do not involve soggy crudités, off-key live bands, or cheap-looking gift bags. While bosses, supervisors, clients, and co-workers can try to suck the life out of you with their day-to-day discord and alleged emergencies, unless they actually require CPR they can be prioritized through career and corporate triage. In other words, though it can feel impossible to try to compartmentalize work, life, fun, health, and doing good, it can and must be done.

For some people, work is also doing good—for example, a doctor who saves lives or brings new life into the world, or a crossing guard who helps students to safely cross the street. For others, work is fun, and they bring that fun and joy into other people's lives—people like rock stars, actors, or event producers. For still others, doing good is their vocation, not necessarily in a Mother Teresa sort of way, but rather in working for a nonprofit organization, developing treatments for disease, or keeping the city streets clean by removing garbage. If you put it all together, we have many different pieces of ourselves, many different relationships in place, and many different ways to choose to prioritize. As our lives get more and more fast-paced, we seem to have less downtime, less time to decompress, less time for ourselves, and much less time to spend with those we love. A common complaint of the modern working person is the quest for work/life balance—both elements are necessary, but at the same time they need to balance out and enhance each other.

I remember watching the repeats of *MASH* on television, where Hawkeye and B.J., the main characters who were surgeons during the Korean War, would sort the wounded soldiers through a triage process. In a nanosecond they would decide who lived and who died—whose wounds were too deep to repair, whose could wait for medical attention, and who required immediate medical assistance.

Plan *and* Prioritize

I'm not a doctor (though I'm known as a heck of a spin doctor and frequently revive brands that are on death's door), and I'm certainly not a nurse (though I regularly nurse clients' and colleagues' bruised egos, and nurture projects from concept to fruition). I am a marketing strategist and consultant who works on high-profile projects and glamorous launches and events. With proper planning and meticulous attention to detail and budget, I can almost always guarantee a close-to-perfect project or event—but, life being life, things can and will go wrong. And that's when it becomes imperative to first reach into your emergency backup plan and then to prioritize your options and reactions.

- ◆ *Always* have a backup and contingency plan in place—a list of emergency numbers; an external and remote computer backup system; a network of friends, colleagues, and mentors; and an all-around support network.

- *Always* be prepared to do things that aren't in your job description. This doesn't make you weak or taken advantage of—this makes you a team player and future go-to girl or guy.
- *Never* blame others for your own mistakes. You'll look malicious and, worse, unprofessional. Take responsibility for your own screwups.
- *Never* let things go from bad to worse. Left unattended, a tiny work hiccup can become a corporate Hindenburg. Try to make things right as soon as you realize that things are veering scarily off course. Ask for help if needed. This doesn't make you weak, it makes you a smart team player.

Things Can Only Get Better

You know that old saying, the rich are different? Well it's never truer than in times of crisis. Whenever a junior mogul, senior celebrity, or seasoned socialite very publicly screws up her partially private life, there's usually an experienced team of trusted public relations professionals waiting in the wings to make things all better. From cooking up alternate versions of the truth to smoothing ruffled feathers, these famed folks employ a mythical tool known as *crisis management*, which is usually more effective than a magic wand and has faster, longer-lasting results and career-reviving properties.

There are a couple of fairly simple and sometimes annoying things to take into account when dealing with unexpected crises. The truth is that in each and every work week some rain must fall, and you won't always have a perky Mary Poppins–style umbrella to protect you from getting soaked (or splattered or battered). As bad as things get—and let's face it, we all know that it can get really brutal at times—you can try to head off disaster at the pass, and if that fails, make like a celebrity and do some immediate and sustainable crisis management. Here are some examples:

Crisis: Family health emergency. If it's not one thing it's another, and that other can frequently involve everything from a son with a bloody nose to a mother-in-law needing a pacemaker.

Comeback: You can't schedule family emergencies, but you can have a contingency plan in place. Every few months take an inventory of your loved ones, closest colleagues, and most reliable friends. Keep a master list at both work and home of emergency phone numbers and alternate contact information, updated doctors' information, insurance policy numbers, and prescription information. Since you're the consummate professional, when the emergency arises you've already broken down all of your work projects and expectations and can estimate the amount and intensity of labor needed to complete each project. Your mind should and will be on your family emergency, but set up a time to check in with your office to manage any expectations or setbacks. Don't be afraid to delegate, and make sure to follow up, but when you're with your loved ones be with them in body and spirit.

Conclusion: After things have calmed down, be sure to thank colleagues and coworkers for picking up the slack. A handwritten card or small gift would be an extra and appreciated personal touch.

Crisis: You're expecting, and while you weren't planning on announcing the news until later in your pregnancy, your burgeoning baby bump or uncontrollable morning sickness has prevented you from keeping the news to yourself.

Comeback: Break the news privately to your boss and then to coworkers, clients, and colleagues, keeping in mind that face-to-face happens first, and e-mail, phone, or long-distance clients can wait to hear the news until later in your pregnancy. Explain but don't apologize for your condition, and do not feel compelled to discuss aspects of your pregnancy that make you uncomfortable—you are still a professional, albeit a gestating one! Know your rights, research the maternity leave policy for your company and state, and begin to set up your own maternity leave plan with your boss, team members, and close coworkers.

Conclusion: It's a sad fact that while countries like Sweden offer 18 months of shared parental leave, the United States is one of the few countries in the world with no formal laws governing maternity leave. Only you can know how much time you need to spend with your newborn. If it feels like it's too soon to go back to work full time, try to compromise by setting up a day or two each week to telecommute.

Crisis: You are the object of malicious office gossip or rumors. *You've* heard it through the grapevine that someone is spreading nasty rumors about you.

Comeback: It might seem overly simplified to say to "Rise above it," especially if these wicked whisperings can somehow negatively impact your career. While your first instinct might be to counterattack, make sure that you know all of the facts before taking action at all. If the rumors are serious enough and you decide to confront the alleged gossipmonger, consider having a third party there to moderate and act as a witness.

Conclusion: Okay, time for another potentially clichéd thought, but in this case, actions really do speak louder than words. Continue to conduct yourself as an experienced and respected pro, and that is the way that you will be perceived—no ifs, ands, or office scuttlebutt about it.

Crisis: You burst out crying at work. It's been the day, week, month from hell and just when you think you've got it covered, you start weeping and wailing like a soap opera actress during sweeps week. While in theory it's more socially acceptable for women to cry, it's never quite acceptable to sob at the office.

Comeback: I remember dealing with a very difficult client last year. While I initially relished the account as a major challenge, as the project progressed my client went from manipulative to downright verbally abusive. After our last encounter, I called my sister to vent and burst out in tears of relief. My sister Kiki (herself a formerly lachrymose lass) said that in her corporate career coaching practice, she regularly has to counsel clients on keeping their emotions in check in the office. While her male clients sometimes are concerned with issues of seeming overly aggressive, her female clients often wish to avoid tears or other signs of perceived weakness. She advises them to mentally and physically prepare for a situation in which tears or aggressive behavior might become an unwanted option, and make a private trip to the bathroom for a quick cry if tears are unavoidable.

Conclusion: Big girls and boys do sometimes cry, but hopefully not while they're at work. If you can, just go. Leave the office, leave the building. Mention your allergies and then sniff for effect and dab at your eyes. If all else fails and you've given in to a good cry, try to minimize the residual damage by applying cold compresses to your eyes, using eye drops to minimize redness, and repairing any eye makeup that's gone awry.

Crisis: A love affair at work ends badly. Boy meets coworker. Boy sends coworker flirty IMs and the occasional bouquet of flowers, shags her senseless (outside of the office of course), and otherwise rocks her world. Boy dumps coworker. Boy moves on. Coworker is a mass of frayed nerves and barely concealed hostility.

Comeback: While everyone's favorite singleton, Bridget Jones, publicly humiliated her cruel ex-boss and former flame, and then went on to great broadcasting success, in real life it's never quite that easy. Caroline Tiger, an expert on modern manners, says that in the worst cases, she'd advise asking for a transfer. "I don't see how anyone can work side-by-side with someone who's just broken their heart, or vice versa, and continue to work at peak performance."

Conclusion: It can be hard to leave your office comfort zone and not only lose your main squeeze but also get used to working for a new big cheese. In the grand old way of accentuating the positive, Tiger advises that you "Turn the problem into an opportunity by spearheading a new project or volunteering to train in a new office—anything that takes you away from your ex."

Crisis: Bad press. They hate you—they really hate you! But wait, it gets worse. Not content to privately hate you, your client, or your product, they've splattered their disdain across every magazine, newspaper, web site, and blog in the free world (and even in some third world countries and isolated convents).

Comeback: If the late Andy Warhol's theory on 15 minutes of fame still holds true, you can choose to simply hide out in your apartment with your two best friends, Ben and Jerry, until the next 14 minutes of infamy have passed. If the situation is serious enough to require an apology or legal counsel, don't go on record with any statement until you're protected. Hopefully, unlike Tom Cruise's buoyant couch-jumping declarations of love, or racially repellent rants by Mel Gibson and Michael Richards, this shouldn't taint your reputation for the long term. But if you're like me, you'll probably want to really accentuate the positive, mix things up a bit, and have some fun at your own expense. Play with the press—instead of fighting fire with fire (which will probably only incite their ire), figure out a way to laugh at this "miscommunication" and paint yourself and company in a positive light.

Conclusion: Take comfort in the veracity of the old adage about any press being good press—it still holds true. Use this opportunity to prove your critics wrong by using your newfound fame to publicly learn your lesson. If your company has been accused of not treating its workers well, institute an employee appreciation policy, highlight what you do well, and for better or worse leverage this moment in the spotlight to convey your long-term positive policies.

CAREER

It's inevitable that no matter how well established you are in your career, you'll face crises of agonizing if not epic proportions. Aba Bonney Kwawu, the president of the Aba Agency in Washington, D.C., believes that being prepared will help you through most tough spots. She relies on these tried-and-true tricks to see her through the most stressful situations: "Plan as far ahead as possible, begin by listing objectives and goals. Program your cell phone with all vendors and crucial contacts in case of emergency. And whatever you do, never, ever look overwhelmed. Be sure to have enough time and staff to make everything run as smoothly as possible."

CORPORATE

Sometimes your job doesn't go quite the way that you expected it to. Corrine Engstrom, a community relations manager for Barnes & Noble, not only has to juggle the tasks of creating programs for groups and schools, but also supervises people who are considerably older than she is. She asserts that while it's difficult to supervise her elders, it's "not as difficult as becoming the supervisor of a person working in an establishment longer than you, no matter what their age." She finds that she tends to get along with older coworkers because "they usually have a strong work ethic and understand we are all here to do our jobs." She also tries to be fun, joke around, and be friendly. "I *ask* people to do tasks, rather than order them to. Helping people with the work always gets respect, and by giving respect to your coworkers you will 99 percent of the time receive it."

COOL

In *The Wizard of Oz* we learned that there was no wizard at the end of the yellow brick road, but rather that each of the deeply flawed characters could find solutions to their biggest problems within themselves. Life isn't necessarily easy, and we each inevitably screw up spectacularly. The key is to find the solutions and keep refining your coping strategies.

Chapter 16

Take Note

Present Yourself Perfectly in Your Phone Messages, Memos, E-Mail, and Instant Messaging

> *Language is the source of misunderstandings.*
> —Antoine de Saint-Exupéry

Express Yourself

OMG. Dont u just h8 it wen ppl use txt speak in biz com? Me 2 :-(

For the uninitiated (some might call you Luddites), the preceding sentence was a fractured cry for help from a businessperson despairing of the wholesale murder of the English language via text message. Blame it on the shortened attention span and limited thumb mobility of those communicating via a host of existing and emerging immediate messaging services available for your desktop computer, your mobile workspace (aka notebook or laptop computer), your cell phone, your pocket PC, and other handheld devices. "Short message service" (aka SMS, text, or txt) is definitely handy, but it can also be tough to decipher and even tougher to shake the habit of obsessively foreshortening all interactions.

In case you're still wondering, that first sentence says, "Oh my God. Don't you just hate it when people use text-speak in business communication? Me too." It ends with an *emoticon*, a symbol meant to convey human emotion—in this case a frowning face to express my displeasure.

Start at the Very Beginning

Etiquette experts everywhere may mourn the near disappearance of handwritten correspondence, but it is in fact in some ways a reason to celebrate. As our methods of communication become speedier and more immediate, so does our ability to leap forward into the great beyond of pleases and thank-yous. Think about it—with the touch of a button or click of a mouse, without changing your location or vocation, you can speedily and eloquently express your thanks, give greetings, or share inspiration, indignation, or elation. You can communicate with your office mate or long-lost classmate, gossip with your best friend in another time zone, or flirt with your significant other in the next room. Whee!

But wait—check that unchecked exuberance at the door. While in theory your newfound freedom of communication allows you to reach out and touch just about everyone, you might want to step back and think for a moment before hitting the "send" key. Before you pen a hastily written point-counterpoint to either the President of the United States or the president of your corporation, think about what it is that you want to say and who you want to say it to—and then think again (and again and again, and once more for good measure). While it's gotten easier than ever to be in touch with both friends and strangers, it can sometimes be like navigating choppy waters when trying to figure out just who to approach and how to approach them, especially when motivated by ire or passion or a combination of the two.

Phone Basics

In 1847 when Alexander Graham Bell invented his "electronic speech machine," what we now know as the telephone, I'm guessing that he had no clue as to the generations of communication devices that would follow. It's almost dizzying to try to keep track of the newest innovations in communication, and the ways in which we use and abuse them. So let's go back, *way* back, and start with basic phone rules.

I'm about to tell you a little secret. I know that I can trust you with it, because I feel we've gotten to know each other quite well over the past few chapters. My phone voice is my secret weapon (well, one of them at least). When at all possible I pick up the phone to introduce myself, to wheedle or cajole a client into a bigger monthly retainer, or just to have a fun conversation with a colleague during a crunch time. My voice mail messages are always warm, friendly, and to the point; my outgoing messages are professional but usually convey a sense of humor. While I feel quite comfortable in mediums ranging from e-mail to instant messaging (IM), it's on the phone that I really rule the wires. There, I said it.

That being said, my medium of choice might really irk someone else. Jim Edwards, a senior editor at *Brandweek* magazine, says that if you want to talk to him, he prefers e-mail, and if he wants to talk to you, he'll just call you on the phone. In his words, "Phone spam is a hundred times more annoying than e-mail spam."

It's important to negotiate communications preferences and defer to the senior person in the business relationship. In other words, if you prefer IM and your boss is a phone person, you'll likely achieve better results (and stay on your boss's good side) by sticking to the phone.

I know you have your secret work weapon, too. Be it your Picasso-like skills with PowerPoint, your uncanny ability to predict clients' likes or dislikes, or your dazzling memos, I'm quite sure that there's one element of your work communication style that sets you above the pack. Here's my best advice: Use your own inimitable power of professional persuasion to make people respond to you.

Now it's time to augment your arsenal with these basic how-tos, with an updated twist.

Repeat After Me

Nearly every shampoo bottle has the same instructions: "Lather, rinse, repeat." Phone messages should have a similar credo. Give your name, phone number, and an idea of why you're calling, and then repeat your phone number again. Speak slowly and clearly, identify your company, and spell your name if it's a toughie. If you zip through your phone number, you're probably making the person have to listen to your message over again—not a very endearing quality at all.

PHONE HOME

Limit your cell phone usage to private areas, or for short and necessary conversations. You know how annoying that woman on the train is—the one who's been on her cell phone for the entire ride? The one who's been talking about her niece's wedding for the last half hour? You're equally annoying to those around you. It's not wimping out to be considerate of the people around you.

BEFORE THE BEEP

When leaving your outgoing voice mail message, take some time to think about who's going to be hearing it. If you're phone communication is limited to work colleagues, then you don't have to be quite as creative—announcing your name, title, and phone extension, with a brief exhortation to do the right thing after the beep, should be fine. If you're at a creative agency, or your company name is a play on words, you can incorporate it into your message as well. My previous book was called *Hello Gorgeous! Beauty Products in America '40s–'60s*, and my outgoing voice message started with "Hello, gorgeous!" People liked it a lot—*if* they knew that I'd written the book, that is. The others were vaguely perplexed though always amused.

The moral of the story? Cutesy rarely works for outgoing voice mail messages, and even when it does, it has a shelf life. My new phone message incorporates the word cool. Shameless self-promotion? Perhaps. But even my outgoing voice mail message serves double promotional duty.

When in doubt, use a variation of the following generic voice mail message. If you plan on jazzing yours up with extra details, write up a script, and remember to listen to your recording afterwards to make sure that you're happy with the end result.

> *You've reached the voice mail box of* _____ *(your name goes here). I'm either away from my desk or on another call. Please leave a detailed message after the tone and I will return your call as soon as possible.*

Now Hear This

When making a phone call, be sure to factor in the person's industry, work schedule, and preferences. For instance, if you're calling someone in the publishing industry, you will probably be out of luck trying to reach them on a Friday during the summer. Fashionistas? Forget about finding them during Fashion Week—and calling them then only highlights your ignorance of their industry.

When you do call, it's your responsibility to identify yourself, your company name, and the purpose of your call. If you have call waiting on your line, dialing certain codes (like *70) before a phone call will disable all incoming phone calls during the duration of the conversation and allow you to devote your concentration to the person you are speaking to, without being distracted.

Up-to-Date

Have you been out of the office on maternity leave? Make sure to change your voice mail message to reflect that fact, and keep it updated as your work status changes.

Hang-Ups

In the colorful and frequently unrealistic world of executives as portrayed on television, a comment is made and then responded to, and then the phone is returned to the cradle with nary a "See ya!" Whatever you do, thank the person for their time, make a follow-up plan if necessary, and politely say good-bye before hanging up.

Hear Ye, Hear Ye

In the cult movie *Office Space* there was a soul-crushing segment about the main character's series of supervisors chastising him about a particular memo. Interoffice documents or letters are generally written forms of communication between coworkers and/or employers detailing crucial or inane elements of your daily work life.

This much-maligned medium can actually be a crucial tool to keep morale up, help a project move along on time, or simply keep everyone up-to-date on corporate policy. A memo might include company news, policy or staffing changes, or other details that affect your work life. While its delivery method may have evolved from mimeographed copy to electronic version, the overall structure and purpose are fairly basic.

The following description of a memo is brief, to the point, and easy to understand—exactly as your memos should be.

Your memo should always include:

- A title, heading, and/or description. This can be as straightforward as:

    Date: _____
    From: _____
    To: _____
    Topic: _____

- A brief summary or explanation. Convey bite-size pieces of relevant information.
- Graphics. It's up to you how fancy you want to get. Bold and underlined salient points may strengthen your point more than illustrated widgets will.
- A call to action. Make it clear if you seek a response or need information.
- Conclusion and/or next steps. Don't just put your memos out there in the ether; let people know what your expectations and timelines are.
- Contact information and/or attachments. Again, make it easy for people to contact you for any follow-up action.

Give Me An "E"

I clearly remember the first e-mail message that I received. It was from a coworker at a Web shop in Silicon Alley, way back in the embryonic days of the Internet. He was sitting at the desk next to mine. (He was also my older brother). Back in those days, few people knew what e-mail was, much less could fathom ever having a need for it or using it on a daily basis. My giddiness at having an e-mail address quickly faded as I realized that there weren't all that many people I could contact with this brand-new electronic method of communication. Fast-forward to today: E-mail seems almost quaint to today's generation of teenagers and other social innovators who rely on instant messaging and the next generation of electronic devices to put them in touch with each other.

Since those heady days, I've gone through a number of jobs and e-mail addresses and learned a thing or two about making yourself heard through e-mail. I've also been constantly amazed at both the professionalism of some and the lack of attention to detail or sheer laziness of others. While for a majority of business professionals, e-mail is very much a preferred method of business communication, don't let the informal feel of the medium signal you to kick off your virtual shoes and forget any of the expected niceties. While we all goof up now and again, it's practically depressing to think about the number of press releases or announcements that I receive with glaring typos and spelling errors.

One of the most professional e-mails I've ever received was from a 12-year-old girl named Emily Weinstein. While I regularly receive e-mail from students and teens from around the world, Emily's message literally stopped me in my tracks. She'd written no more than a well-worded paragraph in which she explained her background, her research on my previous book, a project that she was working on, and a timely and well-versed request for help. Even though I was up to my eyeballs in finishing up this manuscript, there was no way that I could refuse her. In other words, this middle school student had produced a compelling request, one that made me realize that in her universe this project was as important to her as much of the corporate information that comes my way is to me.

Name and Subject

The very first things that people notice about your e-mails are your name and the subject. Of the following two samples, which e-mail would you read first? (And which would you immediately delete?)

From: Sugar Ray
To: Charls
Subject: Luved seeing U!

From: Rachel Weingarten [GTK]
To: Charles Cool
Subject: Great to finally meet you!

Go ahead and laugh at the seeming no-brainer, but you'd be amazed how many people take the informal approach with not only their e-mail addresses but also their choice of subject. When choosing the subject of your e-mail, try not to make it generic. Try to be as personalized or detailed as possible so that the recipient can almost immediately remember who you are and why you are in touch. Use your whole name instead of a nickname (unless you're Madonna, of course). I also include the initials of my company to further jog people's memories. And please, I beg of you, check the spelling of the recipient's name and be vigilant about spelling it correctly in the body of the e-mail.

CHOOSE WISELY

These days there's almost no excuse for not having a personal domain. Even if you're not ready to put up a web site, you can register a domain exclusively for e-mail usage. Here are some tips for using this valuable tool:

◆ When choosing a domain name, opt for something memorable. Don't go for the quirky or esoteric version of your company name or ethos. Choose something that people will both remember and be able to spell.

◆ If your last name is difficult to spell or remember, have your IT person set up your e-mail account with only your first name. If that seems too informal, use a variation of your first and last name.

◆ Have a backup e-mail account for business. You'd be amazed at how many variations and permutations of my name I've seen over the years. For that reason I have a backup e-mail account with the most common misspelling of my name, and yes, I constantly receive e-mails there.

◆ Have a VIP account. If you like to present yourself as the face of your business but don't have time to answer each and every e-mail, have one account that is monitored by an assistant or coworker, and another, secret account that is only available to VIP clients or trusted colleagues.

FOLLOW THE LEADER

Many of us send out e-mails without really giving it much thought. Others are paralyzed by the monumental choices involved in selecting every "Dear," "Hey," or "Hello there." A great rule of thumb in all things e-mail is to pay close attention to the tone and level of warmth, professionalism, and informality or rigid discipline in the correspondences that you receive. While it can be fairly common for e-mail exchanges to get heated up pretty quickly (like a high school romance) and for virtual strangers to be signing off with hugs, kisses, and endless devotion, for the most part business mores remain constant. In a pinch, you can never go wrong with a bit of formality and an underlying core of professionalism.

KEEP IT FRESH

As mentioned in Chapter 3, it's a good idea to create subfolders within your inbox. While you don't have to answer an e-mail immediately, you should try to be timely about your response. A good rule of thumb is to immediately answer any urgent communications, and then to create an e-mail triage in which you move unanswered e-mail messages to folders that reflect their level of importance. It's a good idea to try to answer most messages within three days. If you've dropped the ball on a correspondence thread, don't despair. Briefly explain the reason for your absence, refer to the original correspondence, and inquire as to whether your input or involvement is still needed.

BUT NOT TOO FRESH

If the name Claire Swire is familiar to you, then you've obviously heard or read about one of the well-publicized e-mail indiscretions of our time. Because this book is rated PG-13, I won't go into the specifics, but suffice it to say that in December 2000, a private correspondence made on work time and on corporate e-mail accounts between Ms. Swire and her office inamorato made the interoffice rounds before becoming quite literally the indiscretion that encircled the globe.

If you must go on about private matters, do it on your private e-mail account and on your own time, because not only can your employer get into your e-mail account, they have every right to use this information against you. Millie Martini Bratten, the editor in chief of *Brides* magazine, adds, "You're not only shaming yourself with this behavior but also your employer, whose name and hard-earned reputation are on every e-mail that you send from work."

SALUTATIONS

Unless you know someone pretty well, it's probably wisest to limit your greetings to "Dear" and "Hello," with an occasional "Hey" thrown in for good measure. Signing your emails should be equally gracious, with "Best" or "All the best" working for generic signoffs, "Warmly" or "Warmest regards" to interject a bit of that personal touch, and "Dear Stud Muffin" signed with "Big Sloppy Kisses" reserved exclusively for your significant other. You see where variations on this theme might get confusing?

SIGNATURES

Every e-mail that you send can be an electronic billboard for you and your company; it can also be a great tool to allow people to find you easily. Be selective about what you include on each message. Your name, title, company, contact information, and link to your web site should put your name and position into proper perspective. If you've had a recent accomplishment, feel free to include a line or two at the end of your message. Below your e-mail message, type asterisks or a line to signify where your message ends and your signature begins.

BE SELECTIVE AND BE RESPECTFUL

Whatever your work or communication style, always keep in mind that people are not obligated to read what you send them. Try to personalize your note—ask after their health, congratulate them on a recent accomplishment when appropriate. Spell-checker is your friend—always use it. Don't automatically add a high priority to your notes, because then they don't become a priority at all. Exclamation points can convey perkiness or inappropriate exuberance (though I really like them!).

Gerry Byrne, communications legend and founder of the Quills Literacy Foundation and Quill Awards, doesn't believe in wasting people's time. Every phone call, e-mail, or meeting has meaning and relevance, or, in his words, "It's all about getting to the point." Byrne has admitted to learning the hard way that "time is the most valuable commodity that people have. You don't want to waste anybody's time, and you want to make everything you say or do count."

Instant Messaging/IM

Grasshopper, you must navigate these waters on your own. When a method of communication has evolved from LOL (laugh out loud) to include BMW (be my wife), all bets are off. Those who fear for the future of the English language as we know it will be horrified to know that students in New Zealand were recently granted permission to use "text-speak" on their exams.

Before you lose all hope, consider what Mac Slocum, founder of the Fodder Network, an interactive series of entertainment-related web sites, has to say on the subject. Slocum believes that ideas, even in an immediate media form, require time to become fully formulated. For him, the most interesting communications, from e-mail to IMs, include careful thought and execution.

CAREER

Every phone conversation, voice mail, e-mail, and instant message is a reflection of you and your personal brand. Take the time to figure out your strongest communication skill and perfect it. Write a script if necessary, and update and evolve as needed.

CORPORATE

While your workday might be mind-numbing at times, you are for all intents and purposes being paid to do a job and to do it well. Don't forward chain letters, jokes, or pyramid schemes. Don't send smutty e-mails to your boyfriend. Realize that while you are at work, everything that you say, do, or write can reflect well or poorly on your employer.

COOL

You've worked hard to develop your own style, and following the protocol of your employer, client, or office mates won't dilute that, but rather further reflect your professionalism.

Chapter 17

Let's Hear It for the Boy

Make Your Significant Other Date-Worthy for Work-Related Events

> *The best reason I can think of for not running for President of the United States is that you have to shave twice a day.*
> —Adlai E. Stevenson Jr.

Metrosexual? Retrosexual? Whatever Works for You

A couple of years back there was much hype about the advent of the so-called metrosexual—an übergroomed, überstylish, completely heterosexual guy who wasn't afraid to publicly declare his love for designer labels and embrace his inner product junkie. Suddenly, men were coming out of their cosmetic-crammed closets and regaling anyone who would listen with tales of miraculous spa treatments and age-defying eye creams.

The cosmetic industry raced to produce guy-friendly products that included updated drugstore favorites, quirky male treatments, and a lot of repackaged versions of tried-and-true classics. While men were once limited to grooming their facial shrubbery, they were suddenly presented with new and improved ways to primp. Scores of new product lines emerged. The overwhelming launching of thousands of new products (1,000 new men's products were said to have been launched from 1999 to 2003) ran the gamut from Anatomicals to Zirh, selling hundreds upon hundreds of products. Encouraged by the popularity of television shows like *Queer Eye for the Straight Guy* and tons of media attention, the race was on to become the smoothest guy on the block in more ways than one.

While the Mennen man once ruled the retro roost, today's savvy male consumer doesn't fit any one profile. Thanks to customers ranging from soap-and-water purists to the brand hungry tween-to-college category (ages 12 to 24), to Gen Y (more likely to be open to product launches and future brand loyalty), to übergroomed metrosexuals generally declaring their passion for cult or designer brands, to Gen X former slackers using whatever their significant others have purchased, male grooming products are no longer simply tools of seduction but rather carefully chosen lifestyle-enhancing and status products.

The Survey Says

A couple of months back, I was working on the launch of a new line of grooming products for men. The packaging was slick, the copy was snarky but sweet, and yet for all the millions of dollars being spent on research and development for the line, it seemed to be seriously lacking in soul, or at the very least anything that would attract its targeted demographic. Instead of feeling like we were moving in a new direction, it felt more like a classic case of trying to repackage more traditional or typical elements to sell to another gender. It became a real struggle to come up with the proverbial special sauce that would set (and sell) the brand apart from the pack.

At the same time, I was asked to contribute keynote elements for a marketing conference (I kid you not, it was called simply "The Man Conference") geared to marketing to men, produced by *Advertising Age* and *Maxim* magazines. As if things weren't fully testosterone-charged in my office, I was also asked to appear on CNBC's finance program *On The Money*, hosted by Dylan Ratigan, to discuss the men's grooming industry, specifically Unilever's best selling Axe body spray and Tag, produced by Tag Fragrance Company (the young, hip incarnation of Global Gillette).

While a great portion of what I do is related to the cosmetic industry in general, for those intense months I suddenly found myself immersed in everything related to guy grooming. From formulas to ingredients, advertising, brand hallmarks, copyrights, competitors, evolving brands, and barbershop favorites, I studied it all with a fine-tooth comb. I also drew on our national GTK Good To Know! network. (We have a carefully screened volunteer network of thousands of individuals of differing age, income, sex, region, and social status, who help provide us with invaluable and unbiased market research on everything from entertainment to politics and consumer packaged goods.) We interviewed guys with very clear opinions on how they choose to look, smell, and feel good, as well as my own treasured network of guy friends. We grilled them exhaustively on their product likes and dislikes, buying habits, price point, and more, and here's what these good-to-know guys had to say about male grooming habits:

- Only his hairdresser knows for sure. To tweak an older idiom, a majority of the men we spoke to make grooming purchases based on the advice of their stylist. Barbers didn't have much influence at all, and the purchasing suggestions of female stylists overwhelmingly influenced all grooming purchases.

- Brand lifestyle relevancy trumps brand loyalty. In other words, if it was easy to use and fit their budget or habits, it became the brand of choice.

- Clever marketing campaigns heavily influenced purchases. These men were extremely aware that they were being marketed to, and they admitted that their decision making was influenced by everything from packaging copy to editorials in their girlfriends' magazines, print advertisements, Web presence, and television ads.

- Price wasn't as important as quality, perceived value, scent, or results. Even for the men who preferred bargain brands or cited savings as a major attracter, quality was a determining factor.

- Attracting a romantic partner, while a major driving force, was not the primary reason behind product usage, but rather took a second place to the feelings evinced by the product itself. Feelings were cited most often by men in the late 20s age bracket, who described feelings ranging from power and potency to clarity of thought and improved attitude. Overall, and shockingly to this marketer, attracting a sexual partner was barely in the top five reasons for 30-somethings, while it topped the teen and college categories.

◆ Fear of aging and fear of seeming irrelevant in the business arena are prime motivators in choosing grooming products. Again, while we anticipated this in our gay survey subjects, we were amazed at how many on the C level (i.e., executives—CEOs, CFOs), while they would not entertain thoughts of cosmetic surgery and initially mocked cosmeceuticals, nevertheless wrote follow-up e-mails asking for advice on everything from eye creams to tooth bleaching systems.

◆ Hollywood and the celebrity aesthetic were *not* a defining ideal of attractiveness, desirability, or even virility for these men—quite the opposite, in fact. While sports figures topped the list of desired levels of male sexuality and prowess, a majority of the men polled cited more successful friends and members of their peer group as the desired ideal.

◆ The thing that most of these men would never do? Wax their male parts a la David Beckham.

So there you have it. Would any of these guys don false eyelashes to disguise their graying lashes, as one Hollywood stylist suggested? Doubtful, because while they are comfortable adding to their basic grooming routine, on the whole they want to look and feel great but never silly. While millions of people in the world have come to rely on cosmetic surgery and invasive techniques for a quick fix, on the whole I prefer to think that unless it's an extreme case, most men and women can look amazing without resorting to going under the knife.

Eyes on the Guys

A couple of years ago I was working on a project with a former NFL star turned high-profile entrepreneur. From a distance he looked great: every hair in its place, not a blemish on his face, quietly expensive

Metrosexual? Retrosexual? Whatever!

Italian silk tie, perfectly creased pants—you get the picture. At the end of our first meeting, he motioned me to come over and talk to him for a minute or two. As I got closer, I became mesmerized by his appearance. His hair was obviously (and poorly) colored; he was wearing an orangey foundation that seemed to only highlight the concealer under his eyes, thereby drawing attention to his mascara . . . I can't continue, it only gets worse, but let's just say that his lip stain would better have suited a 12-year-old girl than a man in his mid-40s. In all honesty I can say that he was likely wearing more makeup than I was.

One more story, and then I'll get to my point. As I've mentioned before, I've been blessed to have some of the most incredible and generous people in the world as my mentors and advisers. Several years ago, I was to attend a meeting with a high-powered executive who eventually became a mentor and then a dear friend. It was a steamy, late-August day with the kind of industrialized, stultifying heat and humidity that only New York City seems able to produce. I waited for my meeting, shuffling around miserably, trying to sneak in a blast of icy air from the open store doorways. Though I was waiting for only a few minutes I felt my hair wilt, my clothing become sodden, and I'm sure that my mascara had melted into my lip gloss. There was not a single person on the street who wasn't wilted looking—except for John. His hair was perfect, he wore a suit and tie in that excruciating heat, and his shirt was so blindingly, snowy white that I was grateful to be wearing sunglasses to protect my eyes from the glare. He was so sure of himself, so together, that to this day I'm convinced he had trained his sweat glands to work only on his leisure time.

Two extremely powerful, attractive men with completely different ideas on how to look great in a professional setting. One tried so hard to hang on to his youth that he appeared to be almost comical, while the other was so secure, so very much his own person, that he had figured out how to look perfect even under the most extreme weather conditions (I later found out his system involved a shower, shave, and several changes of clothing at work).

Ten Sneaky Ways to Look Great

Back in my makeup artist days, I would sometimes work with male models in addition to the glamazons. What was always interesting to me wasn't the fact that they were more obsessed with their trim waistlines than most women I know, but rather just how adept they were at disguising their flaws and enhancing their attributes. For the record, I don't mean with simply the well-placed sock. I was frequently asked to airbrush on six-pack abs and—well, I probably shouldn't tell you the rest.

I don't think you need to polish or buff or in any way try to look like a male model, but these 10 tips might just make you look and feel better about yourself.

1. For a really close shave, wait until after you've showered and your pores have opened somewhat from the steam.
2. If you prefer the slightly unshaved look, use hair conditioner on your stubble to keep it softer and save your smooching partner from beard burn.
3. If your eyes are puffy after a night of too much excess, press two spoons against the baggy areas—even better, chill the spoons first.
4. Don't use foundation unless you're a pro—it will look fake and crepey. Instead, use a tinted moisturizer in the lightest possible shade. If even that is too dark for you, cut it with your regular moisturizer.
5. Men's faces are exfoliated on an almost daily basis because of shaving. If you feel you must scrub, stick to your forehead and nose.
6. Apply an extra-moisturizing face mask or intensive moisturizer before you travel; it will help to combat the drying effects of air travel.
7. Mind your cuticles. Rub olive oil into your ragged nail bed to smoothe out your ragged cuticles.
8. Soften the obvious lines around your mouth by also dabbing the area on top of your lips with lip balm. Mind not to overdo it, because if overused, lip balm can clog the pores around your mouth, causing blackheads.
9. If you find that you sweat too much but don't want to resort to drastic measures like shaving your armpits, consider investing in a groomer (sort of like a shaver with attachments) and trim the hair under your arms and on your chest (and other areas of your choice).

10. While many men have discovered the joy of the eyebrow wax, they usually tend to look overplucked or allow their brows to be trimmed too thin. Feel free to pluck or wax stray hairs that cause a unibrow, and trim any longer hairs, but don't feel compelled to prune brows into submission.

Ten Tips from a Style Expert

Some men, like New York City–based attorney Jeff McAdams, have a very clear sense of the personal style that works for them. McAdams is usually clad in some variation of his signature color green. His style can best be summed up as a cross between a Norman Rockwell painting and a 1980s new wave band. For men who don't have quite such a well-defined style, Sean Krebs, fashion editor at large at *Genre* magazine, shares some of his best style tips for guys. Sean is a style expert who has worked in the fashion industry for over 10 years for brands such as Burberry, Fendi, Missoni, and Gap.

Top 10 Men's Style Tips for the Career and Corporate Cool Guy

   1. *De-pleat yourself.* Sean is fairly emphatic about insisting that you rid your wardrobe of all of your suits with pleated pants, since pleated pants are not flattering on anyone. According to Sean, nothing will make you look more dated than fussy, unflattering, pleated pants. Even if you spent a fortune on them, it's time to kiss them goodbye. "If you can't part with them, keep them in your mother's attic—maybe in another twenty years they'll be back in style."

   2. *Be the man in the gray flannel suit.* Take a cue from Cary Grant in *North by Northwest*: A gray flannel suit (with a flat-front trouser, of course) is perfect for any situation you might get yourself into (and need to get out of quickly). Continue to follow Grant's lead by pairing it with a crisp white shirt and a solid, charcoal-gray silk necktie.

   3. *Necking.* Contrary to what politicians think, neckties actually do come in other colors than red. There is a whole world of colors, stripes, patterns, and styles to choose from. Take a serious look at them and experiment. Also try experimenting with different knots (Windsor, half Windsor, four-in-hand) and shirt collar options (spread, pointed, button-down). Just because you're wearing a shirt and tie doesn't mean it has to be boring.

4. *Stylish but casual Fridays.* Casual Friday doesn't mean wearing the pants from your suit with a faded golf shirt or your college sweatshirt, nor does it have anything even remotely to do with Hawaiian board shorts or flip-flops. Sean suggests that you invest in a few pairs of flat-front khakis, but don't limit yourself to only basic khaki. Instead, buy one pair in a true khaki color, one in stone, and also try a pair in navy blue or dark brown. As for what to wear with your khakis, buy some great-fitting polo shirts with long or short sleeves.

5. *Be a mane man.* You don't have to spend a fortune on a great haircut, but it is a good idea to find a barber or stylist who takes your features, bone structure and lifestyle or profession into account. Get your hair cut or at least trimmed once a month. Sean advises being "especially mindful of the hair at the back of your neck—a mullet is never a good look in the boardroom." To keep your cut fresh between visits to the stylist, consider shaving the tiny, fine hairs at the nape of your neck for that freshly cut effect.

6. *A case for briefcases.* It's time to throw away that battered and worn-out messenger bag that you've had since college. Consider buying that pricy leather briefcase that you've been eyeing for years. It's an investment piece that will only get better looking with age (just as you will—unfair but true, you lucky bastard).

7. *Find your sole mate.* Splurge on a pair of great leather lace-up shoes, because let's face it, those slip-on loafers with a low vamp can be as deadly as the pleated pants you've just eliminated from your wardrobe. Remember to keep your shoes unscuffed, polished, and the soles in perfect condition. A trip to the cobbler will save you money in the long run by adding more life to your shoes.

8. *Moving right along* . . . Go to the gym, go for a run, skip dessert—do something to keep your body in shape. Your clothes will look better on you, not to mention what it will do for your health and self-esteem.

9. *Blaze new trails.* Every man should own a cool blazer (not just the jacket that is part of your suit) and a pair of dark denim boot-cut jeans (a boot cut is universally the most flattering fit). Wearing them together with a button-front shirt is the perfect foolproof outfit for drinks with friends and/or dinner with a date that you're desperately trying to impress. (The first time I met Sean, he was wearing a fabulous charcoal patterned Burberry jacket paired with a crisp button-down shirt and perfect-fitting jeans. And no, he wasn't trying to impress me—he just makes looking good look effortless).

10. *Underneath it all* . . . Sean insists that you "always wear an undershirt—my father said to never trust a man who doesn't."

Just Ask Him

Okay, so those are the impeccably groomed, superstylish Sean Krebs's top 10 style tips for men. But what about when you see a guy who looks really good and you're just dying to find out where he got those pants? Should you shuffle your feet and get all goofy about it?

Quite the opposite, says Rob Gould, a strategist with Portland, Maine–based VIA Group. Gould lived and worked in Boston and London before moving to rustic Maine, and he suggests that if you're curious about the accoutrements of another man, be it "his great shoes, the fact that he never has a stupid haircut or always looks healthy and fit, accessorizes well from his glasses to his watch or messenger bag or briefcase," just ask him how he does it. He admits to having male colleagues ask him about his haircut or shoes in the most hushed and almost reverent voices, "like I hold a state secret."

As for guys who run around wearing black socks with white tennis shoes, or worse, mandals (man sandals) and socks? Clueless guys tend to remain clueless and unbothered until someone (usually a significant other) announces that it's time for a style makeover. What about guys who feel that they're too short, or that their spare tire keeps them from wearing great clothes? Jason Rappaport, founder of J. Raffiani, has found a niche designing neckties for the more than 30 million American men who are under 5'8". Rappaport, who falls into that category, says that most people are shocked to discover his real height, even when standing next to him, because of his larger-than-life attitude. Finding clothing and accessories that suit your shape and size will keep you looking irresistible instead of like you're trying too hard.

Face to Face with Your Fears

So you've got some great ideas on style and on bridging that awkward gap when you see a guy wearing the hoodie of your dreams, but now here comes a major hurdle—your first visit to a spa. Men are flocking to spas like never before. Enrique Ramirez, spa director at Face to Face Day Spa, located in the Flatiron district in New York City, says that 85 percent of his spa's patrons are men. While a spa treatment is supposed to be relaxing, men do not always know how to behave in spas, which can be kind of awkward and embarrassing for them, not to mention really uncomfortable for those around them. Here are 10 tips for guys from the Face to Face Day Spa, with all the information they'll need before heading to the spa:

1. *Have a close shave before a facial.* Although by no means a major requirement, it does make a difference to your facialist. A smooth beard area gives the aesthetician the opportunity to treat any signs of razor burn, ingrown hairs, or neck irritation caused by use of an old razor. To avoid irritation, though, don't shave immediately before heading out for a treatment; give your skin a couple of hours to calm down before going for a facial.

2. *Arrive 10 minutes early to your appointment.* Many spas require that you fill out an intake form before your scheduled treatment; you might be asked about medical conditions, allergies, or treatment preferences. Arriving early gives you enough time to fill out the form and have a stress-free check in. It also gives you time to change, freshen up, or decompress.

3. *I see London, I see France*—at the spa, I may or may not see your underpants. Shy guys have a chance to keep on your tighty whities or go commando during a massage or body treatment. Whatever you choose, it will be fine with your professional spa technician—no need to explain!

4. *Shower before a massage.* Another case for arriving early: Most spas have amazing showers. Getting there early gives you plenty of time to hit the shower, and a squeaky clean scent will make your masseur want to rub instead of run!

5. *The tipping part:* You've been rubbed, massaged, exfoliated, or otherwise pampered within an inch of your life. Be sure to show your appreciation to your spa technician with a 15 to 20 percent tip. Your spa technician will appreciate your generosity and will take extra-special care of your face next time you're in the spa.

6. *Hold the phone!* Spa owners and aestheticians work hard to create a soothing, relaxing, and mellow environment to help soothe your frazzled nerves and tame your tension, and nothing ruins that calm like the annoying and piercing sound of a mobile phone. Show that you're a guy with good manners and shut it off.

7. *Don't apply body lotion before waxing.* Okay, squeamish guys stop reading now, hirsute honeys do continue. Smooth, clean skin will make your back waxing less painful and make it easier to remove the strip wax. Also, it's very important that you inform the technician if you are using Retin-A or Accutane, as this will prevent an awkward moment when your skin is being removed along with your hair.

8. *Keep voices down when entering the spa.* Calm and reflective tones are welcomed! You're not at the Super Bowl.

9. *Be open with your spa technician.* Inform your technician of any bodily, mental, or skin issues or imbalances such as allergies, medications that may affect your skin, torn ligaments, claustrophobia, and so on, so that they can customize your massage, facial, or nail treatment.

10. *Don't work out after a spa treatment.* You've just paid all that money to relax your muscles. Why would you want to then go and tense them up again? Also, sweating before showering off any body oil from the spa treatment can cause clogged pores, leading to breakouts.

CAREER

It's been said many times that clothes make the man. These days so do his haircut, subtle cologne, and unscuffed shoes. Spending time on your appearance doesn't make you wimpy. It makes good sense for you to look your best.

CORPORATE

While your business may have a strict dress policy, you can always distinguish yourself in subtle ways. Perhaps you favor diving watches with your buttoned-up suit, or pocket squares that contrast with your socks. You can look perfectly professional while also celebrating your little quirks.

COOL

There's nothing like a well-groomed guy—hair shiny, soft, and not too crispy from product; jaw cleanly shaved (so that beard burn by proxy isn't an option); and that irresistible, shower-fresh smell of clean soap or just a hint of cologne. Bottom line? While we like a guy to take care of himself, we don't like it to turn into an obsession or hours of man maintenance. Even Cindy Crawford has said of her husband, the delectable Rande Gerber, that she's okay with his grooming routine as long as it doesn't take longer than hers does.

Chapter 18

Little Black Book

Some Top Secret Resources You'll Need to Succeed

> *The secret of being a bore is to tell everything.*
> —Voltaire

Top Secret

Take a minute to think about your personal style. Come on, indulge me for a minute and give yourself a mental once-over, taking in every detail. Instead of simply touching on the immediate features that strangers might notice, try to give some real thought to the complete package. Whether you realize it or not, on some level you're making calculated daily choices about how you choose to present yourself to the world.

Let's start with your hair—both cut and color. Is it long, unstyled, and the same way you wore it in high school, or do you wear a trademark razor-sharp bob? Is your color all natural or do you studiously touch up your roots? Do you favor subtle highlights from an expensive salon or over-the-top platinum blonde streaks from a drugstore kit?

What about your jewelry? Do you consider a strand of pearls to be the only accessory for every outfit you own, or do you change your jewelry to suit your mood? I tend to favor very bold earrings—I don't particularly care if teeny, tiny, ladylike studs are all the rage, I'm obsessed with having things that sparkle or dangle gracing my earlobes. I'm equally obsessed with accessorizing. I love unusual or conversation pieces that are quirky or are souvenirs from my travels—they help me incorporate a little bit of magic into my everyday life.

What about the fashion trends that you do or do not choose to follow? Is *Vogue* magazine your bible? Have you at any point eagerly purchased and then worn without irony a cape, bubble skirt, leggings, or stiletto heels? Do you favor comfortable clothes for every occasion? And if so, are you a jeans and T-shirt kind of gal, or do you only wear cashmere lounging pants?

Exhaustive but true—every single detail, from the scent that you spritz on every morning, to the playlist on your iPod, the restaurants you frequent, cosmetic brands you love or hate—well, there's a lot that goes into making up Brand You.

Not All Top 10 Lists Are Created Equal

While you're usually open to new tips and suggestions, over the years you've developed a clear-cut sense of your likes and dislikes. There are colors that you wear (black comes to mind) and colors that you'll probably never wear (does anyone look good in peach)? You probably have a favorite lunch spot, be it a trendy boïte or a cozy sandwich joint, and that one crazy over-the-top restaurant that you eat in only on special occasions. (And if you're a foodie, I'm guessing that you wax rhapsodic over the sushi at one joint and the wine list somewhere else, and the perfect crepes available only on the third Sunday of months ending with a consonant.) Like most well-informed individuals interested in expanding their horizons and refining their consumer palettes, you probably spend a good deal of time perusing the latest news, views, and reviews for information on the best of whatever's new and exciting.

The initial concept for this chapter was to offer a definitive list of the best of everything: the best hairstylist, the of-the-moment eaterie, the reigning designer du jour—you get the idea. However, like much of our incredibly fast-paced and evolving lives, one or several definitive offerings might not be relevant to your life on a longer term. For that reason, I've tried to judge some of the best by a different standard.

The web sites, hotels, restaurants, and resources listed here are recommended not because they are of the minute, but because they have distinguished themselves and also stood the test of time. For the most part, any of the web sites listed have been in business for two or more years. The hotels are not so hip it hurts, but rather provide exquisite service, have quirky décor, or offer excellent amenities.

Since web sites change so quickly, I have chosen to include only classic sites that distinguish themselves not only on great service and selection but also based on the longevity factor. For a regularly updated and evolving list of useful web sites, please visit www.careerand corporatecool.com/blackbook.html. In any event, these are some of the classics, but since tastes and times differ radically, now would be a great time for you to start forming your own little black book of your favorite resources, restaurants, and relevant services.

Beauty/Fashion

Starting with clothing, I like *Billion Dollar Babes* (www.billiondollar babes.com) and *Top Button* (www.topbutton.com) for fabulous fashion and sample sale events, and *ShopBop.com* (www.shopbop.com) for fun fashion and great selection. *Sephora* (www.sephora.com) offers a great gathering of beauty necessities online or off line, and on the other side of the pond, *Space NK* apothecary (www.spacenk.co.uk) is the only way to go.

Henri Bendel is one part old-world glamour, one part socialite's closet, one part Edith Wharton novel. My favorite for cosmetics and accessories, it's located at 712 Fifth Avenue in New York City. For great casual and work wear, try J. Jill (www.jjill.com). I like *Ted Baker* (www.tedbaker.com) because I can rarely resist a man with quirky enough taste to really rock Ted the right way.

When building your wardrobe, try to include fabulous cashmere pieces. *N. Peal* (www.npeal.com) and *Belinda Robertson* (www.belinda robertson.com) are two of my favorites.

Shirise in Chicago (www.shirise.com) doesn't just have a great selection of chic shoes, but also excellent customer service.

Everyone talks about *Kitson* (www.shopkitson.com), but *Lisa Kline* has everything from cute shower caps to over the top pocketbooks; check www.lisakline.com for locations.

You have to have loads of patience at *Century 21 Department Stores*, but you can pick up designer pieces at a fraction of the retail costs. Visit www.c21stores.com for locations

If Judy Jetson and Jennifer Lopez had collaborated on their idea of a perfect mecca for beauty, they might have come up with the *Rita Hazan Salon* on Fifth Avenue in New York. The white, chrome, and turquoise decor mixes Middle Eastern touches with modern hardware and retro detailing. There are cozy areas to chat and network; areas for manicures, facials, and VIPs; and more than anything, there's chocolate! Rita Hazan Salon is at 750 Fifth Avenue, 11th floor, in New York (www.ritahazansalon.com).

The *Andre Chreky Salon* does everything possible to pamper you, from pastries to piano music—oh, and they do a great job on your hair too. Andre Chreky is located at 1604 K Street NW in Washington, D.C. *Umi Salon*, at 75 Newbury Street in Boston, can help ease you through your highlights from hell; it has some of the best color correctors in the country. *Skintology* in Manhattan's Chelsea district looks pretty small from the outside, but once inside you'll be amazed by the incredible attention to detail and impressive 4,000 square feet of beautifying. Try the chocolate raspberry scrub—you'll look and feel delicious!

I am blessed with many gifts, but perfect hair is not one of them. The best blowout of my life, though, was by *Alyn Topper*, he of Bravo's hit series *Blowout*. I could swear that he sneaked some extra hair in there, it was so voluminous, shiny, and downright cute—but nope, it was all due to his talent. Alyn tends to work on both coasts, so consult his web site at www.alyntopper.com to find out where he'll be next. *John Frieda Salon* in Barbados (at Sandy Lane) offers the classic haircuts you'd expect, with a little added fun.

Gifted

When you're looking for just the right gift, try these unusual places:

- ◆ *GoodyBagGifts*. When only a custom-created gift or goody bag for your events or corporate gifting will do, go to www.goody baggifts.com.
- ◆ *SavvySkirts*. When you need a semi-customized gift for a girl-friend, try www.savvyskirts.com.

- *Tiffany & Co.* Because sometimes only the little blue box will do: www.tiffany.com.
- *Red Envelope.* You'll find a great selection and great service at www.redenvelope.com.
- *Stremmel Gallery.* The building itself is an exquisite frame for the contemporary treasures within. Located at 1400 South Virginia Street, Reno, Nevada 89502; www.stremmelgallery.com, telephone (775) 786-0558.

Good Things

These are some of my favorite nonprofit organizations:

- *American Forests.* How can you not love an organization that plants trees for environmental restoration? Find them at www.americanforests.org. Equally cool is their Famous & Historic Trees program (www.historictrees.org) which researches and documents trees that in some way or another are a part of history—because said tree either was written about, was painted, or grew nearby during a historical occurrence.
- *The Quills Literacy Foundation.* The Quills focus' is on the importance of books and reading, and their related awards ceremony is like the Oscars for books, only instead of long acceptance speeches you can just read the book for yourself. (www.quillsliteracy.org)
- *Rails-to-Trails Conservancy.* On the good deed-o-meter this organization ranks way up there with coolest concepts. Rails-to-Trails reclaims unused railroad tracks and uses the materials to create a nationwide network of running paths, biking trails, other healthy outdoor environments. (www.railtrails.org)

Health/Nutrition

For lots of health information, try these web sites:

- AOL Health Channel (http://health.aol.com) offers health news, medical information, a directory of local health services, and health care tips.

- *WebMD* (www.webmd.com) has tons of health information and medical news.
- *The National Women's Health Resource Center* (www.healthy women.org) gives clear, concise, free health information for women.

News and Schmooze

Here's a wide range of information sources—the news and much more!

- *CNN.* Sign up for CNN's breaking news email at www.cnn.com.
- *Eonline.* Gossip without an excess of snark or adulation (www .eonline.com).
- *PopBitch.* Please don't e-mail me on Thursday mornings when I'm trying to figure out the blind items. Sign up for a weekly newsletter at www.popbitch.com.
- *Wired.* Tidbits and info on technology and more, at www .wired.com.
- *Internet Movie Database.* Better known as IMDB, this site has tons of fun information about films, actors, and behind-the-scenes buzz (www.imdb.com).
- *GameFly.* Get your favorite video game rentals delivered to your door (www.gamefly.com). Movies more your thing? *Netflix* has all of the popular films but also hard-to-find foreign and indie films (www.netflix.com).
- *Popdex.* Like a web site popularity contest (www.popdex.com).
- *Television Without Pity.* For TV addicts everywhere, the ultimate online water cooler. Get plot details, comments, and more at www.televisionwithoutpity.com.
- *The Onion.* But it *could* be true! (www.theonion.com).
- *Daily Candy.* Always entertaining, www.dailycandy.com has competition from *The Stylephile* (www.thestylephile.com), a great daily newsletter from the publishers of *Variety* magazine.
- *Style.com. Vogue and W* magazines together in one place—can't beat that! (www.style.com).

- *The Sartorialist.* I'm not a huge fan of blogs. I do, however, worship the Sartorialist (http://thesartorialist.blogspot .com/).
- *Chowhound.* Reviews! Boards! Features! It's every foodie's favorite web site (www.chowhound.com).

Yummy

Ah, food! Am I predictable to insist that you rush to *The French Laundry*? Mere words cannot describe the great feeling and great dining experience, at 6640 Washington Street in Yountville, California. Or for a change, check out *Zin* restaurant in the heart of wine country, which offers dishes featuring home grown produce by Chef Jeff Mall, the son of a farmer and whose motto is "If I can grow it, why buy it?" Zin is located at 344 Center Street in Healdsburg, California. *Willi's Wine Bar* in Santa Rosa specializes in small plates of food paired with great wine, but more than anything the atmosphere and great vibe will keep you coming back time and time again 404 Old Redwood Highway.

If price is no object and you really want to impress a client check, out *Thomas Henkelmann* at the Homestead Inn, 420 Field Point Road, Greenwich, Connecticut (telephone 203-869-7500). It's a fabulous inn, with gracious hosts and a great experience. Private dining rooms are available too.

For the breakfast of champions, it's a toss-up between my all-time favorite, *Norma's*, at Le Parker Meridien in Manhattan; *The Bunnery* in Jackson Hole, Wyoming; and *Mi Tierra* in San Antonio, Texas. Norma's boasts that $1,000 frittata, but you needn't skimp on rent to enjoy the most fabulous breakfast ever—from tiny starter smoothies, to yogurt decorated with orchids, and omelettes and crepes that should be canonized, I'm never quite sure if the presentation or taste is superior. With the views that The Bunnery has, they could serve swill and melba toast and no one would care. It's a toss-up though between their hearty soups and breakfast delicacies, and oh, their famous O.S.M. bread. The Mexican Hot Chocolate alone is worth a trip to Mi Tierra. For a completely different take on breakfast, try *Campagne* restaurant in Seattle—but expect to skip lunch!

Norma's at Le Parker Meridien, 118 West 57th Street, New York; telephone 212-245-5000.

Jackson Hole Bunnery, 130 North Cache, Jackson, Wyoming; 307-734-0075.

Mi Tierra Cafe Y Panaderia, 218 Produce Row, San Antonio, Texas; info@mitierracafe.com.

Campagne, 86 Pine Street, Seattle, Washington; 206-728-2800.

I'm a born and bred New Yorker, so listing all of my favorite eateries wouldn't be fair to any of us. *Blue Water Grill* on Union Square always tops my list. Its soaring ceilings, jazz downstairs, and loads of seating choices from clubbier upstairs to people-watching outdoors make it worth a visit. Oh, and the salmon? Always divine. Located at 31 Union Square West, New York (telephone 212-675-9500), Blue Water Grill is one of the B.R. Guest properties, a chain of quirky restaurants with great food and excellent extras; learn more at www.brguestrestaurants.com. Their *Dos Caminos* makes fab frozen margaritas. Family-owned *Barrolo* has great Northern Italian cuisine and a garden area worth discovering, at 398 West Broadway, New York (telephone 212-226-1102; www.nybarolo.com).

Tops for veggie food in my opinion is *The Green's* in Brooklyn. The Chinese vegetarian menu is extensive, and the lunch menu is ridiculously affordable. I once told a vegetarian client to order five lunch specials so they wouldn't think I was being cheap with my choice of venue. The Green's is at 128 Montague Street at the Corner of Henry Street. Chances are very good that you might run into me there on Fridays, so do say hello! A close second is the *Zen Palate* chain—the Union Square location (in New York, not San Francisco) is one of my favorites, at 34 Union Square East.

As a born-and-bred city girl, it surprised me when I fell head-over-heels for Grand Rapids (part of the Cool Cities Initiative; www.cool cities.com), Holland, and Muskegon, Michigan's gorgeous beaches, friendly people, spectacular farmers markets, and quirky and interesting culture and galleries. *Bar Divani*, a restaurant and wine bar, could give NYC staple *Morrell* a run for its money with clever appetizers, main dishes, and an extensive wine list. Bar Divani is at 15 Ionia Avenue SW in Grand Rapids, Michigan (www.bar-divani.com).

I tend to avoid spots that seem targeted to tourists in favor of clubby neighborhood joints, but Morrell's extensive wine list never ceases to amaze me. *Morrell* is located in One Rockefeller Plaza, New York. If you've really got time to spend with a wine list, you won't want to miss *Montagna* with its 15,000 bottle list. You'll find Montagna at the Little Nell Hotel, 675 E. Durant Avenue in Aspen, Colorado (telephone 970-920-6330).

Just because you can't spend every day at *The Ivy* (113 N. Robertson Boulevard in Los Angeles) doesn't mean you have to miss out on people-watching pleasure. Expect noise and crowds at *Prime One Twelve*, 112 Ocean Drive, Miami, Florida (telephone 305-532-8112) or at A.O.C., 8022 W. Third Street in Los Angeles (323-653-6359). It can be ego-damaging, though, since everyone tends to look so darn airbrushed. (The latter is not to be confused with A.O.C. in the West Village in New York, at 314 Bleeker Street—stop by for the fabulous outdoor garden!).

Citizen Smith's sleek design plays up the great views of Hollywood's historic buildings and neon signs—hey, and the food's pretty tasty too! It's at 1600 N. Cahuenga Boulevard in Hollywood, California. Legendary chef Wolfgang Puck teamed up with architect Richard Meier on *CUT* at the Beverly Wilshire. Be warned though, CUT is a steakhouse for serious carnivores, at 9500 Wilshire Boulevard, Beverly Hills, California. For the best Belgian Fries ever (not for vegetarians though—hence the name), head for *Duckfat*, 43 Middle Street, Portland, Main (www.duckfat.com).

Il Mulino's first location was in New York's Greenwich Village, but two decades later this cult favorite for Italian specialties (their Langoustines are legendary) has locations in Japan, Puerto Rico, and Washington, D.C. Visit www.ilmulino.com for locations. Just around the corner from the White House, *The Occidental Restaurant* is known as the place "Where Statesmen Dine." A rich history (check out the photos on the walls) and a great menu make it a must visit spot, at 1475 Pennsylvania Avenue NW, Washington D.C.

I spent one of the best birthdays of my life in Belfast, Ireland, part of the time enjoying live music at the historic *Kitchen Bar*, and the rest in search of a champagne cocktail—not easy to find while pub hopping in Northern Ireland. Kitchen Bar is at 16-18 Victoria Square (www.thekitchenbar.com). I finally found a rose petal champagne cocktail at *Sugar Room/Potthouse*, 1 Hill Street, in Belfast.

I keep humming that Istanbul/Constantinople song—whatever you call it, you do not want to miss *Tugra* at the Çiragan Palace. Feel free to stare at the exquisite decor and outstanding views, but pay attention to the delicious food, too! Ciragan is at Caddesi 32, Istanbul, Turkey (www.ciraganpalace.com); personal wine tastings are available on request.

Now that we know that chocolate is actually good for us, it would be a shame to indulge in anything less than the best. No preservatives are used in Godiva's G collection. Not much of a problem really, since it's doubtful you'll be able to wait that long before eating all of them. Visit www.godiva.com for locations. Godiva does a yearly Valentine's Day diamond giveaway, proving that they truly know what's dear to a woman's heart in more ways than one.

See's Candy is an institution out west with over 200 locations, and their excellent customer service and motto, "Quality Without Compromise," does best-known investor Warren Buffett proud. Find a location at www.sees.com. The only people who see more chocolate than *Max Brenner* would have to be Oompah Loompas. Before you dive into all of the chocolatey goodness at this candy shop/restaurant, you might want to try out a few of the individual truffles and sauces sold in the front of the store at 841 Broadway, New York. *La Maison du Chocolat* does things to cocoa that are hard to believe, but always delicious to eat (www.lamaison duchocolat.com). You might not have heard of *Bodega Chocolates*, but you are likely to become addicted to their chocolate-covered pretzels (www.bodegachocolates.com).

When *Rice To Riches* opened, I quickly took all my friends there because it didn't seem like a restaurant that sold gourmet rice pudding would stand the test of time. Thankfully, I was wrong. You haven't lived until you've tried their Sex, Drugs and Rocky Road. Rice To Riches is at 37 Spring Street in New York City (www .ricetoriches.com); they deliver locally and ship anywhere in the United States.

The Suite Life

Time now for the best hotels and destinations. I spend a lot of time in strange beds—get your mind out of the gutter, I meant at hotels when I'm on the road. I usually tend to opt for an immediate massage to help combat jet lag.

One of my favorite hotels ever is conveniently located in one of my favorite cities in the world. The *Glasshouse Hotel* in Edinburgh, Scotland, has so many tiny well-thought-out extras (like a Scottish thistle on your pillow, a cozy "snug" or private area to have a free nightcap) in addition to the exquisitely designed rooms and private terraces that it's hard to zero in on just one. If I had to, though, I'd refer to the calling card given to guests with their contact information at the hotel. I still get a cheap thrill when I look at the card hanging on my bulletin board that says "Ms. Rachel Weingarten in Residence." Wish I was. The Glasshouse Hotel is at 2 Greenside Place, Edinburgh (www.theetoncollection.com).

In Dublin, Ireland, a city filled with great hotels, history, art, and culture, the *Merrion Hotel* combines the best of all of those things in a series of attached Georgian townhouses with a private art collection, exquisite rooms, and a fabulous private courtyard. It's located on Upper Merrion Street, Dublin 2, Ireland (www.merrionhotel.com; telephone 353-1-603-0600). The *Sagamore Hotel* in South Beach puts a newer spin on the concept with original artwork in each room, at 1671 Collins Avenue, Miami Beach, Florida. *The Four Seasons Resort Scottsdale* at Troon has a gallery and artists in residence. While visiting I commissioned a painting by artist John Geryak, but the vistas are picture perfect in their own right. The hotel is at 10600 East Crescent Moon Drive, Scottsdale Arizona.

The *Malmaison* hotels are all pretty quirky and great for a last-minute escape. The one in Oxford just happens to be in a converted prison: 3 Oxford Castle, Oxford, England telephone 01865-268-400).

Just because you can't afford a second, third, or fourth home doesn't mean that you can't vacation in one. From townhouses to antebellum mansions, the pristine, private, *Rosemary Beach* community has its own spa and stylish shops, and offers rentals for vacations, events, or weddings. For more information, contact Rosemary Beach Cottage Rental Company, www.rosemarybeach.com; telephone 888-855-1551). For a completely new take on luxury travel, the *Regent South Beach* is a condominium hotel, giving you the opportunity to live in or rent out your luxury suite (www.the regentsouthbeach.com).

The *Grand Targhee Resort* in Wyoming boasts over 500 inches of powder coat annually (www.grandtarghee.com, telephone 800-827-4433). Kit yourself out for your ski trip in style at Gorsuch, with locations in Aspen, Vail, and other ski friendly spots, or online at www.gorsuchltd.com.

I've spent more time in more hotels in Paris than in any other city or country that I've visited. For all-time luxe, nothing quite beats the *Crillon*, though the *Regina* comes close. (Crillon, 10 Place de la Concorde, Paris, France, www.crillon.com, crillon@crillon.com; Regina Hotel, www.regina-hotel.com, reservation@regina-hotel.com.)

It's hard to find somewhere in Venice that doesn't have an exceptional history or view, but none beat the provenance of the *Hotel Gritti Palace*, which directly overlooks the Grand Canal and was commissioned in 1525 as the palace for the Doge of Venice at the time (http://gritti.hotelinvenice.com).

For pure fun, some hotels offer novelty suites or concepts, from ice hotels open only several months each year, to James Bond, Linda Evangelista, and Ernest Hemingway inspired suites. For information about the *Ice hotel* in Canada go to www.icehotel-canada.com. The *Ariau Amazon Towers* is a hotel complex situated on the treetop level of the Amazon River—if nothing else, staying here will provide you with conversation fodder for a lifetime (www.ariautowers.com). Taking anthropomorphization to new levels of chic, the Room Mate Hotels have designed rooms with custom themes and personalities to match (www.room-matehotels.com).

While I'm not generally a huge fan of theme hotels, I find the *Library Hotel* on 41st Street and Madison Avenue in Manhattan to be irresistible. Rooms feel more cozy and clubby than you'd expect. Each room comes stocked with books and a film library, and you can also request a room that best suits your mood—anything from poetry, classics, and botany, to erotica (www.libraryhotel.com).

What was that statistic about single men in Alaska? If you don't find your own version of *Men in Trees* you can at least see the most exquisite countryside in style with *Alaska Railroad* (www.alaska railroad.com). It's a toss-up as to whether the bar at the *Tribeca Grand* or the *Soho Grand* is cooler. Though the service can be uneven, both have great chocolate martinis (the dirty martini is unexpectedly strong—consider yourself warned) and the best macaroni and cheese on the planet. Both are perfect for cozy meetings or after-work flirtations—especially when you're not sure if it's a meeting or a flirtation! Tribeca Grand is at Two Avenue of the Americas, New York (www .tribecagrand.com); Soho Grand is at 310 West Broadway, New York (www.sohogrand.com).

Want to avoid the typical hotel experience? *The Parker Company* will help you locate the Italian villa of your dreams (www.theparker company.com; telephone 800-280-2811). *Small Luxury Hotels of the World* has over 400 exquisite hotels in over 65 countries (www.slh.com, telephone 212-953-2064). Whoever coined the phrase "God is in the details" must have had Cathi and Steve Fowler of the *Honor Mansion* in mind. The Fowlers leave nothing to chance—from the breakfast newspaper and biscotti delivered to your door, to the in-room glass-enclosed fireplaces, to the sinfully creative breakfasts. The Honor Mansion is at 14891 Grove St., Healdsburg, California. For a one-of-a-kind event, try *BallyWalter Park* (that's castle to you and me), a spectacular historic family residence in Northern Ireland owned by former Irish whiskey marketer Brian Mulholland, the 6th Baron Dunleath (his business card says simply, "The Lord Dunleath") and his lovely wife

Vibs. The renovated space boasts an area known as the Gentlemen's Wing and another known simply as Pleurisy Passage.

For a completely incomparable experience, head to the *Portmeirion Village* in Wales, in Gwynedd (pronounced like Ms. Paltrow's first name), off the coast of Snowdonia (www.portmeirion-village.com). Or to see more of the raw and exquisite Welsh countryside, book a stay with *Welsh Rarebits*, which brings together over 50 of the most unique small hotels, inns, and bed and breakfasts, each with a unique take and atmosphere (www.rarebits.co.uk). In addition to hundreds of castles, Wales also has one of the most innovative walking/biking trails through Snowdonia national forest, and some of the best vegetarian cuisine I've ever had.

For design at its best, the *Avalon Hotel* in Beverly Hills mixes retro mid-century design aesthetics with bold modern style, including George Nelson lamps, Isamu Noguchi tables, and chairs inspired by Charles Eames (www.avalonbeverlyhills.com).

I'm convinced that I felt the benevolent spirits of the Rat Pack while staying at the *Wigwam Golf Resort and Spa*; I'm further convinced that I could have fit my entire apartment into my luxury suite. The Wigwam is at 300 E. Wigwam Boulevard, Litchfield Park, Arizona.

The *Whiteface Lodge* in Lake Placid, New York, seamlessly combines new and rustic, exposed beams with world class food, and a skating rink, movie theater, tennis courts, and more (www.thewhite facelodge.com).

For those who favor gardens, *Eleven Cadogan Gardens* is set in a private garden square in Chelsea, London, and identified simply by a small "No 11" placard. This jewel box contains everything from world-class amenities to an on-call personal trainer and more (www.number-eleven.co.uk). Located 90 miles outside of London, *Cotswold House* overlooks a seventeenth-century market square in Chipping Campden, Gloucestershire, in the heart of the Cotswolds— one of the more beautiful garden areas of England. The townhouse hotel is anything but traditional, though, and offers everything from cashmere throws to mood lighting and luxury suites (www.cotswold house.com).

So maybe you can't spend a night in the Taj Mahal. You can, however, stay at the dreamlike white marble and mosaic *Taj Lake Palace*, which was built in the middle of the eighteenth century and spreads across a four-acre island in the middle of Lake Pichola, Udaipur, Rajasthan India (telephone 91-294-2528800; e-mail lakepalace.udaipur@ tajhotels.com).

If you had to envision paradise, you might imagine something that looked like *Curtain Bluff*, Antigua, only with a 4,000-square-foot spa—and yoga (telephone 268-462-8400; e-mail curtainbluff@ curtainbluff.com).

Too tired or overwhelmed to pack for your trip? *Luggage Forward* will pack, pick up, and deliver your luggage (http://luggageforward .com/ or call tollfree 866-416-7447).

Pamper Time

I am a shameless spa addict. Please don't make me choose my favorites, it's just too cruel. Well, okay, I'll try.

Some years ago I went to the *Turnberry Spa* in Ayrshire, Scotland. I expected to relax with massages and facials. Instead, before I even had time to unpack, much less acknowledge my jet lag, I was careening about in an off-road vehicle, steering straight down terrifying drops, and negotiating boulders and riverbanks—all while driving on the wrong side of the road. That was followed by a flurry of shooting (targets), archery, and golf on the windswept links on the Irish Sea, along with other outdoor activities. The perfect massage that I had anticipated was practically a letdown compared to the exhilaration of everything else Turnberry had to offer (www.turnberry.co.uk).

I think tying for top spa spot would have to be the *Ojai Valley Inn & Spa*, situated on over 220 acres in Ojai, California. Though it's been around for over 80 years, the Ojai Valley Inn seems more like a well-kept secret than an of-the-moment escape. From the rustic and luxurious room details (oh my god, the bathtubs!), to the world-class spa services, to the sheer beauty of the location, to the incredibly attentive staff, to the absolutely most delicious huevos rancheros that I have ever had for breakfast, this is truly one of my favorite spots on earth (www.ojairesort.com). Be sure to pay attention to Ojai's famous "pink moment" at sunset, when the entire valley lights up in a dazzling display of a natural play of light and shadow.

The *Ritz Carlton* at Dana Point in Laguna Niguel, California, is one of those rare over-the-top luxury hotels, paired with family-friendly services and breathtaking views (the hotel is on a 150-foot bluff), and quite frankly the outdoor cabana massage with a view of Catalina Island wasn't too shabby, either. It's located at One Ritz-Carlton Drive, Dana Point, California (www.ritzcarlton.com). I'm a bit obsessed with *Lilianfels Blue Mountains Resort & Spa* in Katoomba, New South Wales, Australia (or maybe I just like saying *Katoomba*), but it's hard to believe that such exquisite beauty still exists in the world—and the spa services are fairly awesome as well (www.lilianfels.com.au).

The dry climate in Arizona must be the inspiration behind all of those world-class spas with skin-drenching treatments. The architecture of the *Arizona Biltmore Spa & Resort* was inspired by Frank Lloyd Wright (while you're in the area, why not visit one of his masterpieces, Taliesen West?). The signature treatments include body scrubs with native ingredients like Saguaro blossoms. You'll find this spa at 2400 East Missouri Avenue, Phoenix, Arizona. If the only agave you've had has been courtesy of too much tequila, it might be time to check out *Agave, The Arizona Spa* at the Westin Kierland which draws on the 12 species of local agave plants in its treatments. Find it at 6902 East Greenway Parkway, Scottsdale, Arizona (for more healthful treatments, ask for a consultation that integrates the principles of Eastern medicine). For a desert oasis at the other end of the world, the exquisite *Sheraton Moriah Dead Sea* hotel and spa is situated on a private beach of one the world's most celebrated healing spots. Dead Sea minerals are used to treat everything from eczema to age rough skin. Call (972)(8) 6591591 for more information.

I won't swear to it, but I am convinced that there was a wee bit of alchemy involved with the La Prairie Caviar Firming Facial—there was a hand and foot treatment, delicate massage, and overwhelming sense of bliss. The *La Prairie Spa* also had incredibly thoughtful details, like small jewelry boxes in your locker for your trinkets. It's located at the Ritz-Carlton Hotel at 50 Central Park South in New York.

Esthetician to the fashionable set *Joanna Vargas* doesn't just refresh your skin with her gentle touch and signature three-step Triple Crown Facial—she actually jolts it back to a younger state, or something like that, with a diamond peel and more to fade the look of lines and sun spots (Joanna Vargas, 501 Fifth Avenue, Suite 707, New York). If you want to refresh the look of your skin, and invasive procedures just aren't your thing, *Sleek MedSpa* offers treatments to fade age spots and more. Treatments are quick, easy, and only a teensy bit uncomfortable. Check www.sleekmedspa.com for locations.

If you find that you just can't face the day (or face the face in the mirror!) *Exhale Day Spa* offers a "Power Facial" sure to get your complexion back on track. This is no pampering facial, but rather an intense skin makeover. Find locations at www.exhalespa.com. To really destress visit the Ouachita mountain valley, otherwise known as Hot Springs National Park. Legend has it that Native Americans revered the area as a neutral place where all tribes could bathe in peace. Visit www.hotsprings.org for more information on legendary Bathhouse Row. Or, for a more modern spa experience, visit *Turtle Cove Spa at the Mountain Harbor resort*; if the pure air doesn't inspire you, the world-class treatments will (www.turtlecovespa.com).

And because sometimes the journey really is the destination, *Schiphol Airport* in Amsterdam has a mini Rijksmuseum, and the bathrooms are really quirky looking, with murals and unique decor (I've not seen them firsthand, but apparently the men's urinals are each individually decorated), and one of my favorite concepts ever: public art all over the airport. For a more comfortable airport setting, *Oasis Day Spa* has a satellite at the JetBlue Terminal at Kennedy Airport in New York.

CAREER

Living well really is the best revenge, so instead of trying to prove how cool you are to others, commit to discovering and unapologetically spending time at your favorite spots. Jill Simon of GreenRoom in New York creates sometimes cozy, sometimes spectacular spaces for clients like the Sundance Film Festival. Her business motto? "Living well on location."

CORPORATE

We've all become professional adrenaline junkies, taking less time to relax and spending more time competing with each other and with ourselves. When going on holiday, choose the place that soothes your soul or satisfies your craving for cool, but don't go just because someone else thinks it's cool. Rather, cultivate your own little black book of new and favorite destinations.

COOL

For the most part, I've spent most of my life living in Brooklyn. Did I apologize for being an outer borough girl before 718 became the desired area code? Not even remotely; instead, I half tongue-in-cheek named my first production company Bridge and Tunnel Productions after the pseudo-negative connotations that living in an outer borough evinced with city dwellers, most of whom were Midwesterners by birth. The coolest spots don't have to be the newest, the most expensive, or the hardest to get into—they just have to be the ones that make you feel great. While it's fun to read other recommendations and best-of lists, it's even more fun to create your own.

Chapter 19

The Career and Corporate Cool™ Hall of Fame

Famous CEOs, Entrepreneurs, and Film Icons Who Have the Style We Covet—Because Money, Power, and Influence Don't Guarantee Personal Style

> *You get whatever accomplishment you are willing to declare.*
> —Georgia O'Keeffe

Let's face it, our obsession with looking great at work (and everywhere else) and modeling ourselves after the "it" girls of the moment isn't exactly a brand-new trend. In days gone by, women of a certain ilk were judged by their ability to marry well and carry off elaborate costumes including painted faces, powdered wigs, and whalebone corsets; these eventually gave way to nylon-encased gams and matching shoes, hats, and handbags. Men were initially evaluated on the size of their purse, and their manly calves ended in foppish high heels, until they evolved to wearing natty fedoras and crew cuts. When suffragettes fought for women's right to vote, they did it while clad in lavishly decorated hats, worn with ankle-length gowns that covered their corsets and bloomers. In more recent times, braless *qiana*-draped and gaucho-clad women of the 1970s roared their way into the business world. Corporate women of the 1980s tucked their womanly curves into linebacker-size padded-shoulder power suits, paired with shirts with ornate floppy bows (a more feminized version of a tie), sneakers the size of SUVs, and athletic socks.

Fashions come and go, but the desire to emulate the most fashionable members of our society, especially in the workplace, is timeless. William Shakespeare famously opined on the fickle tides of fashion when he observed that "The fashion wears out more apparel than the man." (Then again, this was a guy who regularly wore doublets and leggings to work.) In our own time, we mostly look to the rich and famous or so-called tastemakers to influence our style, and our own sartorial selections are heavily influenced by what celebrities are or are not wearing.

Hollywood is built on artifice, and for that reason it isn't really fair to the rest of us that our society deifies models and celebrities. If you stop to think about it, the famous ones' sole purpose for being is to be constantly charming and entertaining, with an enormous side order of decorative. In other words, it is practically part of a celebrity's job description to be slim, sparkly, and seductive, and it's a job that they take very seriously—well, most of the time.

If you ever study the starlets on the red carpet in their carefully crafted couture frocks, perilously high stilettos, and borrowed million-dollar baubles, it's almost mind-boggling to wonder how some of them got it so right, while others perpetually get it so very wrong. (Icelandic Pop star Bjork comes to mind—she of the swan-shaped evening gown worn to the 2001 Academy Awards ceremony.) After all, these famous folk have posses of "ists" carefully crafting their larger-than-life personas. From high-priced styl*ists* choosing their clothing and accessories, to makeup art*ists* artfully painting their faces, to hair styl*ists* who tame and tease their tresses, to anal*ysts* propping up their frail egos, to public*ists* ensuring that for better or worse they remain in the public eye. (Not to mention the medical professionals kept on speed dial to deal with everything from unexpected blemishes to pesky laugh lines and dreaded tummy bulge.) Shocking, then, to realize that the perpetually fussy, mussy, and multilayered Olsen twins actually pay someone to advise them on their particular brand of rubbish-bin chic.

Excess and plastic surgery aren't limited to the celluloid set, though, but also run rampant for more ordinary folks. Nose jobs were once the exclusive domain of those with truly horrific honkers, while breast implants, liposuction, and tummy tucks were reserved for top-tier celebrities. In our own times, some consider implants to be appropriate "sweet sixteen" gifts, while wrinkles, laugh lines, or frown lines are instantly frozen with Botox, with sometimes garish results. It's fairly common for women and men of a certain age, tax bracket, or highly publicized profession to nip, tuck, and tweak their previously gracefully aging visages into identical plasticine masks.

All of this frivolous plastic surgery is reminiscent of movies like *The Stepford Wives*, where women in a fabricated suburban town were replaced with robotic doppelgangers, which were presumably the idealized version of a wife and mother. What this aggressive pursuit of perfection neglects to address, though, is that it's a lot harder to stand out when you look, dress, and act exactly like everybody else.

Humorist Mark Twain, while best known for his acerbic wit and punchy prose, always stood out from the crowd by virtue of his shock of white hair, trademark snowy mustache, and uniform of a white linen suit. He famously declared that "Clothes make the man. Naked people have little or no influence on society." While that's not entirely true in our post-Baywatch cum thongs and Brazilian bikini wax culture, the original premise of "you are what you wear" remains. Let's face it, there's a reason that clichéd lines like "Clothes make the man" and "Dress for success" are part of our vestment vernacular. In the immortal words of ZZ Top, "Every girl's crazy 'bout a sharp dressed man." Amen to that, not to mention that a majority of us still tend to swoon over a man in uniform. From longing for summer, when the hot UPS guys break out their brown shorts; to swooning over Richard Gere in pristine dress whites sweeping Debra Winger off her working-class feet in *An Officer and a Gentleman*; to pre-jumping-the-couch Tom Cruise and the always crush-worthy Val Kilmer in *Top Gun*, Hollywood and the rest of us tend to go all gooey when encountering a man in a uniform.

While a majority of starlets (much like teenage girls) tend to adopt the identical uniform of skimpy clothing and oversized sunglasses, for better or worse, many more tend to try to set themselves apart from the boobs-and-Botox crowd. Fashion critic Mr. Blackwell, he of the dubious credentials and voraciously followed annual best/worst dressed list, regularly puts everyone from celebutantes to CEOs in their proper place. He annually chronicles the spectacular sartorial successes and freaky fashion faux pas of the rich and infamous.

If we subscribe to the assumption that clothes do in fact make the (wo)man, at work a well-cut suit, a custom-made shirt, and the right shoes, shades, or signature accessory, are the details that set you apart from the corporate pack. Mega entrepreneur Mark Cuban, owner of the Dallas Mavericks, might be able to get away with his own particular brand of schlumpy chic (if all else fails he can just distract us with the contents of his wallet), but the rest of us seem to have to try harder to set ourselves apart from the corporate clique's sense of chic.

If you look the part and are more put together than the rest of the business bunch, you'll likely exude more confidence, and chances are that people will perceive you to be at the top of your game. It isn't about whether you've got more jingle in your jeans than they do—it's about looking, feeling, and acting like you do.

It shouldn't be an all-consuming or painful process to look and feel outstanding in your work or social environment. If fashionista wannabes had their druthers, there would be an instant formula for looking fantastic, and it would read something like this:

Take pants or skirt
+ add shirt or sweater (liberally dose with timeless accessories)
and voila! Instant fashion icon.

Unfortunately, real life doesn't quite work that way. Bill Gates may be the original captain of industry, but his ill-fitting wardrobe leaves much to be desired. With all his zillions of dollars you'd think that he'd have realized that rumpled suits, grotty ties worn at odd angles, and geeky glasses are woefully mid-1990s computer geek chic. Johnny Depp may have a perpetual sexy glint in his bittersweet chocolate brown eyes, but take away the wardrobe and makeup crew and he most resembles someone's oddly dressed bachelor uncle with his pale skin, penchant for floppy fedoras, and ill-fitting zoot suits.

But it isn't just Johnny. Hollywood has its share of the bold and the beautiful, the sexy, sophisticated, and downright scary. For every sleek and exquisite Halle, there's a mishmash of micromini-clad Britneys and Christinas. For every coolly chic Chanel-clad Grace Kelly offspring like Princess Caroline of Monaco, there's a freaky circus chick like her younger sister Princess Stephanie. For every perfectly pressed, just-out-of-a-box Bill Clinton there's a slightly frumpy, helmet-haired Hillary Clinton—and the list goes on. In other words, if great fashion sense requires balance between accessorized and overdone, the celebrity world is a balance of good, great, and oh my god!

Fashion critics are frequently full of sound and fury but ultimately signify nothing more than the urge to classify the hierarchy of the fittest (and hottest). After all, self-proclaimed celebrity style mavens Joan Rivers and Steven Cojocaru are themselves in dire need of immediate and ongoing fashion mentoring. For that reason, I will avoid the finger pointing and coy mocking of the Monday morning fashion quarterback, and instead affectionately offer up the following list, in no particular order, of famous folks in the Career and Corporate Cool Hall of Fame (or shame). These are famous people whose looks suit their station in life, their career, and their personal path. They're so good at being themselves, and they seem so comfortable in their own skins. We may not want to bring Dave Navarro home to meet our mothers but one can't help but admire his uniquely Navarro-esque ornate facial shrubbery and coal-black fingernail polish.

Meet the new inductees into the Career and Corporate Cool Hall of Fame. Some get it right, some should keep trying, and some we all adore for being so miserably misguided. They may not be strictly corporate, but their personal, professional, or political style sets the bar high for the rest of us. We may not love them solely for their fashion sense, but also for the unique way that they inspire us to make our own mark on the world, fashionably or otherwise.

They follow, in no particular order (drum roll please).

OPRAH WINFREY

Oh, Oprah, we've stuck with you through thick and thin (and thick and thinner, and sorta thicker and close to thinner). We loved you in spite of your circa 1980s turquoise pantsuits and doorknocker earrings. We adored you through your mousse and hairspray days, through your skinny jeans and scary lipstick. We love you because you're like us. You're not perfect—far from it, but you just keep trying. You have good days and bad days, and your style is constantly evolving, much in the same way that you are. We cheered you on when you Slimfasted your way toward a size 8, and we felt your pain as the pounds crept back.

We love you most of all for being the anti-Barbie, a living, breathing, dress-up doll who experiments with styles, trends, and color with a conscience and doesn't always get it right—but keeps on surprising us.

MARTHA STEWART

Why, Martha Helen Kostyra, how you've changed! You went from being a shy New Jersey girl to a model turned stockbroker, incarcerated icon, and role model. You goofed, big-time, but you always looked great. While wearing a handbag worth several thousand dollars to your arraignment might not have been the brightest career move, you redeemed yourself by wearing *that* poncho when you got your get-out-of-jail card. You retained your dignity, class, and decorum throughout your highly publicized ordeal. Your understated "I'm a tough woman, even though I favor a muted palette and Hermes handbags" sense of style still reigns supreme. In many ways, we want to be just like you when we grow up (only without the indictment).

DAVID LETTERMAN AND JON STEWART

Boy, oh boys, how you light up our nighttime television screens. With your sharp wit and even sharper suits, it's a toss-up which one of you is our favorite. You both bring an old-fashioned sense of style to the small screen, with modern touches. Dave, we forgive you your white socks and erratic hairstyle; and Jon, your rubbery face and puppy-dog eyes don't hide your sexy good looks. Gentlemen, you've effectively revolutionized the concept of "desk jobs" and each of you epitomizes Career and Corporate Cool at its late-night best.

GEORGE CLOONEY

Am I shallow to jump on the George bandwagon and include someone so obviously swoon-worthy? Perhaps, but let us consider the facts. As the offspring of a media family (father Nick Clooney was a radio and TV personality, and gifted chanteuse Rosemary Clooney was his aunt), gorgeous George could have gone the Randy Spelling/Tori Spelling route and coasted on his family laurels by appearing in sitcoms and movie-of-the-week docudramas. Instead, he not only developed a sometimes preachy social and artistic conscience (and yes, we do forgive him for his appearances on *The Facts of Life*), but he has looked marvelous throughout. Clooney reminds us of the great ones, from Cary Grant and Clark Gable to a younger Sean Connery. He smolders, but never blazes. He is a man who laughs often and has the sexy laugh lines to prove it. He's always perfectly groomed, clad, and coiffed, and I strongly suspect that he smells as good as he looks.

CATHERINE ZETA JONES

While we're on the subject of old Hollywood glamour, let us salute CZJ. It's rumored that she's years older than she admits to, but we're more than enamored with her timeless looks. With her womanly curves, throaty laugh, and fabulous wardrobe, Ms. Jones exudes attitude, sexuality, confidence, and movie starness. Her natural charisma brings to mind the heady chemistry of Bogey and Bacall or Tracy and Hepburn. She is unapologetic about her modest roots in Wales, and yet she epitomizes Hollywood glamour at its best. And for that we are grateful.

ANDREA JUNG

Picture this: You are the chairman and chief executive officer of Avon Products, a multibillion-dollar global cosmetic company. As the child of immigrants, you learned to speak Mandarin Chinese as a child, and you are more than a bit adroit at tickling the ivories. You've managed to overcome your childhood beliefs about the inferiority of women, so much so that you currently manage a team of over 45,000 salespeople. Throughout, you maintain perfect poise, gleaming hair, and stylish suits. You seek balance in your life, preferring to spend your nights with your family and holding sacred your monthly girls' night out. You undoubtedly embody the most chic and stylish aspects of the American Dream.

JACQUELINE LEE BOUVIER KENNEDY ONASSIS

Though she's gone, her style lives on. No hyphenated names for this classically stylish miss. Jackie was feminine but never frail, timeless but never trendy. While she was most famously known for the men in her life—her father, John Vernon Bouvier III; first husband, U.S. President John F. Kennedy; and second husband, Aristotle Onassis—she was never eclipsed by them, but rather added her own magic to their strong public personas. She went from a life of privilege to that of sophisticated First Lady whose every accessory, nuance, and fabric choice were eagerly emulated by women throughout the world.

From her trademark pillbox hats to her Chanel suits, to her casual costume of black sunglasses worn as a headband paired with simple pants and boatneck T-shirts, Jackie's style was often imitated but never quite as effectively recreated. At her funeral her son, the late John F. Kennedy Jr., spoke of his mother as being most remembered for her "love of words, the bonds of home and family, and her spirit of adventure."

PRINCE FREDERIK AND PRINCESS MARY OF DENMARK

What, you were expecting Lady Diana? While some might not consider attending state functions and cutting umpteen ribbons to be much of a career, these thoroughly modern 30-something-year-old royals do it with style. Raven-haired, Australian-born Mary tends to favor couture evening gowns, stylish hats for state occasions, tailored jackets, and floaty skirts. Frederik looks like a long-lost member of 1980s pop group A-Ha, and it doesn't actually matter what he wears to work, he's that pretty. Okay, to be fair, he looks equally sublime in his military garb, tux and tails, or casual cords and shirts.

ANDRE 3000

Indeed, it's hard to pigeonhole the personal style of this eclectic hip-hop honey, but Andre 3000, né Andre Benjamin, seems to meld old-world appreciation for impeccable tailoring with a fresh new sense of style. While fellow rapster Diddy (aka Diddy, P.Diddy, Puff Daddy, Sean Combs) favors a more tentative palette, Andre 3000 pairs bold patterns, exquisite details, and a love for interesting accessories into his mega fashion mix.

RAHM EMMANUEL AND MICHAEL BLOOMBERG

These two challenge the accepted notion that all politicians favor ill-fitting cheap polyester suits. As the chairman of the Democratic Congressional Campaign Committee, Emmanuel not only has the coolest name in politics, but he also seems to possess a quasi hipster *Rat Pack* swagger and sense of style. He never has a hair out of place, and I'd definitely admire the cut of his jib if I had even an inkling of just what that means.

As for Mayor Mike, being a billionaire bachelor politician must definitely have its downside (though for the life of me, I can't quite figure out what it is), but this fashionable flesh presser seems to have bypassed the curse of frumpy former New York City Mayor Ed Koch. Instead, Bloomberg is always turned out in subtle but spectacular suits, and on less formal occasions he favors soft suede jackets and casual slacks.

Now if only the rest of Congress would follow suit, America would indeed be the beautiful.

RICHARD BRANSON

Before you go crying out accusations of me being a billionairist, hear me out. Sure, Branson isn't known for his spectacular taste in jackets or trademark eyeglasses frames, but his style in everything that he says or does is uniquely his own. From the name of his company (Virgin, since he was brand-new in business) to his faded ginger hair and beard, to his scruffy casual style, Branson personifies the successful self-made man. He seems to be unpretentious and unassuming, so much so that Virgin offered personalized Christmas phone call greetings from Branson himself last year. (And yes, as a matter of fact, I did sign up for one. What a rush to hear his less-than-posh accent wishing me a merry one and exhorting me to visit London in the coming year.)

Branson doesn't seem to take himself or his brand too seriously. He's a mogul who still seems to have the common touch and knows how to touch people, while having fun.

OSCAR DE LA RENTA AND TOM FORD

Before you start complaining about the fact that fashion designers, by virtue of their chosen profession, *must* look and dress better than the rest of us mortals, allow me to say two words to you: John Galliano. And if that doesn't have you convinced, let me follow up with two more: Karl Lagerfeld. While all four of these style supertalents drape women with fabulous frocks, only Oscar and Tom look as great as their clients do.

These two designing men from two completely different generations embody fashion without being frivolous, freaky, or fey. Mr. de la Renta seems almost too good to be true, with his old-world manners, luxury homes, and timeless personal style. Mr. Ford, on the other hand, takes cutting-edge simplicity to new extremes. He even admits to wearing mascara when necessary—though always in a low-key and tasteful manner. Both of these designers truly seem to love women (in their own way) and the female form, but unlike the campy Mr. Galliano or the increasingly Michael Jackson-esque Mr. Lagerfeld, these two seem to enjoy draping themselves in timeless luxury as well.

So there you have it—the best of the best. They look good, they sound better, they live well, but more than that, their individual style embodies who they are both personally and professionally. They don't scream out to be noticed, but rather use their unique attributes to sell not only their brands, but themselves by extension.

Now Donald Trump, and the rest of you who are in dire need of an extreme makeover, you didn't really think that you were going to get off that easily, did you?

In the spirit of good karma, I'll try not to mock these fashion don'ts too mercilessly, but will rather try to gently suggest ways in which they might come forward into the fashionable light.

Okay Donald, we'll start with you. Unless there are no mirrors in your myriad homes you must surely have seen what is growing out of your head. We can no longer take you seriously as a businessperson with that reddish/pinkish cotton candy disguised as hair wrapped around your formidable head. You will look equally daunting with a good haircut. For a while it was Bono whose look was worse than yours. Yes, he's a rock icon and an altruist to boot, but ye gods, the pastel glasses, the lank shoe-polish-black hair, and worst of all, the cowboy hats? Bono, dear soul, even youngish rock stars must age gracefully (look at that darling Mick Jagger from the Rolling Stones— he still snarls, but he does it with style). You've finally gotten a haircut, but there is still time to lose the shades, and opt out of the Schwarzenegger-like coal-hued hair.

And as for you, Mr. Governator, you're looking a bit overly buff for politics. Sure, America's chunkier than it's been in decades, but your alarmingly larger-than-life physique, along with your giant, eerily white chompers and taut complexion make us afraid, very afraid.

An honorable mention to:

Tina Fey: For demonstrating both wit and specs appeal

Susan Sarandon: For proving that sexy doesn't stop at 50+

Sophia Loren: Who as a septuagenarian pin-up girl proves that sexy doesn't stop at 70+ either

Diane Sawyer: For being always and appropriately elegant

Ann Richards: Who never confused feminine with frivolous

Judy Chicago: For turning feminism into art

You: Because I have no doubt that we could all learn a thing or two from your personal style. Send your best business or style tips to rachel@careerandcorporatecool.com.

CAREER

You'd think that earning zillions of dollars and having a coveted career in the spotlight would also automatically grant you the power of perfect taste. Well, Mr. Blackwell's annual worst-dressed list makes it glaringly obvious that that just isn't true. Console yourself with this thought: Just because they have more money than you do doesn't mean that they have better taste than you do.

CORPORATE

I know there are times when your own job sucks, but it could be worse. Imagine if it was actually your job to look beautiful, and if you got paid based only on the ever-shrinking size of your waistline and your expression-proof brow.

COOL

If you compare yourself to the rich, famous, and fabulous and then feel that you are lacking in some way, then I must insist that you also compare yourself with every other person that you encounter. Obviously, this is a waste of time on all counts. Measure yourself by your own yardstick of expectations and not by an unrealistic vision of what you should or shouldn't look like.

Chapter 20

The 23 Rules of Career and Corporate Cool™

Twenty-Three Ways That Good Business Meets Great Style

Keep cool and you command everybody.
—Louis de Saint-Just

Rules Not Meant to Be Broken

When I began working on this book, I thought I had a very clear idea of what I'd say, just how I'd say it, and what sage advice I would share—but, like much of my career, that changed drastically albeit organically along the way. If I've learned one major lesson in my professional life, it's that it is inevitable that shake-ups, hiccups, dizzying highs, and stomach-dropping lows will show up along the way. The key to dealing with the ups and downs is to figure out how to ride those crazy waves, to learn that it's okay to lose your breath as long as you hang on for dear life, and to pay close attention when possible because, just like in *The Brady Bunch*, there's always a valuable lesson to be learned (hopefully a lesson that doesn't involve a bad perm or polyester bell bottoms).

Okay, who am I trying to kid—there is more than one lesson to be learned. As I've fumbled and soared over the years, I've either heard or learned by osmosis some basic and unexpected concepts stressed repeatedly. Since I've always been an innovator more than a follower,

I've also figured out some of my own. And so I present to you the 23 rules of Career and Corporate Cool.

Rule 1: Give Back

You don't have to pledge half of your salary to charity, but you should incorporate charitable giving into your business plan, because it feels good, because it's the right thing to do, because somewhere along the way fate has been kinder to you than to someone else. Because you have gifts, talents, or finances that can help someone else out, and even if you do it for the tax deduction you're still making the world a better place.

I try to create a charitable component to each and every project that I work on, and choose a partner with a like theme, to raise awareness or raise funds. Elizabeth Woolfe, Program Director of Fashion Targets Breast Cancer, the charitable arm of the Counsel of Fashion Designers of America founded by fashion designer Ralph Lauren, cautions against jumping on the cause-marketing bandwagon for the wrong reasons, or for doing good just for the sake of positive press. "The fundamental law is about really meaning what you do. It's a serious and substantial commitment, not just a marketing tool. It's not the size of the commitment or amount of donation. It's about carefully vetting the choices, not just jumping in on the cause of the moment, because consumers see through that, and once they see that it's not a deeply felt commitment they're on to the next thing."

Rule 2: Play Nice

I'm not suggesting that you opt for a strictly Pollyanna-like ethos at all times, but rather to be equally kind to people that you meet on every level of the corporate structure. It's always a great idea to be nice to the people you encounter on your journey through life.

Some people feel they're too important to be nice to the little people, or that it's beneath their dignity to accord to every receptionist or personal assistant the same respect they would offer their higher-ups. Big mistake. First of all, these gatekeepers can literally hold the keys to the kingdom of your future relationships and interactions with their boss. They can make or break your potential relationships by conveniently forgetting to pass your calls along, neglecting to forward crucial information your way, or setting up appointments at a time that is always inconvenient for you. Conversely, they can go out of their way to whisk you in front of the right people at the right time.

You also never know who's going to be demoted or promoted, and you may suddenly find yourself in the awkward position of trying to curry favor with the person that you've ignored or talked down to for years. Rob Walker, a contributor to the *New York Times Magazine*, puts it this way: "You need to treat both your peers and those below you on the totem pole with respect and grace; your colleagues and the people under you—the interns, the assistants, the person who you might think is a loser—both as part of your lifelong goal and because it's good for you."

RULE 3: DEFINE YOUR SPECIAL SAUCE

Face it, there are bound to be too many other people to count who *in theory* do exactly what you do. But you in fact are the only person who can bring your own experience, quirks, talents, and personal style to everything that you say or do. Most people think that the special sauce in a McDonald's Big Mac is just a variation on thousand island salad dressing, and yet that gooey orange sauce of mythic ingredients is one of the enduring elements that sets Big Macs apart for the carnivorous pack. Ben Feldman, CEO of SnapTotes.com, calls this "finding your brand's genius," and he suggests "finding the unique position of your brand, focusing on quality, image, and making sure that you do the best job of it."

RULE 4: DON'T WASTE PEOPLE'S TIME

If you believe the old adage, time is in fact money—or at least a crucial and irreplaceable intangible asset. No one is suggesting that you be rude or brusque (kindly refer to rule 2), but rather figure out what you want to say, the deal that you want to propose, the assets necessary to bring said deal to fruition—either financial or in kind—and clearly explain your proposal and value proposition. If a busy executive offers you 10 minutes of her time, you don't want to spend 9 minutes of that fumbling to make polite conversation. If she agrees to read your e-mail or proposal, make sure to get to the point and make a convincing case for yourself in the first few sentences.

Christopher Laird Simmons, the president of California media company Neotrope, reviews and distributes thousands of press releases each year through his Send2Press Newswire service. Simmons offers these three tips for effectively and immediately communicating your message, based on the most successful press releases:

1. Convey originality, either in a new product or in an idea that has broad or niche appeal to the audience of any specific media outlet
2. Tell the story at a glance in that first crucial 15 seconds.
3. Use supporting materials like a good photograph or supporting web site.

RULE 5: BRAG (BUT DON'T BELIEVE YOUR OWN HYPE)

You may not know this about me, but many years ago I made my acting debut on the Broadway stage with Sir Ian McKellen. Granted, about 30 other audience members were on stage with us, but if acting were my chosen profession you can be sure that I would include this in my CV.

Contrary to popular belief, you may be the most brilliant, talented, and supremely innovative person in your chosen field, but your success story will not miraculously land you the corner office, coverage on major news media, and a miniseries inspired by your all-around fabulosity. Face it, we live in media-saturated times, and everybody seems to have their own publicity-generating machine. Figure out who needs to know, what they need to know, and then make sure to let them know.

Keep a notebook in which you track your weekly, monthly, and quarterly successes, so that you can refer back to specific details if someone else tries to claim credit, and also when negotiating raises and bonuses. If it's necessary for your boss to know that the account winning idea was yours, send her an e-mail expressing excitement over the new project and explaining your excitement at having your concept be the one that sealed the deal. You'll not only remind her what makes you a unique asset to her team, but you'll also have a dated record of your concept.

At the end of the day, realize that while it's an imperative part of your job to promote yourself and your successes, the worst thing that you can do is believe your own (manufactured) hype.

RULE 6: LOVE WHAT YOU DO AND DO WHAT YOU LOVE

There is enough in life that is excruciating (global warming, e-mail scams from Nigeria, the unbearable cacophony emerging nightly from the apartment of my talentless and deranged flute-playing neighbor). For example, your vocation shouldn't be torture—it should be fun. I'm not suggesting that every minute of every day will be a joy, but work can be more than just paying your bills.

If you haven't found your professional passion, keep looking, or find the individual qualities present in your existing job that make it worth doing. Nearly every satisfied and successful person that I spoke to in the context of this book chose *fun* or *personal passion* as the major descriptor of their career. Money often followed, but a deeply rooted enjoyment and personal passion was the top motivator.

Jerrod Blandino, the co-founder of Too Faced cosmetics, says that "once you find that gift that you can be passionate about you need to craft it, feed it, pay attention to it." It becomes "not something you have to do but rather something that you get to do."

RULE 7: HAVE A PERSONAL SLOGAN

Every major corporation has not only an internal guidebook with company rules and ideals, but also a catchy marketing tagline that sums up their mission, brand heritage, and past and future business ideology. Your personal slogan doesn't always have to tie into your professional one, but it should in some way define the businessperson you are or would like to become. Jillian Kogan, Director of Production Events and Concert Services at MTV Networks, is fond of saying: "Don't take a job—make a job." Multifaceted Sandra Payne, of the New York Public Library, is also a visual artist whose bold jewelry designs speak volumes without the need for any kind of verbal personal declaration.

For years my unofficial slogan was "How the hell did I pull that off?" Until I became comfortable in my professional skin, I would shake my head in amazement at the kudos I'd receive after some of the more astounding or spectacular launches, projects, and events that I produced. These days, my slogan is somewhat tongue-in-cheek, and it's based on the concept of loving what you do and doing what you love. I'd love to tell you my slogan, but at the risk of even one person taking it seriously and not realizing that it's more of a euphemism, I'll leave out a key word. My slogan, "You gotta get paid or you gotta get ____," usually gets a laugh when I share it with people, but those with a professional passion usually understand exactly what I mean.

Work isn't only about the hefty paycheck, though that's always an amazing incentive. Good work can also be charitable acts, mentoring, volunteering, or working with clients who can't necessarily afford your services, but they have such a great concept or product that you commit to helping them anyway. If I'm not collecting a juicy retainer, I want to be sure to be having so much fun and getting so much personal satisfaction with a project that it far outweighs the hours of commitment and sweat equity.

RULE 8: HAVE A PLAN AND ALTER IT AS LIFE AND WORK EVOLVE

Way back in the dizzyingly optimistic days of Web 1.0, venture capitalists and angel investors would invest in embryonic companies with little more than an URL, fund them for millions of dollars, and then be shocked when said venture failed spectacularly. If the initial bust-up taught us anything, it's that having the dream isn't quite enough. Even if your business is self-funded, it's a good idea not only to establish your mission and goals but also to evaluate the gritty and potentially damaging upheavals that might occur down the road, and then to prepare for those unexpected eventualities.

Business plans aren't only for entrepreneurs, though. I firmly believe that you don't need to have a 50-page document with due diligence, but it's important to have even a sheet of paper that marks a timeline of successes to date, goals, objectives, and even rewards. It will allow you to take your own pulse over the years and see if you're still on the right track about your career, or if you've veered wildly off track or are ready to change careers entirely.

RULE 9: BE RELEVANT AND STAY RELEVANT

I seem to recall basketball coach Rick Pitino once using the analogy of pioneers to stress the vagaries of embarking on groundbreaking ventures. Pioneers lead the way, stumble in, and discover uncharted territories, but they are also the ones who usually end up with arrows through their hats (or, as in the case of groundbreaking inventor Nikola Tesla, declared to be mad scientists). While it's a real rush to have a great idea, having an idea isn't enough. Nurturing the idea, planning a strategy for your concept and execution, and building in a long-term approach that includes room for growth and loads of wiggle room, will ensure that you succeed in the long term instead of simply paving the way for the next generation of explorers who succeed you by figuring out the right way to do things.

Some years back, everyone was astounded by the sheer simplicity and genius behind online networking site Friendster, which aimed to link people through their networks of friends. Through a series of shortsighted or simply unfortunate decisions Friendster faltered, while sites like MySpace and YouTube dominated the field. Some owe the success of the latter to their covert familial or professional connections, but the bottom line is that these sites not only tapped into an existing need but built in room for tremendous growth and brand extensions.

Keith Nowak, the media relations manager for Nokia, has created what he calls his "History Wall" to give newer employees an idea of the classic design elements in older Nokia products. In this way he visually conveys to his coworkers one of Nokia's brand hallmarks that "good design is always good design."

RULE 10: CREATE AND USE A SUPPORT SYSTEM (VIRTUAL OR OTHERWISE)

We all tend to mock the long, rambling speeches made at awards ceremonies where people thank everyone from their agents, publicists, and deity of choice, to their manicurists and dog walkers (though they sometimes forget to thank their spouses). Nevertheless, we all do rely on so many key people to help us get through the day-to-day grind.

Over the years I've been fortunate enough to build a brilliant network of friends and colleagues, and I'm grateful to be able to publicly acknowledge many of them in the credits to this book. On the television program *Who Wants to Be a Millionaire?* contestants were allowed to tap into their carefully screened network of knowledgeable friends to help them with tough questions in different categories. In your professional life, friends who share your background, or colleagues with a similar work style, ethics, or pet peeves, can help to add an unexpected perspective to your issues, assist you with problems, reassure you that you're right, or help you to ease out of awkward situations when you're completely wrong. Mentors can offer feedback on your career choice or major upheavals, or offer another perspective on a situation. Don't only go to them for advice, but offer them support and encouragement as well.

RULE 11: STAY IN THE LOOP

Whatever field you're in, chances are that there's a trusted source of information and gossip that you should be tapping into. Read industry and trade journals and web sites, and subscribe to related podcasts and "really simple syndication" (RSS) feeds. Be sure to educate yourself on the ins and outs and upheavals occurring throughout your industry and related industries.

More than that, read newspapers, visit popular web sites, talk to your in-the-know friends, and be sure to make yourself aware of current events, popular culture, and diversions. Of course you'll go through crunch times when you'll barely feel like brushing your teeth, much less like brushing up on your knowledge of cultural affairs in France. But sometimes the make-or-break moment in a professional relationship is the one in which you're able to offer an educated comment on what concerns your colleague most.

RULE 12: COOL IS WHAT YOU MAKE OF IT

It isn't too hard to separate the people who are so hip it hurts from those who are naturally, effortlessly, and inherently cool. While we all love to try new restaurants or chic cocktails, most of us understand that sustained cool isn't an accident, but rather an evolution of style over years of experience.

I was introduced to the actor Oliver Platt at a dinner party in his honor celebrating his opening night on Broadway. Please understand, one of my gifts is my ability to schmooze just about anybody from nobility to nine-year-olds, but a lifelong crush on Platt had me blushing and stammering like an idiot. When I was finally able to compose myself enough to talk to him, I mentioned having a lifelong crush on him, to which he replied with a bemused expression, "Why on earth would you have a crush on me?" As charming, talented, and witty as he was, he had the most self-deprecating and sweet attitude, which just added to his overall coolness.

RULE 13: FOLLOW UP

It isn't enough to make a great impression, a great pitch, and a great proposal. If you let the momentum die, you'll never get to the next level, and you'll certainly never close a deal. It isn't always easy to follow up after meetings, but it is crucial.

After a meeting or pitch, be sure to leave with firm plans and a clear understanding of what the next steps are, and then be true to your word and follow up. Even if you come away with a no, you'll have shown that you are a person who completes the cycle of each proposal. It also reinforces your reliability and professionalism and tells the other person that you don't shy away from the tougher aspects of project work, but rather can see even the tiniest details to the end. I cannot tell you how many times I dreaded calling someone to follow up on a niggling detail that then led to more business or priceless feedback.

But how do you find the balance between following up and being too pushy or annoying? Todd Leopold, the entertainment producer for CNN.com, receives a lot of cold calls and pitches on a daily basis. He explains it this way: "If someone e-mails me and I respond in a positive way, then I've invited them to get back in touch with me, and their follow-up is fine." If he responds negatively, though, he doesn't want them to push their point.

RULE 14: OFFER SERVICE WITH A SMILE

Bad or nonexistent customer service is practically an epidemic in corporate America today. Many companies don't just cut corners or farm out customer service to overseas vendors, but they do away with it altogether.

Of everyone that I spoke to or interviewed in the context of this book, none impressed me with their near religious zeal for great customer service like Craig Newmark, founder of Craigslist, who spends several hours each day personally answering e-mail and dealing with customer service issues. He's gracious enough to credit CEO Jim Buckmaster (Newmark found his resume listed on Craigslist) with doing a stellar job at running the company and allowing Newmark time to personally attend to complaints. When asked to define the best part of his job, Newmark answered, "Really helping people."

Your business is as good as your word of mouth. Your customers have myriad choices, and yet somehow they've chosen you. Go the extra mile, do little things to show that your clients matter. Great customer service can make or break your business, and in today's frenetically paced economy the last thing that you want to do is to encourage your customers to vote with their feet.

RULE 15: BE A SUPERHERO (IF NOT A ROCK STAR)

Though I can't necessarily leap buildings at a single bound, or blink my eyes or twitch my nose and produce a five-course meal (or, more useful yet, a five-year marketing plan), I am in fact blessed with superpowers. Don't believe me? Ask someone who hates to talk on the phone what they would give to be able to casually pick up a phone and fearlessly call total strangers, from the president of a television network to the CEO of one of the largest banks in the world, and within a matter of minutes be chatting and laughing like best friends and planning a time to meet. Or ask a painfully shy person about how they dread even team meetings or how they pray for the ability to brazenly address a roomful of colleagues. You see, my superpowers may not have been imparted by the bite of a radioactive spider, but nonetheless, they add a kinetic and branded energy to my professional persona.

I have no doubt that you have superpowers, too (no cape or tights required), and while you may take them for granted, the rest of the world may soon be clamoring for your talents. What do you do better than anyone else? How can you hone that skill to become a superhero in your field? Not all industries require rock stars, but they can all use the highly polished skills of corporate superstars.

And in case you're wondering, being a rock star isn't always what it's cracked up to be. Ben Deily, a creative director at the VIA Group in Portland, Maine, is also a former member of 1990s alternative band the Lemonheads. Deily sounds weary when he talks about the overwhelming aspects of being part of a popular band. When asked what it feels like to live the reverse of most people's daydreams, Deily offers the anecdote that though he was only in his 20s at the time, he was always more of a quirky or old soul, and that fellow indie rocker Juliana Hatfield once gave him a pin that read "Middle-Aged and Proud of It." While he still dabbles in the music world with his new band, the Varsity Drag, he's satisfied with his place in life.

As for those of you who still dream of tripping the light fantastic, Deily advises that "nothing external can substitute for at least trying to do or be what you always wanted to be." So while there's still hope for you and your masses of adoring fans, this guy who credits his grandfather with inspiring his sartorial sensibilities is for the most part happy to leave the manic world of band life behind to be "a rock star of the business world."

RULE 16: FIND A NEMESIS

Betty had Veronica, the Rolling Stones had the Beatles, and Cinderella had her evil stepsisters. While superheroes tend to have archenemies with evil tendencies who desire to take over the world or at least change weather patterns drastically, in life it can sometimes be a better idea to have a nemesis. Your nemesis doesn't actually have to be someone that you hate; it can be a total stranger, former schoolmate, or casual acquaintance. I know people who track their own success rate based on the rising or falling star of their nemesis.

Your nemesis can act as a road map for your own career. Her highs can inspire you to aim for greater things, and her lows can help you to reevaluate your own actions and activities.

RULE 17: STAY ON PEOPLE'S RADARS

Much of my business is built on word of mouth, which is exactly the way that I like it. I prefer to have someone come to my company because I've been highly recommended by a satisfied client—it can cut through a lot of the getting-to-know you period and get to the fun or challenging stuff sooner.

Instead of simply opting for a once yearly holiday card, I try to stay in people's minds, either by remembering their birthday or hobby and sending appropriate silly gifts, or through clever and fun seasonal mailings. I can also usually track three new pieces of business each year to each seasonal mailing. More than any of that, it's a fun way for me to interact with past or current clients, brighten someone's day, and let them know that I've been thinking about them, whether we're currently under retainer or not.

RULE 18: ONE FOR YOU, ONE FOR ME

I can't begin to tell you just how many people I know or have worked with who will disappear for a year or two and then resurface just in time to ask for a spectacularly huge favor. I'm always happy to help people out, but I reserve that extra effort for friends and colleagues who are willing to reciprocate.

Along those lines, don't martyr yourself and always be the one doing the giving (looks pointedly at self). People like to feel needed and, more than that, they don't want to feel as though you're building up a store of brownie points and will crush them at some point with a request for a monumental favor.

RULE 19: PAY ATTENTION AND BE CONSISTENT

A lot of my business savvy is just natural instinct; a lot comes from watching closely and learning from outcomes and then learning how to predict future outcomes. A former friend without a strong grasp of the English language used to refer to me as a "noticer" when I pointed out minutiae about the people around us and then predicted their future behavior and actions.

In my business life I pay close attention to those around me, their likes, dislikes, quirks, throwaway comments, and success rate. I learn from what they say or do or forget to say or do. I learn from their temper tantrums and very thoughtful actions. I learn most of all that to be successful in business, one must frequently lose one's ego in favor of the common good or client.

When you let people know that you're paying attention to more than just their likes and dislikes, their success or failure rates, you're also saying without words that you are someone who sticks around. They learn to rely on you and your consistency, and even if they don't work with you the first time around, they feel confident knowing that you've weathered industrywide ups and downs and lived to tell the tale. I can't tell you how many times potential clients rejected initial pitches only to revisit them and sign on as regular clients a year or so later.

RULE 20: BE GENUINELY ENTHUSIASTIC

I am a person who tends to get very excited about what I work on. This is easy to do, since my company will not work with clients or products unless we're excited about them or think they can improve the world in some way.

Many years ago I was chatting with a former business mentor and daydreaming about the day that I could send employees to meetings in my place. My mentor said that he hated to disappoint me in my reverie, but that people would want to work with *me*—because they want to work with me personally, not simply my company. He explained that my genuine enthusiasm was something that was impossible to fake, and nearly impossible to replicate.

Even on his off days, the highly energetic Vijay Uppal, a political campaign worker from San Diego, is committed to his cause. Instead of staying home or giving in to self-doubt he tries to make a difference anyway. "If I don't give 100 percent effort because I don't feel well or am tired, I have missed an opportunity to have even the slightest impact on someone's life."

Don't be embarrassed to rave, and don't hold back if you're really enthused about working with someone or on a particular project. It will make people want to work with you more if they believe that you love their product as much as they do. And if you're not feeling it? Don't try to fake it, just do the best job that you can.

RULE 21: TRUST YOUR GUT

You're going to hear a lot of different advice about a lot of different business topics over your career. While most people mean well, only you can really know what's right or wrong for you and your long-term success.

Russell Barnett, brand manager at Winery Exchange, tends to "listen to my bellybutton," which never steers him wrong on the toughest challenges. Carter, Aaron, and John aren't a boy band but rather the three founders and C-level executives at Built NY who cooked up the innovative idea of neoprene cases for everything from wine totes to laptops. While some might caution against taking on even one partner, this triple threat has managed to make their three-way partnership work harmoniously despite advice to the contrary. They credit their successful partnership to their shared goals and "core foundation" around which their business was built. Or, as John says: "We have strengths and weaknesses that complement each other well." The three were confident enough to trust their instincts and form an atypical partnership that has proven to be hugely successful.

RULE 22: DO THE RIGHT THING

Corporate America has always been riddled by scandals and schemes of epic proportions, and yet, more than anything else, creating and retaining your most basic set of ethics will not only strengthen your business but your community and the world, according to Professor R. Edward Freeman, co-director of the Darden Business School's Olsson Center for Applied Ethics at the University of Virginia, one of the world's leading academic centers for the study of ethics. Freeman says many people mistakenly believe that "business is doing whatever you can to get ahead. Business is about working together to create value that none of us can do on our own, to create value for those who have a stake in what you do," including your clients, your employees, your community, your investors, and the world.

RULE 23: SAY THANK YOU

Never underestimate the power of a thank-you note. Over and over, I've heard people talk about their great disappointments, which frequently involved not feeling appreciated, not having their actions acknowledged by people they had helped. If you can, send a handwritten note. Otherwise make a phone call, send an e-mail, text message, or any other form of correspondence. Thank the people who have bought you a gift, made a significant introduction, gone out of their way to help you out, or gotten you through a tough time. If appropriate, send a gift that really expresses your appreciation.

And before I forget:

Thank you!

Conclusion

The pain of parting is nothing to the joy of meeting again.
—Charles Dickens

And Now I Fear the End Is Near

This book has been a major part of my life for the past few years or so. But who am I kidding? The concept of Career and Corporate Cool has consciously or unconsciously permeated nearly every minute of my professional life in one way or another. I've never followed a traditionally accepted career trajectory. You know the drill—college; first job, first dress code, and cubicle; second job, better dress code, and bigger cubicle; and so on. I've never followed the prescribed dress or behavior code, either, but have instead found my own way to express, develop, and play up or play down my signature personal fashion and business style.

I'd love to really impress you and say that I've always known what my ultimate professional path would be; that I was one of those hyperorganized and disgustingly goal-oriented teenagers who years before college had a checklist of milestones to be reached and conquered on my way to the corner office. But I was none of those things, and I still am not. I spent my school years in an artistic and dreamy state punctuated by constant work of one sort or another—babysitting, designing clothes, teaching art or woodwork at the local Y, working at my mother's store, even substitute teaching. Instead of attending college right out of high school, I started working when I was 17 and went to school at night. I always thought that I fell into things, but now, years later, I realize that I was, as is my natural wont, trusting my gut instincts to guide me on the winding path to finding my vocation and passion, which, lucky for me, have turned out to be one and the same, and ever evolving.

I initially meandered along multiple career paths, which took me from working as a receptionist at a dermatologist's office to general office work, to public relations, to makeup artist and beauty expert, to cosmetic development for celebrity brands, through a detour in professional baking and founding a mini muffin business, to greeting card and graphic design, to Internet pioneer, to event planning and production, to writing for magazines and becoming a weekly beauty columnist for a Scottish newspaper, to running professional networking events internationally, to marketing and strategy consulting and writing books, to becoming known as the go-to gal for all things business etiquette related—otherwise known as Ms. Biz Manners—and slowly, sometimes painfully, and often thrillingly, evolving into the multifaceted professional that I am today.

When I was working late hours at the dermatologist's office, did I ever dream that the tricks of the trade that I picked up behind the scenes would someday help me in my work in the cosmetic industry? When as a teen I worked on beading and freehand drawing on my first (and only) line of denim clothing for a New York designer, did I imagine that years later when I produced New York City Fashion Week events I'd be able to integrate key design elements into the conceptualization of each event? When I toiled at understanding how to break down and even code and program web sites in the dawn of the Internet, did it ever occur to me that years later I'd more easily be able to grasp nebulous technological concepts and innovations and integrate them into project work for clients? When I worked with celebrities and politicians on launches, or partnered on projects that never came to fruition, did I envision creating long-term, lasting friendships and partnerships that would propel my career much further than any one project could?

Nope, not even remotely. Yet somehow all of the things that I've done or worked on have gelled to transform me and sharpen my skill set and bring more value to everything that I do. Trust me, I didn't always love my miscellaneous jobs, but I always forced myself to take some key knowledge from each situation, which I still tap into on a recurring basis.

When I first started working, I had no defined path, goals, or objectives other than earning enough money to buy cute clothes and makeup. I never was able to tap into an existing network of well-connected friends or friends of friends in high places because I don't come from that lifestyle or background. Instead I had to keenly hone and constantly refine my powers of observation and integration—and thus was born the concept of *Career and Corporate Cool.*

I hope that by now you realize that Career and Corporate Cool is a concept that is far from one size fits all, but rather a lifestyle, a mindset, an empowering series of tools and observances to help you to define your core competencies and dazzling personal brand hallmarks and integrate them into Brand You.

You are more than your educational or work background. You are more than your hip mailing address or the impressive title on your business card. You are more than the color of your skin or timbre of your voice. You are more than your greatest past successes or stunning failures. You are far more than your fun vacations or perfect moments. You are more than your workout routine, work life, and more than your personal life too. You are all of these things and more. Only you know what it took to get you to this point in your life, a point of great pride, comfort, or success, or the complete opposite—a time to shake things up or move on.

As with most things in life, enjoying your journey toward Career and Corporate Cool is as important as achieving that goal—and I, for one, intend to keep savoring every single minute.

Index